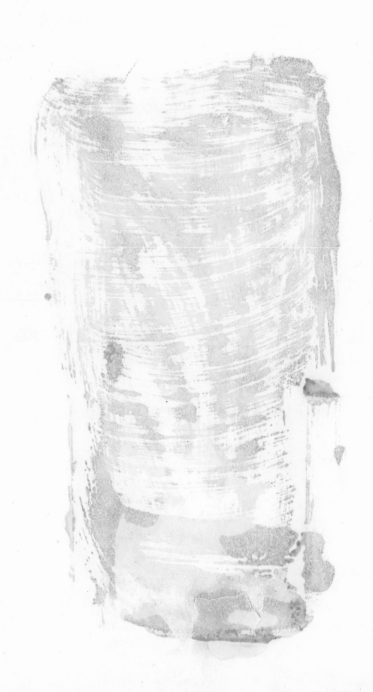

THE BACKGROUNDS AND TRADITIONS
OF OPERA

The Backgrounds and Traditions of Opera

By Ruth Berges

South Brunswick and New York: A. S. Barnes and Company
London: Thomas Yoseloff Ltd

OR 7/75

© 1961 and 1970 by A. S. Barnes and Co., Inc.
Library of Congress Catalogue Card Number: 73-114859

A. S. Barnes and Co., Inc.
Cranbury, New Jersey 08512

Thomas Yoseloff Ltd
108 New Bond Street
London W1Y OQX, England

ISBN: 0-498-07672-5
Printed in the United States of America

For Marisol

CONTENTS

List of Illustrations   9
Preface to the Second, Enlarged Edition   13
Preface   15
Acknowledgments   17

Part One: Opera as a Part of Life

A People's Opera   23
The Unanswered Question   32

Part Two: A Look at the Composer

Venetian Pioneer   41
The Enduring Charm of Pergolesi   48
The Ideal Beloved   54
Napoleon of Opera   58
Melody Magician   65
Sicilian Orpheus   72
Rossini's French Operetta   76
The Man Meyerbeer   80
Benvenuto Berlioz   86
In Wagner's Shadow   102
Gothic Swan Song   108
No Opera, No Wife   113
Tchaikovsky and his Operas   120

Part Three: A Look at Others: Librettist and Cataloguer

Arabella's Fathers   131
Koechel Listing. . . .   137

Part Four: The Play's the Thing

Genoveva—A Forgotten Opera   143
The Devil's Domain   150
Dumas, Son of Duval   156
The Marriage of North and South   161
No Name for Iago   166
The Abyss of Reality   171

Part Five: History and Legend

The Three Riddles   177
Orpheus and his Lyre   185
Carmen's Ancestors   189
Antecedents of the Mantuan Court   195
The False Dimitri: Hero or Villain?   199

Part Six: Myth and Reality: The World of Wagner

The Fabled Swan   211
Under the Rhine   217
Brünnhilde's Heritage   222
Worms and the Nibelungenlied   228
The Love Potion   233
Under an Open Sky   237
The Making of a Hero   241

Selected Bibliography   247
Index   259

LIST OF ILLUSTRATIONS

The following illustrations appear as a group after page 38
An opera performance at Rome's Baths of Caracalla
Cavalleria rusticana at Verona's amphitheatre
Milan's La Scala Opera
The San Carlo Opera in Naples
Grace Bumbry as Lady Macbeth
Alfredo Casella
Ildebrando Pizzetti
Ottorino Respighi
Clemens Krauss
A scene from *Capriccio*
A bust of Jean Philippe Rameau
Cavalli's house on the Grand Canal
A scene from *Ormindo*
Another scene from *Ormindo*
Erice, the old nurse, in *Ormindo*
A scene from *Le nozze di Figaro*
A scene from *Die Zauberflöte*
A scene from *Don Giovanni*
A scene from *Fidelio*
Rita Gorr in *Médée*
A scene from *Médée*
A scene from *La Vestale*
Maria Callas in the title role of *La Vestale*
Carl Maria von Weber

The following illustrations appear as a group after page 128
A scene from *Der Freischütz*

A bust of Gioacchino Rossini
A scene from *Oberon*
A scene from Act II of *Il barbiere di Siviglia*
A scene from Act I of *Il barbiere di Siviglia*
A scene from Act II of *Le Comte Ory*
The drinking song from *Le Comte Ory*
The opening scene of *Le Prophète*
The council chamber scene from *L'Africaine*
The prison scene from *L'Africaine*
Giacomo Meyerbeer
Hector Berlioz conducting an orchestra
Benvenuto Cellini's statue of Perseus
A scene from Act I of *Béatrice et Bénédict*
A scene from Act II of *Béatrice et Bénédict*
Franz Liszt
Johannes Brahms
Clara Schumann
Brahms' house at Bad Ischl
Johann Strauss and Brahms
Brahms' grave in Vienna

The following illustrations appear as a group after page 140
Three Italian comedy figures in porcelain
Gaetano Donizetti
The Donizetti monument in Bergamo
Heinrich Heine
Vincenzo Bellini
Bellini's birthplace
The Beethoven monument in Vienna
Johann Wolfgang von Goethe
A scene from *Fidelio*
A room in the Brentano country home
Jacques Offenbach
E. T. A. Hoffmann
A scene from *La belle Hélène*
A scene from *Eugene Onegin*
Another scene from *Eugene Onegin*

The following illustrations appear as a group after page 174
Hugo von Hofmannsthal

Richard Strauss
The final scene from *Arabella*
Ludwig Alois von Koechel
Wolfgang Amadeus Mozart
Robert Schumann
Friedrich Hebbel
Scene of the Walpurgis Night
Charles Gounod
Gustaf Gruendgens as Mephistopheles
St. Richard with his sons, Willibald and Wunnibald
St. Walburga
Alexandre Dumas the younger
Marie Alphonsine Duplessis
Mademoiselle George
The house in Roncole where Verdi was born
The house where Shakespeare was born
A scene from *Otello*
Giuseppe Verdi
Verdi and his librettist, Arrigo Boito
Another scene from *Otello*
Georg Büchner
Alban Berg
Franz Kafka

The following illustrations appear as a group after page 208
Friedrich von Schiller
Giacomo Puccini
A scene from *Turandot*
A scene from *Orfeo ed Euridice*
Christoph Willibald von Gluck
An ancient Hebrew coin, and a modern Israeli coin
Apollo's birthplace, the island of Delos
Illustration from a medieval Hebrew manuscript
Georges Bizet
An etching of a gypsy caravan by Jacques Callot
An eighty-year-old Spanish gypsy
A Yugoslav gypsy
Hindu gypsy women and children
Gypsies in Seville
King Francis I of France

Château de Chambord
A scene from *Boris Godunov*

The following illustrations appear as a group after page 246
Richard Wagner
Porcelain tureen from the swan service
Porcelain platter from the swan service
A scene from *Lohengrin*
Wagner's original sketch for *Das Rheingold*
A scene from *Siegfried*
Neptune on a sea monster by Severo da Ravenna
Church portal with scenes from the Sigurd legend
Swedish rune stones from the Viking era
A scene from *Die Walküre*
A Viking burial mound from the Iron Age
Martin Luther
Lindenfels in the Odenwald
The Odenwald Lindelbrunnen where Siegfried was slain
A mural from Runkelstein Castle in South Tyrol
A scene from *Tristan und Isolde*
A miniature showing King Marke about to kill Tristan
A scene from *Die Meistersinger*
Hans Sachs
The riot scene from *Die Meistersinger*
A scene from *The Flying Dutchman*
The Hall of the Grail, from *Parsifal*

PREFACE TO THE SECOND, ENLARGED EDITION

Nine new chapters and appropriate illustrations have been added to this enlarged edition of *Opera: Origins and Sidelights.* The subject matter of the new chapters is of kaleidoscopic variety, considerably broadening the scope of the first edition's operatic origins and sidelights.

The additional material, comprising more than one fourth of the present book, throws further light on opera in Italy, France and Germany during various periods in history essentially through composers significant at—and in some instances representative of—their time. In a sense they are the makers of opera, the avant-garde, those who shaped and reshaped it, rather than those whose works form the standard repertoires of the major opera houses today. There are chapters on such diverse composers as Cavalli, Spontini, Rossini, Meyerbeer, Berlioz and Cornelius. There is even a chapter on a nineteenth-century non-opera composer with an attempt at explaining why he desisted from music drama. The entirely new first part of the volume is devoted to opera as a part of life, as exemplified in different ways by an entire people and an individual composer.

Here then is *The Backgrounds and Traditions of Opera,* not only an expanded, more comprehensive and diversified book, but also, it is hoped, a more interesting, colorful and improved volume.

Ruth Berges

PREFACE

THE FASCINATION OF OPERA LIES IN ITS DIVERSITY. APART FROM ITS primary function of entertainment, opera offers a variety of other stimulation. As an artistic form of expression, it is all-inclusive. Is there another art form in which a blending of vocal, choral, and orchestral music as well as poetry, drama, and the dance can be found? Opera is a treat for eye, ear, emotion, and intellect.

An active interested mind will probe even beyond these obvious entertainment and cultural values into the background of an opera. Like the other arts, in particular the drama, but on a more elaborate artistic scale, opera encompasses all concepts of life and humanity, good and evil, beauty and ugliness, legend and reality, past and present. Whatever its message, it is easily comprehensible because it appeals directly to more than one sense. And the grandeur and richness of an artistic enterprise such as opera arouse interest and curiosity beyond what is actually seen and heard.

How much, for instance, do we know about the composer or the librettist? Or what do we know about Mozart's devoted cataloguer, whose mysterious initial, "K.", appears so persistently next to every Mozart composition? Who are Brünnhilde's real-life ancestors? What are the origins of the *Walpurgisnacht* in *Faust?* How important is the love potion in *Tristan und Isolde?* Would the tragic hero and heroine have fallen in love without it? Carmen is a gypsy; where did gypsies originally come from? How typical is Carmen of them? What part do nature and primitive nature rites play in *Die Meistersinger?* What is Verdi's attraction to Shakespeare? Who is the prototype of the Duke of Mantua in *Rigoletto?* Of what significance are the three women in *The Tales of Hoffmann?* How autobiographical

15

is this opera? How much did the composition of an opera mean to Robert Schumann? What personal yearning did Beethoven express in *Fidelio?* How are the common ideals of Georg Büchner and Alban Berg ultimately expressed in *Wozzeck?* What is the significance of the water, gold, and dwarfs in *Das Rheingold?*

Every opera may pose any number of questions to the opera lover or student. Pondering these and finding answers to them is illuminating and gratifying, further enriching the listener's and viewer's enjoyment.

This collection of varied essays seeks to answer some such questions. The book does not presume to be comprehensive. It is not even representative of the operatic repertoire. It is simply a beginning, the outset of a pilgrimage through opera-land, where I have sought and chanced upon interesting and enlightening treasures.

RUTH BERGES

ACKNOWLEDGMENTS

Acknowledgment is made to *Opera News*, New York, for permission to reprint the following articles, some in altered form: "The Unanswered Question"; "Venetian Pioneer"; "The Ideal Beloved"; "Napoleon of Opera"; "Melody Magician"; "Sicilian Orpheus"; "The Man Meyerbeer"; "Gothic Swan Song"; "No Opera, No Wife"; "Arabella's Fathers"; "Koechel Listing . . ."; "The Devil's Domain"; "Dumas, Son of Duval"; "The Marriage of North and South"; "No Name for Iago"; "The Abyss of Reality"; "Orpheus and his Lyre"; "Carmen's Ancestors"; "Antecedents of the Mantuan Court"; "The Fabled Swan"; "Under the Rhine"; "Brünnhilde's Heritage"; "Worms and the Nibelungenlied"; "The Love Potion"; "Under an Open Sky"; and "The Making of a Hero." "A People's Opera" appeared originally in *Musical Courier/The Music Magazine* in a slightly different version and is reprinted by permission of The Summy-Birchard Company, Evanston, Illinois. "Rossini's French Operetta" was first published in *The American Record Guide*, New York.

THE BACKGROUNDS AND TRADITIONS
OF OPERA

Part One
Opera as a Part of Life

A PEOPLE'S OPERA

ITALY IS NOT ONLY THE COUNTRY WHICH GAVE BIRTH TO OPERA; ITALY
and its people are also most naturally and popularly associated
with opera. Here nothing like the Piccinni-Gluck controversy in
Paris or Wagner's battle against the opposing German romantic
school could have disturbed operatic development. Although there
were conflicts of minor nature, opera in Italy flourished unper-
turbed along its own course, a unifying force creating and main-
taining its unique traditions. Since the Italian language itself is
like music, once it was welded to melody and grew into opera,
this form of musical expression became immensely popular, over-
shadowing all others. The voice predominated while the orchestra
remained secondary.

In Italy opera belongs to the masses. It does not cater to an
aesthetic-minded cultural elite or minority. Italians are an emotional, impulsive and easily excited people who express their approval or criticism in the theatre without inhibitions. Judgment
is not pronounced by a chosen few but arises from the ranks of
the people. Italians demand that opera arouse their feelings, and
from the depth of their emotions they respond. Small wonder that
in eighteenth and nineteenth-century Italian operatic history the
forbidding figure of the censor repeatedly appeared: opera in addition to being the Italian's entertainment also provided his social
life and voiced his political grievances.

Although public reaction basically has not changed much
throughout operatic development, the inception of opera was totally different from what we think of as Italian grand opera today. When in the late 1590's a group of aristocratic Florentine

intellectuals was experimenting in joining words to music, it was trying to recreate the Greek theatre. Out of this circle's attempts grew Jacopo Peri's *Dafne* (1597) and *Euridice* (1600). Italian audiences—at that time the aristocracy, though as ebullient as the masses—soon tired of the *recitativo secco* accompanied by chords on the lute or harpsichord. Claudio Monteverdi's orchestral innovations as well as introduction of arias stressing music over words were welcomed. His *Orfeo* (1607) and *Arianna* (1608) were immediate successes. He continued with the masterpieces *Il ritorno d'Ulisse in patria* (1641) and *L'incoronazione di Poppea* (1642), written especially for the first opera houses in Venice.

It was Alessandro Scarlatti in Naples who, in Edward J. Dent's words, "before 1700 . . . had gathered up all that was best of the tangled materials produced by that age of transit and experiment, the seventeenth century, to form out of them a musical language, vigorous and flexible as Italian itself. . . . Lesser composers contributed their part to this great work but . . . the main glory of the achievement is certainly due to him."

Scarlatti's operas and libretti, however, were strictly conventional. Although mythological subjects were replaced by historical personages, the characters, always unbelievably high-minded, might politely disagree operatically but never really acted like human beings. The number of opera houses was growing rapidly throughout Italy; yet the endless posturing of *opera seria* became tedious. By the beginning of the eighteenth century only the aria and its singer retained significance, and even the singer could not render the static action more dramatic. But as the leading female parts were sung by *castrati,* who were highly trained musicians, these singers could enhance operatic art by adding their own embellishments to the arias. For a while the *castrati* reigned supreme, but eventually prejudices, and a papal prohibition which kept women off the stage, lapsed, encouraging the rise of the *prima donna.*

In 1720, the Venetian aristocrat and composer, Benedetto Marcello, assailed current operatic conditions in his satiric volume *Il teatro alla moda,* in which he cleverly gave instructions to all involved in the production of an opera. He advised the singer always to keep his mouth half-closed and to clench his teeth, to do everything possible to keep the audience from understanding him. When he addressed his partner, Marcello suggested, the singer should in between greet the occupants of the loges or smile at the orchestra so that the audience would not forget that he was Alipio Forconi, the famous *castrato*, and not Prince Zoroaster whom he happened to be playing. When he was not busy singing, he should converse with his colleagues.

A large number of Italian opera librettos came from Pietro Metastasio, who was court-poet in Vienna. As Metastasio was all powerful in the theatrical world and well liked by society, opera composers—less to be reckoned with than singers—never raised objections to the repetitious librettos. But Count Giacomo Durazzo, intendant of the Vienna opera, decided it was time to challenge the Metastasio formula of virtue, impeccability and nobility. He was tired of the state of opera, like the public—which, however, managed to amuse itself otherwise during interminably boring stretches—and recruited Ranieri Calzabigi, a friend of Casanova's and a bohemian remarkably like him, to write a text for Christoph Willibald von Gluck. Gluck, who by adoption and training had become an Italian composer, had been composing along standard lines on Metastasio librettos, among others. Durazzo was less interested in skillful, fluent counterpoint than in dramatic expression which, fortunately, was Gluck's forte. To his composer-librettist team he added the ideas of the ballet-master Gaspare Angiolini. Opera was to consist of music, dance, mime and dramatic action. The year of the opera revolt was 1762 when *Orfeo ed Euridice,* the new, reformed opera, was first presented. Only the role of Orfeo was retained for a *castrato* while the happy ending was a concession to Metastasio. The Greek dramatic ideal which the early Florentines had sought to recreate once more had been approached.

Naples, meanwhile, was developing its own operatic form, the *opera buffa,* which had grown out of the popular *commedia dell' arte* and was more to the taste of the masses with its rough, farcical fare and intensely local, colorful atmosphere. First making their appearances as intermezzi between the acts of an *opera seria,* these little operatic gems with their sparkling *recitativo secco* and short, delightful arias and duets featured the tenor, formerly the villain, as the hero, while the bass, once totally neglected, now assumed an important *buffa* role. A fine example of *opera buffa* is Pergolesi's *Serva padrona*.

Opera seria, in spite of Gluck's reforms, declined in favor. Its chief proponents—Salieri, Cherubini and Spontini—were active mostly outside Italy. The newly derived comic form through the subsequent efforts of Piccinni, Paisiello and Cimarosa expanded and flourished in eighteenth-century Italy.

The acme of this development was scaled with Rossini's comic operas. Music was established supreme over text. Yet Rossini was craftsman enough to make the best of a dramatic situation, whether comic or tragic. His melodies were so contagious that *"Di tanti palpiti,"* from *Tancredi,* first produced at La Fenice in Venice in 1814, was immediately sung by every Venetian, *gondoliere* and aristocrat alike. His popular *Barbiere di Siviglia,* at its 1816 premiere in Rome, raised a riot, partially manufactured by Paisiello supporters who castigated Rossini for writing an opera on a subject that the older, experienced Paisiello had used twelve years before. Moreover, Rossini had permitted Manuel Garcia to sing to Rosina a serenade of his own instead of the one Rossini had composed. The public was infuriated. However, the second night, when Rossini's aria was sung, a courteous, attentive Roman audience received the work enthusiastically.

The competition and snobbery that developed among opera houses of different Italian cities is well illustrated by *Il Turco in Italia,* which Rossini composed for Milan's La Scala in 1814. The Milanese promptly rejected the work as "scraps left on the plate by the Venetians," because to them it seemed to be just an inversion of the successful *L'Italiana in Algeri,* previously written for Venice's Teatro San Benedetto. The opening drum roll of *La gazza ladra* (1817) caused a sensation in Milan. After the overture, for the first time in La Scala's history, everyone began to talk, and a conservative student threatened Rossini with assassination for his revolutionary ideas.

By that time many changes had occurred in *opera seria.* The *da capo* aria and the *castrati* had disappeared. But the public still clamored for happy endings, even in operas like Rossini's

Otello. Singers were as demanding and capricious as ever. One *prima donna* was known to insist that her first aria contain the words *"felice ognora,"* which were especially suited to display her vocal technique. It is a credit to Rossini that he persisted in having his arias in *Elisabetta, regina d'Inghilterra* sung exactly as he had written them, without embellishments. Another singer refused to sing unless his first entrance was on horseback or on top of a hill; he had to wear a helmet with white feathers six feet high. As the singer was most important, certainly to the audience, the poor composer had to acquiesce. Performances were long, often with a ballet interspersed between the acts. The premiere of Verdi's *Rigoletto* in 1851 was followed by a ballet in five acts called *Faust.* Spectators thought nothing of visiting the gambling rooms or one another during a performance. Refreshments were served while secondary singers sang their arias (*aria di sorbetto*). Rossini was more amused than angered by these customs and instituted no reforms beyond placing some curbs on the singers.

Another prolific *opera buffa* composer was Gaetano Donizetti. Upon hearing that Rossini wrote *Il barbiere di Siviglia* in two weeks, Donizetti, who required only eight days for *Maria di Rohan,* commented, "The lazy fellow!" Much in Donizetti's scores is fresh and exuberant, in particular in *Don Pasquale,* which has come down to us as the last *opera buffa.*

One of the first occasions at which the public associated opera with patriotic sentiment during the years leading up to the *risorgimento* occurred in Venice at the premiere of *Belisario,* composed by Donizetti for the carnival season of 1836. After the performance, several Venetians carried Donizetti home on their shoulders. Forming a torchlight procession behind him, the people sang an aria from the opera as a new patriotic song.

Together with Donizetti, Vincenzo Bellini is considered the bridge to late nineteenth-century opera. Though Bellini has been criticized for his weaknesses in counterpoint and orchestration, his pure and simple melodies are commendable and surely were an impetus to the era of great singing. He not only fell in love with his leading sopranos but wrote music which gloriously displayed their voices. Giuditta Pasta, Maria Malibran and Giulia Grisi sang brilliantly in *La sonnambula* and *Norma*. *I Puritani* was written for Grisi, Giovanni Battista Rubini, Antonio Tamburini and Luigi Lablache, a distinguished cast which subsequently became known as the *Puritani* quartet. Bellini's chief innovation was the two-women opera, *Norma,* which was widely hailed, perhaps particularly because it required the talents of two exceptional female singers. However, the sensitive, gentle Bellini, possibly overwhelmed by Donizetti's resourcefulness and resenting his superior technique, did not venture beyond the operatic conventions of his time.

It was Giuseppe Verdi's greatness as a man and musician, his simplicity coupled with strength of character and determination, which enabled him to enforce the composer's will on the performers, developing some changes in the grand opera tradition. He put an end to semi-improvised opera. He did his utmost to create credible characters. Voices became clearly associated with characteristics. The baritone was the dominating, acting character but not the lover (Iago, Giorgio Germont). The tenor, outwardly glowing, was actually weak and acted upon (Otello, Alfredo Germont). He became most effective in concerted action with the lyric soprano. Verdi insisted on faithful vocal, orchestral and dramatic presentations. At one time he would not tolerate Banquo's ghost in *Macbeth* being played by someone else but the singer who had sung Banquo. "Banquo must have the same face when he is dead as when he is alive," Verdi explained. He was also the first to introduce the modern art of conducting to Italy, replacing the mere time-beating *maestro al cembalo* or first violinist.

Verdi's sincerity and integrity won him support. His musical genius rallied the people's acclaim and adulation. Drunk with ever-intensifying patriotic fervor, they saw in him the symbol of liberation and unification. Unable to express themselves freely, they used opera as a code through which they could give free reign to their strong emotions in spite of tight Austrian censorship.

If Donizetti had previously caused the Austrians embarrassment, Verdi incensed them even more. They became touchy and cautious when Verdi protagonists—Jews, Lombards, Spaniards, Huns and Scots—touched off riots through mere suggestions of patriotism, oppression, exile and nostalgia. With *Ernani*, full of intrigues and plots, Verdi had to pacify Austrian as well as Venetian censors. However, with the exception of very minor alterations Verdi had his way, and it was this opera which first insured him international repute.

Not even Verdi could altogether control or subdue public response. The Italian opera-going public's spirit was indomitable. Though audiences loved him, the premiere of *La Traviata* in 1853 was a fiasco because the leading lady looked too robust to be suffering from consumption. At Parma's Teatro Regio in 1886 a poor vocal performance of *Nabucco* was accompanied by constant whistling and shouting. But during the intermissions, while the house was quiet, sounds of arias, duets and quartets floated from the gallery where the audience demonstrated how it felt Verdi should be sung. Verdi was held in such esteem that in 1893, when he was supposedly traveling incognito to Rome for the first performance of *Falstaff* at the Teatro Costanzi, the mayor of Rome and more than two thousand people waited at the Termini station to meet every train coming from Genoa from early afternoon until close to midnight when the composer arrived. The welcome was so enthusiastic that the seventy-nine-year-old Verdi had to be smuggled through a toolshed to a waiting carriage. Cheering crowds were everywhere; he was unable to retire before he had appeared at his hotel window.

In Verdi's gigantic shadow several other operas have enjoyed successes, among them Ponchielli's *Gioconda* (1876); Mascagni's Sicilian *verismo* piece, *Cavalleria rusticana* (1890); Leoncavallo's *Pagliacci* (1892), based on a true episode; and Giordano's *Andrea Chenier* (1896). Giacomo Puccini's *verismo* operas, with their pessimistic outlook, suffering women and hovering touch of sentimentality, were on the whole well received, except for *Madama Butterfly* (1904) at La Scala, where a large anti-Puccini faction was determined to wreck the performance.

A curious reception was given young Arrigo Boito's *Mefistofele* at La Scala in 1868. Although no Wagner operas had yet been performed there, *Mefistofele* was attacked by the public as being "Wagnerian." After each of the opera's three performances there were demonstrations ending in disorders in the *piazza* outside the theatre. By order of the police chief the opera was withdrawn. Political riots were one thing; disturbances caused solely by music—for the first time in La Scala's history—were not to be tolerated.

Respighi, Casella, Malipiero, Dallapiccola and Pizzetti have continued the Italian operatic tradition. But none of Puccini's popular achievements—though frowned upon by some musicians—have been equaled by these composers.

It is the older masterpieces which are still dear to the Italians; it is the superior artistry of performers which still arouses their emotions and spirited response. Neither Verdi's insistence on the composer's supremacy, nor Arturo Toscanini's conductorial iron discipline have successfully suppressed the traditional Italian exuberance or openly expressed indignation. At La Scala, around the turn of the century, Toscanini waged a relentless war against singers and their cohorts of supporters. The chief issue was the question of encores. Police laws against them had lapsed so that Toscanini had to fight the battle alone. The climactic incident occurred on the last night of the 1903 season, at a performance of *Un ballo in maschera*. In the second scene the audience clamored for an encore from Giovanni Zenatello. Toscanini refused, waiting patiently with his arms folded. When the tumult did not cease, he turned around, flung his baton at the shouting mob and left the theatre. He did not return to finish the performance; in fact, he did not return to La Scala for three years.

But the Italian public will not be overruled and the expression of its displeasure may be violent or humorous. The critical standards of the Parmesans are renowned. In 1929 at the Teatro Regio, a mediocre tenor, who owned a bicycle shop in Rome, sang in *Aida*. At the end of the performance a voice from the gallery called, "You, little man, when you're finished, will you fix my bicycle?" And more recently, a Spanish tenor, who had displeased audiences in *Rigoletto*, found upon leaving that no porter at the station would carry his luggage for him. On the other hand, a purring sound of approval has often been heard at La Scala, for example when Maria Callas would sing a leading role.

In spite of censorship and battles of various nature, Italians have jealously guarded their operatic traditions and through their participation have kept their grand opera vibrantly alive and flourishing. It is not only their entertainment but intensely a part of their lives.

THE UNANSWERED QUESTION

TWICE IN HIS LIFE RICHARD STRAUSS DREW ON HIS OWN EXPERIENCE
for operatic inspiration. The first time he transposed to the stage
an episode from his personal life. *Intermezzo,* a "bourgeois
comedy," realistically portrayed himself and his wife in sharp
misunderstanding and on the brink of divorce because of a case
of mistaken identity. The opera was conceived as a light, trans-
parent work, in which the characterizations emerged comically
human and true to life.

In the second instance Strauss chose a subject consisting of
ideas rather than incidents, symbolic personifications rather than
real personages. This time his professional experience served as
the prime inspiration. In 1934 Stefan Zweig had suggested to him
as an operatic theme Abbate Giovanni Battista Casti's *Prima la
musica e poi le parole.* Zweig was charmed by the title, but found
the libretto itself useless. It had been set to music by Antonio
Salieri and was performed as a companion piece to Mozart's *Impresario* at its Vienna premiere in 1786.

Five years elapsed before Strauss seriously occupied himself
with the possibilities of the Casti title. In the intervening years,
while writing *Daphne, Friedenstag* and *Die Liebe der Danae,* the
idea had remained dormant in his mind, but it was too stimulating and challenging ever to be quite rejected or forgotten.
Surely every operatic composer—with or without his librettist—
had at some time during his career endured the ancient rivalry
between word and music. Strauss was captivated by the idea of
somehow presenting such a controversial contest on the stage.

Initially he felt that he actually did not want to write another opera. As the idea ripened, he had visions of a theatrical prologue after Goethe with clever, witty dialogue: "I should like to do something exceptional, a treatise on dramaturgy, a theatrical fugue." It was Clemens Krauss who persuaded and helped the composer to bring the subject to life and transform it into an opera. The scenario and text gradually emerged from correspondence and discussions between Strauss and Krauss. Even the title, *Capriccio—A Conversation Piece for Music,* grew out of a lengthy exchange between the two musicians.

Strauss' imagination was kindled, his wit sparkled, his sympathy warmed. Supported by the experience and wisdom of a lifetime, he was young once more, a beginner, eager to experiment. Seeking and exploring new means of operatic expression and presentation, he originated a novel style with *Capriccio.*

This process suggests a parallel to Verdi who at about the same age, his reputation well-earned and secure, had begun to experiment. *Falstaff* was an innovation, his first comic opera, written, as he claimed, only for his own amusement. Verdi suddenly stripped opera of many of its nineteenth-century romantic trappings to which he himself had more or less adhered during a long and successful career. He turned from black and white histrionics, from mediocre librettos stretched to accommodate his music, to multi-shaded realism, earthiness, the affecting foibles of human nature, all magically touched by humor and sympathy. Now text and music became partners engaged in a dialogue. Words grew meaningful and the music spoke with endless vocal and orchestral color and variety. Without a care for his public, Verdi indulged in creating in Falstaff a character close to his heart, one he could understand and love.

Similarly, Strauss felt certain that *Capriccio* was "no piece for the public, at least not a public of 1,800 people per evening. Perhaps a delicacy for cultural epicures, musically not very significant, in any case not so tasty that the music will help if the large public does not warm up to the text. . . ." Proposing the Salzburg Festival for the work's premiere in 1942, he explained, "I do not believe in its real stage effectiveness in the ordinary sense or in a really successful premiere at a normal court theatre. That is why this extraordinary infant must be presented in a special cradle."

It was a unique opera, something never attempted before. Where in operatic history could one find a work discussing as serious and abstract a question as which should be the prime consideration, words or music? The problem was to lift the work from the level of an aesthetic historical discussion to a human psychological plane. In addition to spirited conversation, a range of emotions and an interaction of characters were required to breathe life into this "theoretical comedy." The choice of Paris in 1775, scene of the historic Piccinni-Gluck controversy, gave the work a basic realism.

The action takes place on the birthday of the young widowed Countess Madeleine, who is to be entertained by her guests. She is courted by the poet Olivier and the musician Flamand. The three main characters are surrounded by figures from the theatrical and musical world: the actress Clairon, a historical figure; the count, Madeleine's brother, an enthusiastic amateur actor and ironic philosopher who is infatuated with Clairon; La Roche, the director, to whose command and will the arts are subjugated; a pair of Italian singers representing *bel canto;* a young ballet dancer; the tragicomic prompter, who can no longer distinguish reality from fantasy or night from day; finally, the countess' eight servants who comment mockingly on the philosophical discussion and the transpiring affairs of the heart.

The characters and their moves cleverly convey the double meaning. Olivier's sonnet addressed to the countess (actually a poem by Pierre Ronsard written in 1578) is set to music by Flamand; it becomes the symbol of word and music unified. The countess is enchanted by sonnet and song. She is deeply moved by the attention of her admirers but to her consternation, through their combined effort, they themselves merge into an inseparable entity; she can no longer think of one without the other. The obvious solution is that they compose an opera. La Roche encourages their collaboration. The count suggests the subject: why don't they compose the events of this day?

Poet and musician appeal to the countess to determine the opera's ending. As their muse and the woman they both love, she is to answer the aesthetic and human question: words or music, poet or musician? The countess debates their merits in her final monologue, but she cannot reach a decision. With a teasing smile she leaves the stage to dine alone. For Strauss had decided that this "sketch about artistic questions" should not conclude with "a happy end, rather everything left in suspension . . . also the personal relationships of the couples: whether the count marries the actress, whether the countess decides for the poet or the musician or neither one of them. In short: a big question mark!"

The inconclusive ending is totally satisfactory. A wealth of opinion has been voiced within a charmingly conceived two-and-a-half-hour conversation piece. Even the characters, essentially stereotypes invented to project ideas, exude life and invite sympathy. They are concerned with ever timely questions about the arts. The lovely countess is caught in a rather delightful dilemma. Her "passionate poet" with the "powerful mind" and musician with the "great spirit and beautiful eyes" are friendly enemies until the forthright director subdues them with his verdict that their works are dead paper unless he produces them. The count who disdains opera is cool and ironic except in the matter of Clairon. He pursues the actress who plays her role with finesse whether in the theatre or on life's complex stage. The dancer and Italian singers entertain, enlivening the controversy by provoking additional darts and daggers. The count suggests that where the dance is concerned, music is only an accessory. Flamand retorts that without music it would not occur to anyone even to lift a leg. The countess professes her admiration for the cheerful Couperin. She believes Rameau to possess genius, but considers his behavior ill-mannered and crude. Flamand favors Gluck—the prophetic successor to the great Corneille. La Roche, partial to the old Italian school, admires Piccinni, "who knows his craft—both rich and poor understand it; it entertains and delights even the man in the street."

In the brilliant "laugh ensemble" and the subsequent "dispute ensemble" all ridicule the director and his flamboyant fantastic productions. His grandiose and grotesque effects submerge and destroy both word and music. Thunder machines instead of an

orchestra! Scenery instead of actors! But La Roche defends himself. What do you youngsters know of my troubles, he angrily
demands. Like them he despises the "tawdry farces" in which the
public takes such pleasure. But where are the works that speak
to the heart of the people?

> Only pale aesthetes stare at me;
> they ridicule the old and create nothing new!

He urges Flamand and Olivier to create the works he seeks. Without men like him, the discoverer of talents, where would the
theatre be?

The countess is the gentle, inspiring muse, but La Roche is the
active force behind her. She enflames and encourages yet hesi-
tates; he speaks with determination, knowledge and experience.
While in all the characters there is a little bit of Strauss, he is
most emphatically—and humorously—present in La Roche. Strauss,
too, in his youth, was guilty of overpowering voices with orchestral
effects, surpassing even Wagner. Then he pruned the orchestra,
searched for new modes of expression to equalize word and music.
He abhorred the fashionable vulgar Viennese operettas of Johann
Strauss, Lehár and their followers that spoil and cater to the
taste of the public.

While he leaves the impossible choice between word and music
to the countess, his ultimate advice is given by La Roche:

> Respect the dignity of my stage!
> My aims are sound,
> merits indelible!
> I fight for the beauty
> and the noble dignity of the theatre,
> and I will live on
> in the annals of its history!

In this last work, Strauss achieved the delicate balance between
music and word, orchestra and singer. A chamber ensemble is
used with only a few appropriate, controlled, full orchestral outbursts. The dialogue sparkles with wit and intellect; accompanied,

followed and elucidated by the lofty, restrained and discreet score, it creates an atmosphere of warmth, humor and sympathy. The opera shimmers with a deep, steady glow and an unexpectedly engaging simplicity. Strauss rated *Capriccio* highly with justification. When after its completion Krauss inquired whether he should start thinking about a new text, Strauss, now seventy-six, replied, "Do you really believe that after *Capriccio* . . . something still better or at least equally good can follow? Is not this . . . the best ending to my theatrical works? I can leave only one testament!"

An outdoor opera performance at Rome's Baths of Caracalla. *Italian State Tourist Office*

Mascagni's *Cavalleria rusticana* at Verona's amphitheatre. *Italian Cultural Institute*

Milan's La Scala Opera. *Italian State Tourist Office*

The interior of the San Carlo Opera in Naples. *Italian State Tourist Office*

Grace Bumbry as Lady Macbeth in the Salzburg Festival production of Verdi's *Macbeth. Austrian National Tourist Office*

Alfredo Casella (1883–1947). *Italian Cultural Institute*

Ildebrando Pizzetti (1880–1968). *Italian Cultural Institute*

Ottorino Respighi (1879–1936). *Italian Cultural Institute*

Clemens Krauss (1893–1954). *Austrian National Library Picture Archive, Vienna*

Scene from Strauss' *Capriccio:* The principal characters discuss the importance of words and music. *Hamburg State Opera*

A bust of Jean Philippe Rameau (1683–1764) and a plaque honoring the composer. *French Cultural Services*

Cavalli's house on the Grand Canal in Venice. *Victoria & Albert Museum*

Scene from the Glyndebourne Festival production of Cavalli's *Ormindo. The American Record Guide*

Ormindo (John Wakefield) and his friend Armide (Peter-Christoph Runge) discover that they both love Queen Erisbe; Nerillo (Isabel Garcisanz), Armide's page, overhears their conversation, in the Glyndebourne Festival production of Cavalli's *Ormindo. The American Record Guide*

Erice (Hugues Cuenod), the old nurse, in the Glyndebourne Festival production of Cavalli's *Ormindo. The American Record Guide*

Scene from the Salzburg Festival production of Mozart's *Nozze di Figaro*. *Austrian National Tourist Office*

Scene from the Salzburg Festival production of Mozart's *Zauberflöte*. *Austrian National Tourist Office*

Scene from Mozart's *Don Giovanni* at Bonn's City Theatre. *German Information Center*

Scene from Beethoven's *Fidelio* in a drawing by Moritz von Schwind. *German Information Center*

Rita Gorr in the title role of Cherubini's *Médée* at the Paris Opéra. *French Cultural Services*

Scene from Cherubini's *Médée* at the Paris Opéra. *French Cultural Services*

Scene from Act II of Spontini's *Vestale* at Milan's La Scala Opera. *Opera, London*

Maria Meneghini Callas in the title role and Franco Corelli as Licinio in the final scene of Spontini's *Vestale* at Milan's La Scala Opera. *Opera, London*

Carl Maria von Weber (1786–1826). *German Information Center*

Part Two
A Look at the Composer

VENETIAN PIONEER

THE WORLD OF OPERA HAS RECENTLY REDISCOVERED ONE OF ITS
founders who reached the peak of his career in Venice more than
three hundred years ago. Opera was flourishing, having been
born as a performing art form about fifty years before in Florence.
Six theatres capable of producing opera were active in Venice
and in 1651 no fewer than five different works by one composer
were being performed simultaneously. Their prolific and esteemed
creator was Francesco Cavalli. Together with Claudio Monteverdi he ranked as the leading opera composer of the period.

The two composers have been evaluated as analogous to
Wagner and Strauss in modern times. Monteverdi, the innovator,
probably was the greater genius. Cavalli was the more brilliant
musico-theatrical personality, who surpassed Monteverdi in further developing and perfecting the operatic form. He enriched the
Venetian stage with such a wealth and variety of outstanding
music dramas that he is recognized not only as the founder of
Venetian opera but also as the lagoon city's most significant
opera composer.

Pietro Francesco Caletti-Bruni was born in 1602 at Crema, an
attractive small town in Lombardy, about forty miles southeast of
Milan. Famed for its resistance to Frederick Barbarossa, Crema
was under the sovereignty of Venice for about three centuries,
until the fall of the republic in 1797. Francesco's father, Gian
Battista Caletti-Bruni, a madrigal composer, served as director of
the Crema cathedral choir for forty years. The boy received his
first musical instruction from his father and sang in the church
choir. When a wealthy Venetian nobleman, Federigò Cavalli, then

the city administrator of Crema, offered to take Francesco to be educated in Venice, the father, who had a large family to support, was delighted and grateful. The boy eventually assumed the name of his benefactor. Thus, in 1617, Francesco came to Venice, where he began his career as a chorister at San Marco's, under the tutelage of Monteverdi, the *maestro di cappella* at the cathedral. Ten years later, the church listed Francesco as a tenor; in 1640, his name appeared—for the first time as Cavalli—as organist at the second organ. In 1665, he was promoted to organist at the first organ, and ultimately, in 1668, he was appointed *maestro di cappella*.

This is the record of Cavalli's official career. But his finest accomplishment and lasting achievement extended far beyond his service in the church. In his creative work, he chose to devote himself primarily to the composition of music drama.

Venice's first opera house, the Teatro San Cassiano, opened in 1637 with Francesco Manelli's *Andromeda*. Two years later Cavalli's first opera, *Le nozze di Teti e di Peleo*, was produced. It is also the first Venetian opera that has been preserved. None of Manelli's, Benedetto Ferrari's or Francesco Sacrati's works are known, and only two of Monteverdi's Venetian operas are extant. In the thirty years that followed, Cavalli composed forty-one operas which continuously kept one or more of Venice's theatres occupied. The musical content of his work was mostly responsible for the rapid dissemination of Venetian opera, not only in Italy but in other countries as well. Cavalli's style was readily adopted by his colleagues and followers. His popularity persisted until the end of the century in spite of the rise of new and younger composers.

The subject matter of the *dramma per musica* of the early sixteen hundreds, as presented to an elite audience of nobles and artists in Florence, had been drawn from classical mythology. Because of their glorification of the Greek gods, these Renaissance works were vigorously opposed by the church. Gradually, as they were performed before a wider and more mixed audience, only superficial resemblances to antiquity remained. Local and modern references were substituted. In Venetian opera, episodes from Greek and Roman history replaced mythology. The hero's name was still derived from Homer or Pindar, but his character reflected the Renaissance or contemporary Italian. His circumstances depicted the intrigues of the Borgias rather than the heroic drama and adventures of the *Iliad* and *Odyssey*. The Venetian public began to demand more frequent changes of scene and eventually more characters and comedy. Thus disguises, festivities, scenes of gallantry and war, and strange adventures were commonly included. Most of the action was carried by sympathetic secondary characters such as nurses, loyal servants, braggart soldiers and, ultimately, buffoons. There were few "good" characters. Noble women of honor might sacrifice themselves for their husbands in distress, but they attained their goals through devious or corruptive means.

Opera's early protagonists, Jacopo Peri and Giulio Caccini, had envisioned the new musical form as a union of poetry and music. Monteverdi pursued this idea by incorporating vocal and instrumental selections, linking them by dialogue, or recitative. In his later works, he adopted a more unified dramatic structure, eliminating as much as possible the earlier self-contained pieces. This was the *dramma per musica* that Cavalli inherited from his teacher and friend Monteverdi and shaped into the form which he first named opera.

Cavalli embraced the concepts of the *nuove musiche*, abandoning polyphony for monody. He was able to achieve the desired musical impact by the simplest means, using apparently common motives based on triads. His phrases were short and precise, simple and clear. He excelled in attaining striking effects—elegiac, grave and comic. His harmonies were penetrating and profound when demanded by the intensity of feeling. His recitative assumed an *arioso*-like character, in order to avoid the strong contrast between ordinary dialogue and dramatic or lyrical sections. Thus he passed gracefully and without harshness from recitative to melody. Adagios and allegros were sometimes juxtaposed as by the later Handel.

Cavalli used choruses sparingly. Self-contained simple songs with variations in several stanzas, described as arias, appeared in isolated cases. Instrumental passages were confined to the beginning of an act, changes of scenes, processions, or perhaps to emphasize a crucial point in the action. Cavalli's first opera contained a *sinfonia,* entitled *"Concilio infernale,"* which in only thirteen measures depicted the powers of darkness. In later operas he developed instrumental movements more elaborately. In addition to Monteverdi's bold harmonies, Cavalli effectively employed chromatic inflections to portray pathetic expression. He skillfully treated the song form called the *lamento,* a melody chanted over a recurring bass motive, or *basso ostinato,* customarily placed at the end of Venetian opera.

In contrast to Monteverdi, who deliberately and ponderously sought the proper expression, Cavalli was a spontaneous and energetic worker, in his animation and haste sometimes even careless, as indicated by his sketchy scores of which twenty-eight have been preserved in Venice's Marciana Library. His schooling under Monteverdi is undeniably evident, but so is his own originality and determination. Cavalli composed from the point of view that in opera the drama should prevail, receiving light and warmth from the music. Although he was disposed toward the severer and nobler forms of composition, he possessed the rare gift of adapting his work to the demands of his Venetian audiences without sacrificing the integrity and refinement of his art. His music was always alive and expressive, charming his public at the various Venetian theatres.

Cavalli preferred certain good librettists of the period, such as Giovanni Faustini, Niccolò Minato and Giovanni Francesco Busenello, one of the great dramatists of the time, who had written the text for Monteverdi's *Incoronazione di Poppea.* Cavalli had a good instinct for powerful dramatic situations. The plot usually was simple. His characterizations, particularly of women, were individualistic and compelling, not because they, as personages, were significant, but because they received stature through Cavalli's musical and dramatic resourcefulness.

Ormindo, one of Cavalli's finest early works, was first produced in 1644 at the Teatro San Cassiano. Set to a libretto by Faustini, it relates the story of Ormindo who falls in love with Erisbe, the beautiful young wife of the tyrant Hariadeno. Ormindo and Erisbe escape together but are caught and thrown into prison. They are brought a chalice containing a poisoned drink with the command that they must die. Ormindo pleads for Erisbe's life, but she, not wishing to live without him, takes the cup, drinks and dies. Ormindo follows her in death. The action culminates in a delightful surprise ending.

This work is particularly noteworthy for its exquisite and eloquent duet, a long and varied selection. It takes place in the prison scene where Erisbe sings a solemn farewell while Ormindo agitatedly intones his lamentation. Gradually he transcends his mournful chant with noble resignation. In the overture, *fermata* motives create tension, broken by an exciting turbulent section. In the vocal solos, there are indications of Cavalli's increasingly complex formations: the main theme is appended by a coloratura part, followed by a development of new motives, without a return to the original theme.

Another notable Cavalli score is *Ciro*, first performed in 1654 at the Teatro San Giovanni e San Paolo. It contains skillful vocal parts and some exceptionally good writing for chorus. This time Cavalli ignored the weakness of the Venetian stage choirs which he usually took into consideration. The prologue of *Ciro* features an interesting theatrical device, anticipating Goethe's *Faust*. It consists of a symbolic discussion of the ensuing drama. Poetry, music, painting and architecture personified are about to complete a new music drama. Curiosity joins them, posing all kinds of questions. The participants relate what they have contributed to the work and in the course of this conversation finish setting the stage before the audience.

Giasone, first performed at San Cassiano in 1649, is probably Cavalli's most famous work. Its recitatives are impressive. Cavalli most successfully used a chromatic progression for Isifile's wailing cry. *Egisto*, composed in 1643 for San Cassiano, also contains many remarkable passages. It bears the distinction of having been performed in Paris in 1646 by a visiting Italian company.

Cavalli, who spent almost his entire life in the service of San Marco, rarely left the city. In 1653, he visited Milan for the premiere of his *Orione* at the Teatro Regio. The following year a journey of longer duration took him to Innsbruck for the ceremonies attending Queen Christina of Sweden's conversion to Catholicism.

The great undertaking of his life began in June, 1660. King Louis XIV of France was to be married to the Spanish Infanta Maria Theresia. The Italian architect Gasparo Vigarani was building a theatre in the Tuileries, and the French emissary, during a full meeting of the Venetian Senate at which the doge presided, requested the presence of Cavalli at the lavishly planned festivities. At the instigation of Cardinal Mazarin, Cavalli was being asked to compose, produce and supervise the performance of a new opera. Venice immediately offered to send along the required singers. At first Cavalli was reluctant to accept the French commission. After he had consented to the project, some of his demands were not met, and he retracted his acceptance. Finally an agreement was reached. Cavalli composed *Ercole amante* and departed for Paris. However, several obstacles hindered a prompt production of the work. There were delays in the construction of the theatre. Mazarin fell ill. To calm the court and placate the composer and the artists, it was decided to present Cavalli's *Xerse,* written for Venice six years earlier, in the Grand Gallery of the Louvre. For the French court, accustomed to opulence in life and art, *Xerse* was a tame work, in spite of a divertissement added by Lully so that the king, himself fond of ballet, and the nobles could dance between the acts. *Xerse,* which was sung in Italian, did not make too much of an impression in Paris. Nevertheless, it was more successful than several previous attempts at introducing Italian opera in France, including visits early in the seventeenth century by Caccini and his daughter Francesca, the famous singer; by the well-known librettist Ottavio Rinuccini; and in 1647 by the composer Luigi Rossi, who came at the invitation of Mazarin to supervise the production of one of his operas.

The death of Mazarin caused further postponements of Cavalli's new opera but in 1662, at last, *Ercole amante* was performed in Paris. Composed to suit the taste of the French, it was a colorful work, rich with choruses and arias. However, the sumptuous production with magnificent scenery and interspersed ballet eclipsed the reserve and refinement which characterized Cavalli's musical style. Disillusioned and weary he decided never to compose another opera, although he did later change his mind. Laden with gifts from the king, he returned to Venice where he was welcomed with honors.

Cavalli resumed his unpretentious life in his house on the Grand Canal. Through the years he had grown wealthy; he employed several servants who were as devoted to him as his fellow citizens, accustomed to referring to him fondly from the very beginning as *"il Cecco della Cà Cavalli."** He was a warm-hearted man who never forgot deeds of kindness. With gratitude he always remembered his patron, Federigò Cavalli, and his family. He had married a widow, Maria dei Sozumeni, who in her will thanked him for his love and fidelity. After her death in 1652, Cavalli's two sisters continued to share his quiet life. As he grew older he composed several pieces of sacred music, among them a Requiem to be sung at his own funeral service. His wish was granted after his death in 1676. He was buried in Venice in the Church of San Lorenzo, but his tomb remained unmarked. His operas are his testament, yet to be fully appreciated.

---

* Frankie from Cavalli's house.

THE ENDURING CHARM
OF PERGOLESI

SIMILAR TO SHAKESPEARE'S LOW COMEDY SCENES INTERJECTED throughout his plays to release dramatic tension, there developed in Naples in the early eighteenth century the custom of performing at first independent arias, then comic intermezzi between the acts of a serious opera.

In spite of Metastasio's textual reforms, the effect of *opera seria* had begun to wear rather thin. Endless recitatives and long-winded moralizing or philosophizing at the most passionate or crucial moments proved anti-climactic and tedious. The public rebelled against the rigid formula of opera and its complex polyphonic music, reflecting aristocratic Venetian and Roman influences. Growing restless and bored, audiences looked with eager anticipation to the relieving little comic scenes that had no connection with the serious work being performed and could easily be shifted from one opera to another. The popularity of the sparkling intermezzo, with its Neapolitan folk flavor and bright simple melodies, quickly spread northward beyond Naples and over the continent.

Although the intermezzo featured only two characters in an ingenuous comic situation, the presentation in its brevity was lively, colorful, and entertaining. With its stereotyped characters and incidents, horseplay, vigorous action and dialogue, and accompanying cheerful music, the brief farce clearly derived from the *commedia dell' arte*. Gradually it became customary to insert between the three acts of an *opera seria* one intermezzo of continuous action in two acts instead of two separate intermezzi. Thus surprised foreigners at-

48

tending an opera performance in Naples were treated to two operas in one. The general appeal and rapid expansion of the intermezzo gave rise to another operatic category, the *opera buffa*.

Of particular significance as a leader in this operatic development is Giovanni Battista Pergolesi. Although he was a follower of the Neapolitan school of Leonardo Leo, Leonardo Vinci, and Adolph Hasse, his own works are noted for originality, spontaneity, and expressiveness. Unfortunately, his life in itself was too fleeting to become very distinguished or noteworthy. Nevertheless, during his lifespan of twenty-six years, he managed to win and maintain a place for himself in the history of music as a composer of intermezzi, comic and serious operas, and sacred music. And had he composed no other work but *La serva padrona*, his fame would rest securely on this one intermezzo.

Giambattista Pergolesi was born a sickly child, the third of four sons to Francesco Andrea Pergolesi, a farmer of Jesi, near Ancona, on January 4, 1710. Probably because he was not expected to survive infancy, he was confirmed when he was seventeen months old rather than at the usual age of six years. Since Giambattista was intelligent and sensitive and exhibited an avid interest in and talent for music, his father decided to let him study. Through the aid of a nobleman, the Marchese Cardolo Maria Pianetti, Pergolesi was sent in 1726 to the Conservatorio dei Poveri de Gesù Cristo in Naples. Here the violin teacher Domenico De Matteis paid especial attention to the gifted boy's progress. His instructors in counterpoint were Gaetano Greco and Francesco Durante.

With Giambattista's entrance into the Conservatorio, his career as a composer began. He wrote first a number of sacred works, among them the oratorios *La morte di San Giuseppe* and *San Guglielmo d'Aquitania*. While his work progressed, there was frequent tragedy in his personal life. In 1726 his only remaining brother died; the following year he lost his mother. When two years later his father remarried, he sought solace from loneliness and sorrow in his compositions. In 1732 his father died; Giambattista was destined to survive him by only four years, occasionally illumined by success or darkened by failure, while his fatal illness, tuberculosis, steadily progressed.

In spite of his misfortunes, Pergolesi, in the Marchese di Villa-rosa's description, was of a cheerful, simple nature, but not prone to jesting. At the conservatory he associated with youths of good character. "He deserves the highest praise for his modesty, for his low self-esteem, for never showing deceit despite praise which especially the older masters of composition showered upon him in his earliest youth. With resignation he succumbed to his premature end," writes the Marchese.

Pergolesi's first *opera seria, Salustia,* was composed in 1731, followed in 1732 by the *buffa* in Neapolitan dialect on a text by G. Federico, *Lo frate nnammorato* (The Brother in Love), a charming tale about an adopted foundling who, after he turns out to be the long-lost brother of two sisters enamored of him, becomes the bridegroom of his formerly supposed sister. This *opera buffa* caused Napoli-Signorelli to exclaim enthusiastically, "Federico and Pergolesi united in one work give us an intimation of what the Athenian theatre might have been if a Menander and Timotheus had worked together." The local note prevails throughout *The Brother in Love.* Typical Neapolitan characters are the servants Venella and Cardella. The score contains some of Pergolesi's most vigorous and buoyant music.

After the earthquake of 1732, Pergolesi was commissioned to write a mass. Its performance was one of the few highlights in his life: it won the praise of the older admired master, Leonardo Leo, who warmly embraced the young composer. From 1732–1734 Pergolesi served as *maestro di cappella* to the Prince of Stigliano, equerry to the Viceroy of Naples. In 1733 he was appointed deputy conductor to the city of Naples. During this year he produced fewer creative works since there were no theatre performances after the earthquake, and no new works were ordered. An exception were the festivities planned for the birthday of Empress Elisabeth Christina, for which he was requested to compose an *opera seria* with an intermezzo. The resulting compositions were *Il prigionier superbo* and *La serva padrona,* both premiered on August 28, 1733.

La serva padrona was an immediate success. Federico had provided the text, a brief psychological study of a scheming young maid, sung by a soprano, who becomes the wife of her grumbling master, a bass. The action opens with Uberto complaining about the poor service: for hours he is kept waiting for his hot chocolate! Admonishing Serpina and the mute Vespone, he soon begins to threaten. Gluck's biographer, A. Bernhard Marx, believed these two arias of Uberto sufficient to ensure Pergolesi's fame.

Serpina, of course, has her own ideas. She tyrannizes and tries to move the old man; she even attempts to arouse his jealousy by having Vespone, dressed as a soldier, woo her. Serpina wins and becomes mistress. The unassuming comic situation with a minimum of plot and its touches of tenderness is strongly brought to life through its mature musical realization. The moving melodies and sprightly recitatives remain indestructibly fresh and vivid. Of Uberto's monologue in the second act, De Villars has said, "It is a recitative that one does not expect in an *opera buffa*, and which must have influenced the composer of *Don Giovanni*."

Music and text blend to perfection; singing often seems to be a simple melodic declamation of the words. Consequently, there is ample variety in the form of the arias. Donald J. Grout has described the musical style as "prevailingly major, rapid in movement, having much repetition of short motifs, a disjunct melodic line, comic effects, wide skips and an infectious gaiety and vigor of utterance, offering much to the tone and gesture of the actor."

Pergolesi's reputation was established. In 1734, the year in which he entered the service of the Duke of Maddaloni, he was invited to Rome to conduct a mass of his own for the celebration in honor of St. John of Nepomuk. Upon his return to Naples, he completed his *opera seria, Adriano in Siria,* on a libretto by Metastasio, together with the intermezzo, *Livietta e Tracollo.* Although the premiere was one of great pomp at which the Emperor Charles VI was present, the performance of *Adriano* proved a disappointment. *Livietta e Tracollo,* however, like *La serva padrona,* has its delightful moments, colored with sentiment and parody, to mention in particular a burlesque on the pompousness of serious opera.

While Neapolitans had simply voiced their disapproval or remained indifferently silent to Pergolesi's most recent work, Romans more violently exhibited their disapprobation of his next—and last—*opera seria, L'Olimpiade,* again on a Metastasio libretto. At the premiere in Rome, one spectator hurled an orange at the composer who, as was customary, accompanied his own work at the cembalo. It was suspected that the Roman school was intriguing against the rising young Neapolitan.

Discouraged and depressed, Pergolesi returned to Naples. None of his *opere serie* had been greeted with much acclaim. Only after several months of inactivity and increasingly poor health did he pull himself together to compose his final *opera buffa*, *Flaminio*, on a libretto by Federico. The story concerns the hero of the title, who had once loved a young girl while she was betrothed to another. Now that she has become a widow he seeks in disguise to win her. The spirited comic situations are in this opera somewhat overshadowed by a more serious and romantic vein. An overdose of sentiment had crept into Pergolesi's former robust style.

The time left to the ailing composer was running out. Yet he was still very young, only twenty-five. His career was just beginning. He was appointed to the important position of organist to the court of Naples. But his consumption became so acute that the doctor prescribed a more favorable climate. He moved to the Capucin Monastery at Pozzuoli, which had been founded by the ancestors of his patron, the Duke of Maddaloni. Here Pergolesi composed his last work, the hauntingly mournful *Stabat Mater*, commissioned by the Confraternity of San Luigi di Palazzo at Naples as an alternative setting of that by Alessandro Scarlatti.

On March 26, 1736, Pergolesi's life was over—the briefest and one of the most tragic in musical history. Ironically, the works by which he is most remembered—his comic operas and intermezzi—convey the joys and lighter aspects of life. Yet though they scintillate with froth and mirth, they are never heartless nor do they ring a false note. On the contrary, through all of them runs the thread of warmth and sincerity.

It was not until 1883—nearly 150 years after his death—that Jesi, the composer's birthplace, properly paid tribute to him by naming its theatre in his honor, with the words, "Giambattista Pergolesi, bold and successful reformer of opera, master of sacred music, the city's music greets you with profound emotion and reverence in this temple of the dramatic arts, where the heavenly melodies of the

Stabat Mater sounded the sorrowful farewell of a chosen soul from this earth. Poor and without comfort did you live, but during your short life fame smiled upon you, a fame which will never perish, be it then that the world return to ancient barbarism."

Since Pergolesi's death, reactions to his work have ranged from utter disparagement to unreserved praise of his achievement. Paisiello claimed that Pergolesi would never have enjoyed such high esteem had he lived longer. Actually, Pergolesi's short life is totally irrelevant to the huge success of *La serva padrona*. Soon after his death the intermezzo was revived and was given numerous performances by traveling companies all over Europe. It staunchly survived the heated 1752 controversy in Paris over the merits of the frivolous intermezzo as compared to the stately operas of Lully and Rameau.

Today, 260 years after Pergolesi's birth, his delightful little operatic *buffa* gems are still appreciated. It appears very likely that his fame will continue to endure.

THE IDEAL BELOVED

"LOVE ONLY, YES, LOVE ALONE CAN GIVE THEE A HAPPIER LIFE—O God, let me find her, her at last, who fortifies me in virtue and who may be mine in honor." This fervent prayer of Beethoven, noted in one of his sketchbooks of 1817–1818, expressed his endless search for a wife. It was a quest never to be fulfilled.

"Now you may help me find a wife," he wrote to his friend Baron von Gleichenstein on March 18, 1809. "If you find a beautiful one there in Freiburg who perhaps honors my harmonies with sighs . . . I attach myself to her in advance. But beautiful she must be. I cannot love anything not beautiful. Otherwise I should have to love myself." Considering his own appearance, it is not surprising that beauty was a prerequisite on his list of wifely virtues.

He did love a number of beautiful women and even considered marriage with a few, but his plans and proposals came to naught. Giulietta Guicciardi, Therese von Brunswick, Therese Malfatti, Bettina Brentano, and Amalie Sebald stirred his amorous feelings at various times. More importance than is properly due has been attached to these women in Beethoven's life because of the passionate and eloquent document found after his death, addressed to the unknown "Immortal Beloved." In spite of biographers' ceaseless speculation and research, the identity of the Immortal Beloved has never been proved with certainty.

Beethoven's views on women and marriage were lofty. "Sensual gratification without a union of souls is and remains bestial," he wrote in an 1817 sketchbook. "One experiences afterward no trace of a noble sentiment; on the contrary, only penitence." Because he had a violent abhorrence of dissipated women, he criticized Mo-

54

zart, whom otherwise he adored, for having used what he considered frivolous subjects such as *Don Giovanni* and *The Marriage of Figaro* for operas.

Unable to find an ideal wife in reality, he finally created her in his only opera, *Fidelio*. On his deathbed he presented the manuscript to his faithful factotum, Anton Schindler, with the words "Of all my children, this is the one that cost me the worst birth-pangs, the one that brought me the most sorrow; and for that reason it is the one most dear to me." The opera is imbued with his dream of marriage as a haven, a harmonious refuge offering companionship and mutual understanding of mind and spirit. Beethoven was able to endow his musical Galatea with all the wifely qualities he admired: kindness, devotion, tenderness, compassion, and courage bordering on heroic self-sacrifice for her husband.

Beethoven's ideal wife emerges as a classic German heroine. His favorite poets were Goethe and Schiller; but while Goethe's heroines tended to be portraits of women he had loved in real life, Beethoven invented a perfect heroine. Such Goethe characters as the chaste Iphigenie, or Werther's adored Lotte, were not enough for Beethoven. He too had loved a number of women, but none of them is recognizable in his heroine Leonore. For a long time he had searched for a suitable libretto. Offered Bouilly's *Leonore*, he immediately found it acceptable as an operatic subject, in spite of the book's weak scenes and painfully trite dialogue.

The idea of conjugal love conquering oppression and torture fired the composer. The plight of Florestan in chains, innocently and hopelessly languishing for years in a dungeon while his wan fellow prisoners hardly dare to dream of freedom—here was a real and moving situation. It demanded compassion of all humane souls in every time and age. Against unjust suffering shone the luminous figure of Leonore, unquestioning in her devotion to her husband. Now Beethoven could glorify in music the state for which he so longed: married life and love. While the great poet translated his life into his work, the life of his contemporary, the great composer, *was* his work.

Fidelio was originally known by Bouilly's title, *Leonore, or Conjugal Love*, which Beethoven much preferred. He reluctantly agreed to the change to avoid confusion with Paër's opera of the same name, and on the same book—but he called the three additional overtures to the opera "Leonore" and not "Fidelio." From the very beginning the character of Leonore inspires admiration. To gain access to the prison where her husband is being held, she has courageously assumed the disguise of a man; she does a man's work in order to carry out her intention of saving Florestan's life. She copes with the embarrassing situation of finding herself engaged to Marzelline. At times feminine fears and doubts about her strength possess her, but she does not despair:

> I am courageous; calmly
> Will I venture down.
> For a high reward,
> Love can endure high suffering.

Outraged by Pizarro's cruel scheming, Leonore sings her great aria, "*Abscheulicher! Wo eilst du hin?*" in which she likens him to a tiger. Yet she clings to her faith:

I will not hesitate, the duty of true conjugal love will strengthen me.
O you for whom I have suffered all, could I but penetrate to the place
Where malice bound you in chains,
To bring you sweet comfort!

Beethoven is most successful in portraying Leonore as she alternates between triumph and despair, first overjoyed that she may enter the dungeon, then dreading that she may have to dig her husband's grave, finally strengthening herself for the ordeal that lies ahead. Nor in her compassion does she forget the other prisoners. She begs Rocco to let them out of their cells for a while so that at least they may breathe some fresh air in the garden.

In the first scene of Act II, Florestan's vision of Leonore bears great resemblance to the final scene of Goethe's *Egmont*, the drama for which Beethoven was to write incidental music only a few years after *Fidelio*. In his opera, however, the vision has a happier outcome: the courageous Leonore soon does appear. Where Clärchen was merely the passive beloved in Egmont's life, Leonore is the heroine, triumphing in her wifely devotion.

In spite of her agitation in the dungeon, Leonore contains herself and continues to hide her true identity. With apparent calm she assists in preparing her husband's grave; she persuades Rocco to give the starving prisoner a morsel of bread and a sip of wine. The climactic moment arrives when she shields Florestan from Pizarro's dagger and then, when the villain does not desist, bravely draws a pistol. The Minister arrives; justice is finally done. To her husband's heartfelt exclamation at how much his faithful wife has suffered for him, she protests modestly, "Nothing, nothing, my Florestan!"

The brilliant choral finale Beethoven devotes to praises of Leonore: "Whoever has won a noble wife, join in our jubilation. To be one's husband's savior cannot be praised too highly." The opening words are from Schiller's *Ode to Joy;* for more than twenty years they remained so meaningful for the composer that in the Ninth Symphony he chose to set them again. A parallel might be drawn between this symphony and Goethe's *Faust,* which culminates in the famous line *Das Ewig-Weibliche zieht uns hinan* (The eternal feminine draws us upward). But Beethoven once again creates his ideal and is more specific: "Whoever has won a noble wife, join in our jubilation!"

At the time he composed the Ninth Symphony, in 1824, Beethoven still sorely missed a wife's companionship, causing him to exclaim, "The terrible fourth floor, O God, without a wife! What kind of life, and a victim of every stranger!" It was no longer likely that he would marry; he was resigned to being a lifelong seeker of ideals that only he could create. It was a last echo of the heroic Leonore—the ideal beloved.

NAPOLEON OF OPERA

SPONTINI'S TRAGEDY WAS THAT HE OUTLIVED HIS FAME. HIS LIFELONG problem, a determining factor of his decline, was his personality. Of the humblest origins, he rose to sudden fame, was accorded the highest honors, but died in obscurity.

Gasparo Luigi Pacifico Spontini was born on November 14, 1774, in the hilltown of Majolati, from whose heights on a clear day one can see in the far distance the blue Adriatic to the east and the imposing mountains of the Abruzzi to the south. The fourth son of simple peasants, he was expected like his brothers eventually to enter the priesthood under the tutelage of his uncle, prior of Santa Maria del Piano in nearby Jesi. Never given to understatement, Spontini recalled many years later, "My parents wanted me to become archbishop."

Gasparo rebelled; he was more interested in the church organ and carillon than in sacred studies. He ran away to a more sympathetic uncle, a musician, and finally received his parents' permission to obtain musical instruction. Local lessons were followed by admission to the conservatory at Naples where at the age of seventeen he was studying counterpoint under Nicolo Sala and later under his successor Giacomo Tritto.

Spontini's small sacred compositions were soon performed in and around Naples. But his main interest was opera. He met and favorably impressed Cimarosa, Paisiello and Piccinni. In the ensuing decade he composed about fifteen operas in the prevalent light Italian style of Cimarosa and Paisiello, dividing his time between Naples, Rome and Florence, where they were performed.

Gradually the impact of revolution and the attendant tumult

and uncertainties affected the young composer. He learned to use political coups to his advantage. Once having risen above the lower classes, he rejected them and democracy which favored them. In 1798, when the liberal-minded Cimarosa refused the offer, Spontini briefly accompanied King Ferdinand I of Naples into exile in Palermo. Ultimately, however, it was the Empire period and the image of Napoleon which most strongly influenced his personality and, consequently, the development of his music. In later years, as a conductor, he acted like Napoleon leading his troops into battle, directing his orchestra with commands such as "*Allez,*" "*En avant,*" and at the end of a rehearsal, "*Au revoir au champs de bataille!*"

It was not surprising then that Spontini turned up in Paris as a voice teacher in 1803. Before long he had antagonized his Italian and French colleagues when some of his early operas were successfully performed at the Théâtre Italien. However, he did not fare as well with new works composed for the Opéra Comique.

Spontini remained undaunted. The French capital had much to offer to an ambitious young musician. He met Cherubini, the respected composer of *Médée, Les deux journées* and *Anacréon.* Above all, he was tremendously impressed with Gluck's *Iphigénie en Aulide,* and became convinced that opera must consist of more than a facile superficial entertainment; it must probe and truly express the human soul and spirit. In this belief, in attempting fuller operatic portrayals, he could project his own dramatic personality. His acquaintance with Gluck's operas finally had the strongest impact on his mature style.

It was Spontini's good fortune that both Boieldieu and Cherubini had declined Etienne Jouy's libretto for *La Vestale,* based on material from Winckelmann's *Monumenti antichi inediti.* Several composers had considered the book a perfect opera text. When Jouy offered it to Spontini, the composer found the material for which his nature and creative ability were ideally suited. Berlioz wrote that Spontini "forgot everything, darting like an eagle on his rich prey. He shut himself up in a miserable habitation, neglected his pupils, and without care of the elementary necessities of life, worked with that feverish ardor, that quivering passion, the sure signs of the first eruption of his musical volcano."

While working on *La Vestale*, Spontini composed a one-act opera, *Milton*, also on a text by Jouy with whom he had become quite friendly. Performed as an *opera semiseria* at the Théâtre Feydeau on November 27, 1804, it was received with much acclaim. Although still cast in the conventional form of Spontini's youthful operas—arias and ensembles connected by recitatives—this composition began to show his concern with creating more serious characters and situations and carefully working out the score. Spontini dedicated *Milton* to the Empress Josephine who named him her *compositeur particulier*. His patronage at court was even more enhanced with his composition of a cantata celebrating Napoleon's victory at Austerlitz. Spontini ultimately needed imperial support to see *La Vestale* performed. Innumerable rehearsals were required, often as a result of the composer's endless rewriting. Even before the premiere, Spontini was being ridiculed for his noisy score, unusual for its day. One story making the rounds told of a physician accompanying his patient to a performance of *La Vestale*, which he had advised him to attend in order to cure his deafness. During the performance the patient suddenly called out, "Doctor, I can hear!" The doctor did not respond; the music had turned him deaf.

Berlioz, who called Spontini the "inventor of the colossal crescendo," reported that the students at the Conservatoire, the chief concentration of Spontini's opposition, had planned at the premiere to yawn and laugh during the first two acts, and put on their nightcaps and pretend to fall asleep at the end of the second act. However, on December 15, 1807, when Spontini self-confidently conducted the first performance of his opera, they were so impressed that they forgot to carry out their plans, joining instead in the public's enthusiastic reception.

Spontini's opponents further acknowledged his brilliant success when a jury consisting of Grétry, Méhul and Gossec awarded him for *La Vestale* the coveted decennial prize founded by Napoleon. At thirty-three Spontini had reached the peak of his creative power. He had continued in the tradition of the great Gluck. In Wagner's opinion: "What Gluck aimed at and adopted as the first principle of his work—namely the most complete dramatization possible of the opera cantata—Spontini accomplished as far as it was attainable." Although his recitatives were modeled on Gluck's, Spontini's melodies, quite naturally, were essentially Italian in character. His love for drama and the grandiose found stirring expression in his large powerful ensembles. His orchestration was more advanced than that of his contemporaries Boieldieu, Cherubini and Méhul. His classical subject, treated sympathetically as lyric drama, was perfectly suited to the taste of the Empire period. Expressive of his own personality, marked by pride, dignity, nobility and military bearing, Spontini's style happened also to coincide with the spirit of the time. His inspiration was ardent and forceful in his dramatic climaxes; his crescendos stunned and overwhelmed; his arias and ensembles were tuneful. But the Empire style was basically conventional and cold. Too much stateliness may turn into a pompous bore. The overall effect of Spontini's work sometimes came dangerously close to being studied and mannered rather than freely and gracefully flowing.

La Vestale enjoyed a huge success—two hundred performances were given between 1807 and 1824. Spontini inspired the respect and admiration of the upcoming generation of dramatic composers. In nineteenth-century romantic fashion Berlioz wrote of the opera's love duet, "It is Italian love, in its furious grandeur and its volcanic ardors." Spontini's German rival Weber thought the dramatic confrontation between the pontiff and the hero "astonishing." And many years later Wagner recommended for study of the tragic genre, "the two Iphigénies of Gluck and then the Vestale of Spontini." Meyerbeer and Wagner as well as other composers were influenced by Spontini, especially in constructing their grand finales.

La Vestale was followed two years later by Fernand Cortez, an opera in which Napoleon was particularly interested because it might well predispose the public in favor of his Spanish war. The libretto was again by Jouy. Like La Vestale it enjoyed a tremendous success. About this time Spontini married Céleste Erard, the daughter of a well-known piano manufacturer. Another opera, Olympie, after Voltaire, performed in 1819, did not arouse much enthusiasm.

Spontini was in his prime, lacking neither appointments nor

honors. From 1810 to 1812 he served as director of the Théâtre de l'Impératrice, formerly the Théâtre Italien, where he presented Mozart's *Don Giovanni*, which he considered the greatest operatic masterpiece. He was appointed court-composer to Louis XVIII for whose coronation in 1814 he had produced a routine festival work. In 1820, however, he decided on a major change in his career. King Frederick William III of Prussia, during several visits to Paris, had been favorably impressed by performances of *La Vestale* and *Fernand Cortez*. Negotiations had been in progress for some time when Spontini finally agreed to come to Berlin as general music director.

His contract stipulated that he produce two operas every three years, a commitment which was far too taxing for his strength and ability. Spontini was a slow and plodding composer who made innumerable revisions up to the time of performance and again afterwards. He did mount and direct magnificent and lavish productions of *La Vestale* and *Fernand Cortez*, and revised *Olympie* to a German text by E.T.A. Hoffmann, a version more sympathetically received. He composed the incidental music for *Lalla Rookh*, a *tableau vivant*, in 1821, which the following year he incorporated into an opera, *Nurmahal*, both for court occasions. A fairy opera, *Alcidor*, was presented in 1825. A new grand opera, *Agnes von Hohenstaufen*, based on German medieval history, was first produced in 1829. None of these works survived for long after their initial performances.

But Spontini's inability to produce further distinguished operas was far from being his only problem. In 1821, Weber's *Freischütz* received its premiere in Berlin, immediately afterwards gaining enormous popularity throughout Germany. Weber's success resulted in the rise of two contending factions: one consisting of a liberal, cultivated and intellectual national group rallying around Weber; the other, more conservative, around Spontini. The king continued to support Spontini who, though highly sensitive to criticism, persisted in his position as an autocrat as much as an aristocrat. Heinrich Heine, reporting on the Berlin musical scene in 1822, admired Spontini's "tall figure; the deeply set, darkly flaming eye; the black curls covering half of his furrowed brow;

the half-melancholy, half-proud line around his lips; the brooding wildness of this yellowish face on which all passions have raged and still rage; the entire head apparently belonging to a Calabrese, which nevertheless must be called beautiful and noble." The conductor Heinrich Dorn remembered Spontini from his Berlin years as a personality inspiring awe, often fear. Possessed by a Napoleonic tenacity, he knew how to overcome all obstacles when it came to producing his own operas with perfection and brilliance.

The Berlin opera was one of Europe's finest when Spontini arrived at the Prussian capital. Its efficiency and quality continued under his leadership although Spontini's opponents claimed that the secret of his success was his freedom to schedule an unlimited number of rehearsals. As a result his performances were always precise, but rigid and lacking in spontaneity; they were colorful and bold, with violent contrasts and extreme dynamics, but delicate shading and natural grace—the human elements—were missing.

Spontini's operas and performances naturally were like him. Ironically it was his character that gradually undermined his reputation. For all his noble and dignified demeanor, he was too blunt and aggressive in promoting himself. He could command admiration and respect but hardly ever affection. He was vain and arrogant. Clara Novello of the music publishing family recalled an 1837 visit with Spontini in Berlin: "His house was a gallery of portraits of himself, alternating with sonnets in his praise, busts of himself, etc., all the way to his own sort of throne room, where he sat on a raised dais in an armchair with his portraits, busts, medals and sonnets all around him."

He quarreled continuously over management details with Count Karl von Brühl, general director of the royal theatres, a gifted man of a patient and gentle nature. The press criticized and ridiculed Spontini. He had the poor judgment to answer the attacks of anonymous letter writers. When Frederick William III died in 1840, Spontini lost his best friend and last loyal supporter. Finally he even offended the new king, Frederick William IV. He was sentenced to a prison term, but pardoned by the king. The catastrophic climax came when the public in no uncertain terms expressed its strong disapproval of Spontini. At a performance of *Don Giovanni* on April 2, 1841, he was received by a hostile, shouting audience. He conducted the overture nevertheless and gave the cue for the curtain to be raised. But nothing happened. Even the theatre's personnel had conspired against him. In silence he left the podium, and soon afterwards Berlin. From time to time he visited Paris, but here too he had been replaced by Meyerbeer and Rossini. He never composed again, gradually turned deaf and lived the last years of his life, frail and defeated, in his birthplace, Majolati, where he devoted himself entirely to philanthropic endeavors.

The recipient of numerous honors in France, Germany and Italy, the once proud and acclaimed composer of *La Vestale* died in Majolati on February 24, 1851, with only his wife at his side to mourn him. He had swiftly conquered and briefly ruled an empire. But while he was still alive, it had already become a memory.

MELODY MAGICIAN

IN LOMBARDY, NOT FAR FROM COMO AND MILAN, LIES THE BEAUTI-
fully situated city of Bergamo. Between the Brembo and Serio Rivers
this mountain town of spires and cupolas rises like a fortress of the
Middle Ages. Streets are hilly; ancient ramparts afford magnificent
views. The city itself abounds in churches and chapels famed for
their beauty, antiquity, and paintings. There are a fourteenth-century palace and a fine theatre. Monuments honor a king, Victor
Emmanuel; a fighter for liberty, Garibaldi; a poet, Torquato Tasso;
and a composer, Donizetti. The composer's monument was erected
in 1897, one hundred years after his birth in Bergamo, by his devoted fellow citizens.

As a child Gaetano Donizetti already showed definite leanings toward the arts and especially music. At the age of nine, the boy
entered the small conservatory in Bergamo which was under the
direction of Simon Mayr, an able Bavarian musician and prolific
opera composer. Because unusual talent and an earnestness to pur-
sue it were so apparent in the pupil, the master was especially concerned with developing his abilities. Gaetano also exhibited dramatic talent and an active interest in the theatre and poetry. Under
the guidance of Mayr he soon excelled in contralto solo singing.
Consequently, after his tenth birthday, Mayr appointed him prepar-
atory teacher in voice and violin classes and at the same time began
to instruct him in the rudiments of harmony. Gaetano, who enjoyed
and admired Italian and German classic masters, diligently learned
to play the piano, organ, flute, and double-bass. Aside from his music he studied history, mythology, Latin, and rhetoric.

After Mayr had given him a sound basic education, he sent Doni-

65

zetti off to Bologna. In 1815, the boy began to study fugue and counterpoint with the former teacher of Rossini, Padre Mattei, at the Liceo musicale. For three years he worked there with his usual perseverance. When he returned home to Bergamo, he was well read, poetically and artistically inclined, a linguist and a Latin scholar, to say nothing of his excellent musicianship.

At home he began to compose, first a number of quartets in the style of Haydn, Mozart, and Beethoven, probably as a result of his early training with the German Mayr and his own admiration for the great composers. His stay at home, however, was not destined to endure. The elder Donizetti, himself a petty government official, decided that his son should study law. Gaetano rebelled. In turn the father demanded that his son make a living by giving music lessons.

Gaetano remained firm. He had been trained as, and was going to be, a composer. His ambition was to write for the theatre; he believed that his background had thoroughly prepared him for it. He was aware of having to compete with famed masters like Paisiello and Cimarosa and the more recently established and accepted favorite, Rossini. Nevertheless he remained determined and confident. Knowing that his father would not understand, and in order to avoid further arguments, he enlisted in the Austrian army.

Once in the army Donizetti began to compose to his heart's content. Fortunately his regiment was stationed in Venice, so that he could take part in the many musical activities of that city. There in 1818 his first opera, *Enrico, conte di Borgogna,* was performed and his reputation established. More operas followed swiftly; in 1822 *Zoraide di Granata* won him an honorable discharge from the service.

Now he was free to devote himself with all energy and imagination to composing for the theatre. Proof of his constant efforts is the fact that by 1831 he had written twenty-eight operas. None of these works showed much original or individual merit; on the contrary, they were obvious and frank imitations of Rossini's style. The master was much admired and those who emulated him shared a reflected glory.

Like the early Rossini operas, Donizetti's tragedies were shallow and superficial. Leading soloists sang brilliant arias with rippling cadenzas, arousing wild enthusiasm on the part of audiences. But it was only entertainment of the moment and left no deep or enduring impression. None of the Italians seemed as yet to have drawn upon the musico-dramatic inventiveness of the German master Gluck, who had reformed opera by breathing into it the drama of human emotion and reality. In the Italian opera of Donizetti, solos were showpieces for singers and often disconnected numbers. The composer seemed unconcerned about leaving the opera without musical development or unity. Nor were librettos based on well constructed plots. The actual words sung were often meaningless. Such ineffectiveness was representative of the poor quality of most of the words of the Italian lyric tragedies. Comedies fared somewhat better. Situations were novel and amusing and the lilting charm of their melodies preserved them.

It was not until 1831 that Donizetti produced his first mature and serious work, *Anna Bolena*. Its creation was the result of a more thoughtful and less casual process. The characters of Henry VIII and of Anne Boleyn were well defined. Introduced in Milan with Pasta and Rubini singing the leading roles, this opera caused his name to become known and spoken about outside Italy. The following year he composed one of the finest comedies of the Italian *opera buffa* repertory, *L'elisir d'amore*, which in turn was followed by a prolific outpouring of melody in 1833, consisting of *Il furioso, Parisina, Torquato Tasso, Lucrezia Borgia* (a revival of which, performed in Paris some years later, was interrupted by the objections of Victor Hugo, who claimed infringement of copyright so that the libretto had to be changed) and, in 1834, *Gemma di Vergy*.

In 1835 Donizetti made his first trip to Paris for a performance of *Marino Faliero*. This opera was unfortunately overshadowed by *I Puritani*, the masterpiece by the pale young Bellini, who was destined to die so young that same year. Donizetti's stay in the French capital was brief. Soon he was back in Naples for the premiere of his tragic *Lucia di Lammermoor*, a huge triumph that secured him the position of professor of counterpoint at the royal music school. Within the next four years he composed *Belisario, Betly, Roberto Devereux, Maria di Rudenz*, and *Gianni di Parigi*.

A memorable year was 1839 when, at the Teatro filarmonico in Milan, Donizetti met young Giuseppe Verdi. This was the beginning of a long, close friendship between the two composers, its course running somewhat parallel to that between Robert Schumann and Johannes Brahms. In both relationships the elder thought highly of the younger's gift and ability and did his utmost to publicize his *protegé*. It is an interesting coincidence also to note that the two older men, Schumann and Donizetti, died comparatively early and at nearly the same age of a similar illness.

A second journey to Paris was made by Donizetti in 1840 for the premiere at the Opéra Comique of the delightful *La Fille du régiment*, which had an enthusiastic reception but did not gain real popularity or a standing place in the repertory until it was hailed as a masterpiece in Italy and Germany. *La Favorite* as well as *Les Martyrs* received their first performances in Paris that year.

Judging from his plentiful production, one would suppose that Donizetti's preoccupation with composing was so time-consuming that his life was exclusively devoted to writing opera. It is true that he did compose with astounding speed and ease, rarely if ever making corrections. He was quick to grasp and absorb and equally agile at creation.

But his life did not consist of work only. Although success and fame had come to him easily and in his youth, he remained modest and unaffected. He became the friend of many artists and scientists and was honored by sovereigns. When he started out on his career, his mind was set on amusement as well as on composing operas. Unlike his serene and serious compatriot, contemporary, and competitor, Bellini, Donizetti lived with burning eagerness, plunging into a life of considerable dissipation. Bellini remained cool in spite of adulation bestowed upon him by beautiful women; Donizetti enjoyed himself feverishly in their midst.

Among the many Roman beauties he courted was Virginia Vasselli. Completely under the spell of her charms, he conceived an ardent passion for her and was overjoyed when she finally accepted his proposal of marriage. Donizetti idolized his wife, a sensible no less than beautiful woman. Their marriage was ideal, completely happy.

Two years passed without a cloud on the horizon. Then Italy was severely struck by cholera in 1837, and the lovely Virginia Donizetti became one of its victims.

Some say that with her died a part of Donizetti, that his great desire for amusement, capacity for happiness, and general interest in life vanished as a result of her sudden death. He was dazed by sorrow: possibly his oncoming illness was hastened by this tragedy.

Meanwhile his success and popularity had been growing. The Milan premiere of *Maria Padilla* in 1841 was another achievement. *Linda di Chamounix*, a work with touches of German influence, performed in Vienna in 1842, earned him royal honors, among them the title of *K.K. Hofkapellmeister*. Early in 1843 *Don Pasquale*, for which Donizetti had helped to write his own book and composed the four leading roles for Grisi, Mario, Tamburini, and Lablache, received deserved salvos in Paris. This was followed by a favorable reception of *Maria di Rohan* in Vienna. Within the same year Donizetti was back in Paris for *Dom Sébastien*, but where the season before the charming *buffa, Don Pasquale,* had delighted audiences, *Dom Sébastien* provoked harsh criticism and proved a sad failure.

The fiasco of this opera, in addition to the tragedy that had cruelly disrupted his ideal marriage and personal contentment, may have helped to account for the paralytic stroke he suffered in 1844. Although he was deeply engrossed with plans for projected works, *Catarina Cornaro*, performed in Naples in 1844, was destined to be his last opera.

When Donizetti began to suffer from hallucinations and other symptoms of approaching insanity, it was suggested that he return home to Bergamo for a rest. Yet even the respite offered by his lovely native city proved to be no cure for the deranged mind of the composer. It was there he died in 1848, deeply mourned by those who had known him and his music.

The talent that had burned so fiercely flickered and went out after a lifetime of fifty-one years, a production of sixty-six operas. They are his monument, a treasure of melody written with fluency and ease. An example of his rapid working habits was the final act of *La Favorite*—considered by many one of his finest—which he composed in one night, some claim in three hours. He worked out the instrumentation of the entire opera in thirty hours. At another time, he wrote *Il campanello di notte* within a week to supply a failing operatic troupe in Naples with an opera to save them from bankruptcy. The charming piece served to fill the house and saved the theatre. At the time of the premiere of *Don Pasquale* in Paris, the German poet Heine commented in one of his musical reports that "this Italian, too, is not lacking in success, his talent is great, but even greater is his fertility, with which he is second to rabbits only."

In addition to the record number of operas Donizetti produced, he had composed dramatic cantatas, church works—including a Requiem for Bellini—and various arias, canzonettas, and duets.

His talent, coupled with his poetic ability, was without doubt one of the richest in the history of modern music, yet his ability was not fully developed, perhaps as a result of inadequate instruction, or success and fame attained too easily and early in life. Thus he fell victim to every fad and fashion of the period. His works lacked style, abounding in incredible paradoxes. They were liked and marveled at for a while, but are now often underrated as monuments of a period of decay in music drama, products of a shallow direction primarily concerned with entertainment rather than artistic truths.

Robert Schumann expressed the general German contempt for Donizetti's work. He considered one aria completely "unmusical"; he regretted that in a city like Vienna, where formerly the court composer had been Mozart, it was now Donizetti. His brief comment on *La Favorite* was, "I heard only two acts. Puppet-theatre music!" and on *Torquato Tasso*, "Again I had enough of that music for years; it was altogether too bad. . . ."

What saved Donizetti was his knowledge of the human voice and of instruments, which enabled him to compose fluently—if not profoundly—to satisfy and please performers and audiences. His innate sense of dramatic effect caused him to create affecting situations. His orchestra was always secondary to the voice and served merely as accompaniment. His greatest and most untroubled talent was apparent in the bubblingly light comic operas of which *L'elisir d'amore* and *Don Pasquale* are most important and best loved.

In the famous trinity of Italian opera, Bellini is known for his lyric sweetness and Rossini for his brilliant and mischievous sparkle. But it is Donizetti, the composer from Bergamo, who is remembered for his humorous and tragic characterizations and the rare creative ability of producing endlessly flowing and graceful melody.

SICILIAN ORPHEUS

"HE WANTED SO MUCH TO REMAIN ALIVE, HE HAD AN ALMOST PAS-sionate revulsion against death; he wanted to hear nothing about dying, he feared death like a child that is afraid to sleep in the dark. . . ."

Thus the poet Heinrich Heine recalls Vincenzo Bellini a few years after his untimely death in 1835. Thirty-four years before, Bellini was born in Catania, the beautiful Sicilian city lying under the dev-astating shadow of Mount Etna. The son of a music teacher and or-ganist, and the grandson of a musician, the boy grew up in a natu-rally musical environment. Under the patronage of the Duchess of Sammartino he was admitted to the Real Conservatorio di Musica at Naples, and later studied with Nicola Zingarelli. Among the youth's favorite composers ranked Haydn, Mozart, Beethoven, Per-golesi, and his contemporary, Rossini.

Once playing Pergolesi's mournful and celestial *Stabat Mater* on the harpsichord, singing the words softly with his small voice, he told his friend, Francesco Florimo: "Is it possible not to weep over this poem of sorrow?" And, as the tears ran down his cheeks, "If I could write but one melody as perfect as this, I would not mind dying young like Pergolesi!" A sadly thoughtless remark for, al-though Bellini was to write countless beautiful and "perfect" mel-odies, he was destined to live only seven years longer than Pergolesi.

His student works met with such success and enthusiasm that he was commissioned to write an opera for the San Carlo Theatre at Naples. Performed in 1826, the opera *Bianca e Fernando* was met by an unusual reception. Since the King, Francis I, was one of the audience, etiquette demanded that the public refrain from ap-

72

plause or demonstrations of disapproval. However, the king himself began to applaud and the enthusiastic audience gladly followed suit. They were delighted, as they had formerly been with his love song *Fenesta ca lucive* and his aria *Dolente immagine di figlia mia*.

One success followed another. The famous impresario Domenico Barbaja invited Bellini to Milan. Here in six months he completed *Il pirata*, which was acclaimed at La Scala.

The adulation bestowed on him after his success, especially by the beautiful women of Milan, did nothing to disturb his quiet nature. La Scala demanded more works but in spite of all pressure he remained serene. Instead of acquiescing to the demands, he decided to perfect his earlier opera, *Bianca e Fernando*, which inaugurated the Carlo Felice Theatre at Genoa.

In 1829 he returned to please the Milanese with *La straniera*. This was followed by two operas which revealed his maturing individuality: *Zaira*, composed for Parma, and *I Capuleti e i Montecchi*, written for Venice.

The pastel enchantment of Lake Como—and love for Giuditta Turina—inspired Bellini in 1831. During this year he created the fully mature melodramatic masterpieces, *La sonnambula* and *Norma*, whose dramatic heights suggest Rossini's powerful *William Tell*, which had been produced two years earlier in Paris.

In *Norma* we find Bellini's sincerity, his broad sentiment. Lacking the versatility of Rossini, he never ventured into the field of comedy. Rossini claims brilliance—bursting with vitality; Bellini, lyricism imbued with solemnity. His output is smaller—deliberate, serious, meditative—almost entirely the result of inspiration, yet he never let his intellect curb his emotions in his musical work.

It was not given to Bellini to break the traditional restricting conventionalities of his time. But though his gentle, pensive soul lacked the revolutionary force, he did much to extend the boundaries. On the whole, the German romantic school represented by Robert Schumann and Felix Mendelssohn was not favorably disposed toward Bellini and the Italian style, considering it soft and weak. On the other hand, their opposing force, Richard Wagner, who struggled violently against Italian melodrama in his efforts to create a German national opera, singled out *Norma* to open the

1837 opera season at Riga. "Bellini is one of my predilections," he declared, "his music is all heart, intimately connected with the words. The music I abhor is the vague and inconclusive kind which neglects poetry and the situation." The care in construction and dramatic progression in the finale of Wagner's *Tristan und Isolde* is not totally unrelated to the final "love death" of Norma and Pollione.

Bellini and Frédéric Chopin became friendly to a degree where they exchanged and compared compositions and, according to Schumann, may thus have influenced each other. Sunny Italian echoes may be apparent in Chopin; but the Pole's brilliance hardly entered Bellini's essentially lyric realm.

Norma—a lyric tragedy—had its premiere at La Scala on December 6, 1831. The libretto is by Giuseppe Felice Romani, based on a drama by Alexandre Soumet. He and Louis Belmontet were the successful collaborators of the tragedy, *Une Fête de Néron*, performed at the Odéon in Paris in 1829.

When Bellini was asked by an admiring Parisian lady which of his operas he preferred, he claimed to have no preference; yet at the query which one he would save were he out at sea and shipwrecked, he exclaimed, "I would leave all the rest and try to save *Norma!*"

After the new production of *Beatrice di Tenda* at Venice in 1833, Bellini finally accepted insistent invitations to visit London and Paris. He loved "to roam all alone along the wide streets [of London] and on the banks of the misty Thames and in the quiet parks which are so beautiful in spring." Enthused about the performance of *Sonnambula* in which Maria Malibran was singing at the Drury Lane Theatre the evening of his arrival, he wrote to Florimo, "The first to come to greet me was Malibran who, throwing her arms around my neck in great exultation of happiness, sang those first four notes of mine: *Ah, m'abbraccia. . . .* She could say no more; words failed her as they failed me."

From London he continued on to Paris, where he was to compose his final triumph, *I Puritani*. Paris adored him—aristocracy and populace alike. On behalf of King Louis Philippe, Rossini presented him with the Legion of Honor. He could hardly remain aloof from the social life of Paris. Heine, who also mentions that his French was worse than poor, describes him as a tall slender figure, with a face of even features, "rather long, pale-rosy; light blond, almost golden hair combed into small curls; high, very high noble forehead; straight nose; pale blue eyes; beautifully shaped mouth; round chin. His features contained something vague, lacking character. . . ." An "expression of pain substituted in Bellini's face for the missing spirit; but it was pain without depth; it flickered without poesy in his eyes; it palpitated without passion about the lips of the young man." After knowing him longer, Heine "felt some affection for him. It originated as I noticed that his character was noble and good throughout. His soul surely remained pure and untainted from all ugly associations. Neither did he lack the harmless good nature—childishness—that we never miss in genial persons, even though they do not exhibit it to everyone. . . . I shall never forget him! . . ."

A bust of Bellini executed by Dantan in 1835 seems to confirm Heine's description.

Bellini's visit to Paris was destined to be his last journey. Overworked, he succumbed to an attack of dysentery and died in 1835 —at the age of thirty-four—in Puteaux, near Paris.

Rossini asked that his heart be preserved; Chopin was present to place his body on the bier. Bellini was buried at Père Lachaise, but in 1876 his remains were conveyed to his native Catania—into the Cathedral where his small fingers had played the organ. His Sicilian compatriots erected him an impressive monument in Catania (by Monteverde) in 1882, inscribed: *A Vincenzo Bellini—La Patria.*

ROSSINI'S FRENCH OPERETTA

IT HAS BEEN SAID THAT THE PROFOUNDEST EMOTION ROSSINI EVER EX-experienced was love and adoration for his mother. Early in 1827 she died in Bologna while Rossini's *Moïse* was in rehearsal in Paris. The spectacular success of this opera hardly mitigated the composer's great sorrow. Two of the singers who participated in the premiere on March 28th related that Rossini, when taking his curtain call after the opera's initial triumph, murmured sadly to himself, "Ah, but she is dead!"

For some time Rossini, then in his mid-thirties and prematurely middle-aged, had been considering giving up his career as an operatic composer. By July, 1827, he had firmly resolved "to retire home from everything in 1830," hoping to enjoy the life of a gentleman. Deliberation over ultimately renouncing operatic composition and the grief sustained by his mother's death probably caused his unusually long delay before he resumed composing. Perhaps this serious, reflective and sorrowful period of his life also decided him to turn—quite unpredictably, possibly as a release—to the composition of his first comic subject in ten years.

No less a librettist than Eugène Scribe was pressed into service to provide the text. It was the dreary task of transforming a one-act vaudeville, written by Scribe and Charles-Gaspard Delestre-Poirson in 1817, into a two-act opera text, simultaneously incorporating several salvaged numbers from *Il viaggio a Reims*, an earlier opera of Rossini's which he had withdrawn after a few performances. The French tenor Adolphe Nourrit, who on previous occasions had furnished invaluable advice to Rossini concerning French singing, was again consulted on musical details. Thus a workable libretto for *Le Comte Ory* was fashioned; Rossini wrote the music in about a month's time.

The story is based on an old Picardy legend about the crusades, originally narrated by Pierre-Antoine de La Place in 1785. Count Ory is a medieval counterpart of Don Juan. Disguised as a hermit seeking to further his amorous adventures he gains entrance to the Countess Adèle de Formoutiers, whose brother together with all the other men of the region is away on a crusade. Unsuccessful, Ory and his companions now dress up as nuns and arrive at the castle where Adèle and the other lonely women are trying to console one another. At the crucial moment the brothers and husbands return; the indignant Adèle relents, decides to forgive Ory, and smuggles him and his friends out of a side door.

Although the plot is slight, the individual situations are amusing and Rossini's musical wit and resourcefulness render them utterly beguiling. This work, the last example of his irrepressible comic exuberance and energy, is handled with such style and grace that the score emerges as one of Rossini's most elegant, delicate and piquant. In the second act Rossini used a theme from Beethoven's Eighth Symphony. His interest in Beethoven is corroborated by the fact that at this time he was studying the Beethoven symphonies with the conductor François Antoine Habeneck.

The premiere of *Le Comte Ory* took place at the Opéra on August 20, 1828, with Nourrit singing the title role. The opera pleased both critics and public, although Adolphe Adam at a later date suggested that audiences did not really appreciate the work until after many performances. It may well be that true connoisseurs—among them Hector Berlioz—were more perceptive to its subtler musical beauties and inclined to judge it a masterpiece, while the general public merely accepted the opera as another of Rossini's engaging comic works.

Le Comte Ory never fared as happily in Italy as in France and probably with good reason. Rossini was no longer simply the acclaimed writer of Italian operas such as the brisk, energetic, comic *Il barbiere di Siviglia* or *L'Italiana in Algeri*. The days when he had started in Paris as the director of the Théâtre Italien in 1824 were past. His goal had been to compose French opera and all his efforts were concentrated in that direction. He studied French and, according to Saint-Saëns' judgment some years later, Rossini's settings were far more skilled than Meyerbeer's, who like Rossini had determined to write French opera. He discarded his former stress on *fioriture* singing popular with Italian audiences but not as well suited to the French language or appreciated by the French. Thus his brilliant vocal acrobatics were replaced by refined but equally light, disarming and delightful vocal lines which took into consideration the more sophisticated French literary sense. Nourrit's intelligence and musicianship proved immensely helpful to Rossini in this respect.

But Rossini had also observed and learned from his French forerunners: André Grétry, remembered for his richness of ideas and his lively and graceful manner of expression stressing declamation in melody; and François Boieldieu, the pioneer of French light opera, in whose *Calife de Bagdad* and *Dame blanche* melodic wit and charm were expressed with a characteristic Gallic lightness and elegance. In turn, Rossini's fresh rhythms, originality in modulation and scintillating orchestration left their mark on a number of his French contemporaries and followers, including Louis Hérold whose *Zampa* produced in 1831 was a variation on the Don Juan theme, and Daniel François Auber, the gentle, reserved, modest composer of light opera, who never attended performances of his own spirited works such as *Fra Diavolo* (1830), *Le Cheval bronze* (1835) and *Le Domino noir* (1837). Auber's style emerged as a happy blend of Boieldieu and Rossini, vivacious, frothy and dashing. The development of French *opéra comique* of which Rossini had suddenly become a major influential exponent eventually culminated most effectively with the bright, dazzling operettas of Jacques Offenbach, so irresistably witty and appealing.

Little did Rossini know that *Le Comte Ory* would initiate a new operatic variation, and even today only a few connoisseurs are aware of the work's special charm and significance. After the first three performances of the opera Rossini withdrew to the country home of his friend and patron, the banker Alexandre Aguado,

where he composed one more work for the operatic stage—his last
—*Guillaume Tell*. Then, true to his word, he retired from operatic
composition to live the life of a gentleman for nearly forty years,
but without ever renouncing his active interest in the music
world, its changes and developments.

THE MAN MEYERBEER

ON THE SURFACE, THE LIFE OF GIACOMO MEYERBEER DEFIES THE TRA-
ditional image of the poor struggling artist. He was rich, his musical studies and career were encouraged, his works received performances and acclaim. His fortunate background, however, did
not guarantee immunity from religious prejudices or venomous
personal attacks. At least partially because of his comfortable circumstances, Meyerbeer became one of the most controversial
figures of nineteenth-century music.

Born Jakob Liebmann Beer in Berlin in 1791, the son of wealthy
and cultured parents, he was exposed to the arts from childhood.
The Beers were known for charitable endeavors as well as hospitality. Among artists who visited and performed at their home
were Ludwig Spohr, Carl Maria von Weber, Muzio Clementi,
Johann Dussek, Angelica Catalani and Henriette Sontag. But
young Beer also gleaned an early understanding of business and
finance and met many prominent figures outside the arts at the
Prussian court and elsewhere through his father's international
transactions as a banker. These connections were later to benefit
the composer.

Young Jakob was educated by private tutors; his musical talent
was cultivated by thorough basic instruction on the piano and in
composition. While still a child, he began to participate in musi-
cales at home; soon he made frequent public appearances. When
he decided on a career in music, his maternal grandfather provided
a considerable legacy, with the stipulation that the boy adopt his
name Meyer. Meyerbeer thus became the first composer of note
who throughout his life had no financial worries. He composed

from conviction rather than necessity without having to adapt or sacrifice his ideas or point of view. If driven by need to compose, his work might have turned out quite differently. It is possible that lack of financial security would have restricted him; on the other hand, poverty might have made him bolder.

Though Meyerbeer grew up in an atmosphere of comfort and harmony, he was well aware of the subjugation of the Jews and their struggle for emancipation. They were denied citizenship, were compelled to pay special taxes and could not own property. At the turn of the century, a Prussian commissioner of justice demanded that the Jews wear a Jewish star. Temporary freedom and equality accompanied the Napoleonic invasion and occupation of Germany. With the gradual resumption of restrictions, it is not surprising that many Jews converted to Christianity, among them Heinrich Heine, Lorenzo da Ponte, Ferdinand Hiller and Ferdinand David. Meyerbeer's diaries report of humiliations suffered because of his Judaism, but he adhered to his religion. At the age of twenty-one, after his grandfather's death, he wrote his mother:

> Yes, if poor grandfather was possessed with a faint glow of consciousness on his deathbed, it must have sweetened his last moments to know that his children would never leave the faith which was so dear to him. Therefore take from me the solemn promise that I shall always live in the religion in which he died. I do not believe that we could honor his beloved memory more through anything else.

Later in life, like his one-time friend and later adversary Heine, he defended himself against anti-Semitic indignities with a brittle, biting sarcasm, possibly acquired from the poet.

Although Meyerbeer is not known to have observed holidays, he was deeply religious. Anniversaries like birthdays and New Year's Day became occasions on which he entered prayers into his diary. On January 1, 1864, the last year of his life, he wrote:

> A new year begins today. . . . May the Almighty bless this year for all mankind, for my beloved ones and for me. May he give us all health and protect us from misfortune. . . . Amen. May God give his blessing.

His piety was closely linked to his philanthropic acts. His naive efforts to accomplish a daily good deed dispute Heine's later accusations charging Meyerbeer with intrigues and miserliness. Like his mother, he often combined the fulfillment of a wish with the vow of a good deed. A diary entry dated May 8, 1848, is typical:

> An eight-year-old beggar-boy approached me almost every day. . . . While my daughter Caecilie was sick in Venice, I had vowed that if Heaven restored her health, I would pay for the education of a poor child. For this I have now chosen this little one, and beginning tomorrow he will be placed in a boarding school . . . for which I shall pay, and where he will be fed, raised and taught a trade. . . .

For an intelligent, well-educated and talented youth like Meyerbeer, France possessed a doubly magnetic attraction. His reaction to Napoleon was no doubt similar to Heine's enthusiasm:

> His image will never fade from my memory. I can still see him on his horse, with his eternal eyes in his marble-like face, gazing down with the silence of destiny on the guards marching by. . . .

Symbolizing the ideals of liberty, equality and fraternity, Paris beckoned brightly as a haven from discrimination and as the obvious fertile ground for artistic opportunity and exposure. "You have known for years," he wrote his father from Vienna in 1814, "that I consider Paris the first and most important place for my musico-dramatic education; you know of my passionate preference for the French operatic stage and know how I long to go there." Many years later, in 1846, after Meyerbeer had tasted bitterness as well as success in Paris, he could still maintain, *"Dans tous les cas je travaillerai pour la France."*

But the road to Paris was destined to be long and circuitous. After having completed his formal musical education in Darmstadt with Abbé Vogler, Meyerbeer heard Hummel play in Vienna and decided that pianistically he was far from ready; further, to really study operatic composition, Salieri advised, he must first go to Italy.

Meyerbeer's visit to Italy, begun in 1816, extended into an

eight-year stay. Imitation of the popular Italian operatic idiom was easy for a man of his ability and training; in spite of exhortations of friends like Weber to return to the German style, Jakob turned into Giacomo and earned a reputation for his Italian operas.

Yet when he finally arrived in Paris in 1826, where without much effort he could have conquered with his Italian style, he chose to go into retirement for several years. He studied French character, art and history, and observed the likes and dislikes of the public. Personal affairs, too, contributed to his temporary withdrawal from creative activity: his father's death, his marriage in 1827, the death of his two children.

When Meyerbeer finally emerged from his seclusion with his first French operas, it was quite apparent that he had shed Rossini's influence in favor of more grandiose theatre, and those who had first lamented his sacrificing serious German art for Italian frivolity now condemned him for catering to French decadence. Meyerbeer had learned that the magical Paris of freedom and unlimited possibilities was also the superficial flamboyant Paris of Louis Philippe. It was basically unmusical; its theatre level was distressingly low; and its operatic attractions of merit were primarily foreign. Bellini was dead; Donizetti's mind was shrouded with insanity; Rossini had withdrawn from composition; Wagner and Verdi were youthful beginners. This interval of uncertainty and expectancy was filled with Meyerbeer's translation of a bizarre and melodramatic period into opera—faintly disguised by historical pageantry, the exotic and the supernatural. Among his severe critics were Schumann and Spontini. Mendelssohn called his music cold and heartless. When Meyerbeer received favorable reviews, he was accused of having bribed the press.

Undoubtedly money was helpful to his career, but it did not assure the composer's peace of mind. He was constantly plagued by indecision and fear. Composing was no easy matter for him. He wrote and rewrote, dreaded reviews and made further alterations after performances. If he had been more self-confident, he might have imposed his will on Eugène Scribe, who provided him with unwieldy, often ludicrous librettos. His brother Wilhelm called him a *Schwarzseher*, an outright pessimist. For a man of his intelligence, he was incredibly superstitious. An irrational fear of the number thirteen possessed him. He would avoid important decisions and sign no contracts on Fridays; he would interrupt a journey not to arrive at his destination on a Friday. Premieres of his operas were emotional crises, probably the most shattering experiences of his life. Having written for his mother's blessing for these ordeals, he would carry her letter over his heart until the suspense was past.

Meyerbeer was a serious man who lived a retiring life devoted to his art. He suffered periodically from an intestinal ailment that worsened with age, making him irascible and eventually bringing on his death. Excessive nervous anxiety surely affected his health. His irresoluteness may have been one reason for his frequent style changes. But beyond his timorousness, he was, deep down, a thoroughly gifted and earnest musician. He possessed a vivid sense of history, a good knowledge of literature, a true feeling for the theatre and an appreciation of beauty. A keen observer, he constantly exposed himself to musical and theatrical performances and studied the trends of real life in the various social strata. Modest in his own habits, he was generous to all, and in his eagerness to be fair to everyone, assumed responsibilities he could not possibly fulfill. Those aware of his weaknesses and vulnerability could easily take advantage of him. Heine was always in financial need; during the times Meyerbeer obliged with considerable sums, the poet was full of praise for the composer and his works. When other commitments made it impossible for Meyerbeer to continue his generosity, Heine's articles and poems turned violently against him.

In 1842, Frederick William IV appointed Meyerbeer *Generalmusikdirector* to succeed Spontini. Through this position he was able to encourage and assist other composers, including Otto Nicolai—whom he named *Kapellmeister*—Félicien David, Liszt, Spohr, Heinrich Marschner and last but not least Richard Wagner whom, once before, in 1839, he had recommended to Dresden. He produced both *Rienzi* and *Der fliegende Holländer* in Berlin. Wagner, in turn, most harshly abused his benefactor, calling him a miserable music maker.

But there was praise, too, for Meyerbeer, whose style was quite his own and remained unique, though his art was eclectic and necessarily summary, containing echoes of past Italian *bel canto* and German dramatic power. Goethe thought him capable of composing a *Faust*. Verdi considered him a musical dramatist superior to Mozart. Musorgsky praised his skill in writing for the stage.

With the rise of Verdi and Wagner, Meyerbeer was quickly down-graded and dismissed. As the herald who paved their way, who preserved operatic continuity from Weber to Wagner and Rossini to Verdi, he bears significance in operatic history. As a man and as a composer, he deserves sympathy and respect.

BENVENUTO BERLIOZ

HECTOR BERLIOZ SOUGHT AND PREACHED TRUTH IN MUSIC AND IM-
bued his compositions with the truth of his own life. The theme
that connects his compositions blends autobiographical elements,
examples of his literary taste and his innovative musical characteristics. Most of his productions are major works, and motives of
early discarded attempts were successfully incorporated into
later mature compositions. These original inspirations and sketches
retained their meaning and timeliness for Berlioz. His taste was
formed early in life; he remained loyal to the favorites of his
youth, the great masters whose influence helped to broaden his
intellect and refine his discernment.

In 1821 when, barely eighteen, he arrived in Paris as a medical
student, Berlioz was a confirmed disciple of Gluck. Fortunately at
this time frequent performances of Gluck's operas as well as of
Spontini's *La Vestale* enabled him to study these works, intensi-
fying his enthusiasm. He was enchanted by the music of Weber,
his German romantic counterpart, particularly as a reformer of
opera. In 1826, when Weber passed through Paris on his way to
stage *Oberon* in London, the young Berlioz, eager to pay tribute
to him, was fated to miss him everywhere: at his teacher Jean-
François Lesueur's, at a music shop, and at the Opéra. A few
months later Weber was dead. Berlioz studied and listened to
Beethoven's music and was overwhelmed, especially by the last
works, which were derided as cacaphony and the works of a mad-
man. As a boy translating his Virgil, Berlioz had been moved to
tears by the tragic heroine Dido; now he was captivated by Juliet
and Ophelia as played on the stage by the visiting Irish actress

Harriet Smithson. His admiration for Shakespeare merged with his love for the actress who had made his heroines come alive. He pursued her with his characteristic ardor and determination until she married him some years later. He was excited and inspired by Goethe's *Faust*. How well he could understand Faust's tireless activity and endless quest and the idea that two souls were harbored within him!

Exposure to the theatre in the capital as well as actual music studies with Lesueur and at the Conservatoire library resulted in Berlioz' decision to drop his medical studies and devote himself entirely to music, in spite of opposition from his family at La Côte Saint André. Several years of study and composition in Paris and a brief stay in Italy after having won the *prix de Rome* followed. Berlioz gradually realized that in Paris success as a composer could be achieved only through the Opéra. But his concept of music drama diverged so sharply from the steadily deteriorating standards of the opera house that he was bound to encounter resistance from the forces in power, which were perfectly content to present dreary, pedestrian, conventional fare as long as paying audiences came. In his youthful idealism and enthusiasm Berlioz believed that once he had surmounted the barriers of the Opéra, he could reform the public taste with good, serious, dramatic works.

His head was full of operatic ideas. He was considering a *Hamlet* but finally settled on the rebellious bandit-hero-artist Benvenuto Cellini. Even then Berlioz' conception of dramatic music actually went far beyond the stage. While he was planning *Benvenuto Cellini,* he wrote his friend Humbert Ferrand, "Music has wings that the walls of a theatre will not allow to unfold." Opera was just one example of dramatic music. Beyond the rigidity of conventional forms were numerous other possibilities to be explored. Beethoven, at the end of his career, had only begun with his Choral Symphony. In January, 1835, Berlioz wrote Ferrand, "If I had time, I would be progressing on another work of which I am thinking . . . a symphony on a new and enlarged plan."

In the meantime Berlioz composed his *Benvenuto Cellini,* a fictitious episode in the life of the Renaissance artist. When he finally succeeded in having the opera performed in 1838, the public was puzzled. A traditional Italian melodramatic subject was being treated as an *opera semiseria* rather than an *opéra comique;* portions of the text were too naturalistic for refined Parisian ears; the overture was too long. With a connoisseur's taste, Berlioz happened to prefer the operas of Gluck, Mozart, Beethoven and Weber, which the public found incomprehensible, dull and colorless. In *Benvenuto* he tried to introduce reforms to enliven his ideal of dramatic music, hoping to make it more easily accessible. Using a loose construction, like Shakespeare or Mozart in *Don Giovanni,* he had his librettists Léon de Wailly and Jules Barbier prepare a series of disconnected scenes, highlighting dramatic conflicts whose essence could be expressed imaginatively and perceptively in musical terms. The music itself was to contain the drama; it was no longer intended to serve simply as an accompaniment.

The public did not respond to Berlioz' reasoning and musical application. *Benvenuto Cellini* failed but Berlioz, who had a reputation as a serious composer, had entered the Opéra with an "Italian" work criticizing the current Italian repertoire as well as the common French product.

In this first opera Berlioz identified strongly with the hero as artist, conscious of both his strength and weaknesses. The casting of the statue of Perseus symbolized the creation of all art through the artist's inspiration and perseverance. But like producing an opera, casting a statue was also a cooperative effort. Berlioz surely had this in mind when he called the opera *Benvenuto Cellini, or the Master-Goldsmiths of Florence.* The solitary artist is depicted struggling against the establishment, risking his life and art for love. The object of his love is Teresa, daughter of the papal treasurer. Benvenuto's rival is an inferior artist, a ludicrous figure anticipating Wagner's Beckmesser. Berlioz' cast of supporting characters includes Benvenuto's artisan friends, a cardinal representing the pope, an innkeeper, a hired assassin, hawkers, pairs of lovers, monks and strolling players. To illustrate the conflicting passions and comic aspects of the situation, Berlioz produced a vibrant score, scintillating with variety, color and rhythm. He wrote nature, religious, love and carnival music as well as guild choruses and recitatives ridiculing bad artists and pompous officials. In a lively, superbly organized and controlled score he depicted the passions and confusions of life with beauty and feeling.

Berlioz characterized his hero as passionate, tender, reflective, violent and melancholy. Benvenuto philosophizes about his destiny; his life, forfeited by murder, hangs in the balance against his art: if he finishes his Perseus by nightfall, he will be pardoned. Benvenuto must overcome the circumstances that are common to every man as well as the obstacles that are particular to the artist. Momentarily he despairs "alone with my struggle, alone with my courage," longing to escape into nature, envious of the shepherd in the mountains. But finally the intensity with which he lives and works claims him. He becomes totally absorbed in his most challenging task; when he runs short of metal he sacrifices earlier works of art to complete his masterpiece. The chorus of workmen repeats its rousing guild song as Benvenuto carves the inscription on his statue: "If anyone harms thee, I will avenge thee!"

Though box office receipts for *Benvenuto* lagged far behind what Meyerbeer's operas realized, the critics after three performances acknowledged certain merits in the work: Berlioz had opened up a new continent; with such powerful music and abundance of ideas his opera was entitled to ten first performances; *Benvenuto* clearly was a masterpiece. Berlioz best understood the shortcomings of his work. Many years later he wrote to his favorite sister Adèle, "I like better than ever that dear old *Benvenuto,* which is more vivid, more fresh, more *new*—that is its greatest disadvantage—than any of my works."

During the composition of *Benvenuto* Berlioz had complained more than once that like his hero he was "short of metal." An unexpected gift made it possible for him to reduce his assignments as a music critic and concentrate on his next dramatic work. After having conducted a concert consisting of his *Symphonie Fantastique, Harold en Italie,* and some selections from Gluck, Paganini rushed to the stage and kneeling at Berlioz' feet declared that Beethoven at last had a successor. Two days later this public tribute was followed by a note:

Beethoven being dead, only a Berlioz could reincarnate him. I who have fed on your divine compositions, worthy of a genius such as yours, feel it my duty to ask you to accept in homage the sum of 20,000 francs, which the Baron Rothschild will remit on sight of the accompanying note. Believe me always your affectionate friend.

Nicolò Paganini

In more than one sense was Berlioz the follower of Beethoven. He was now certainly the foremost orchestral composer. He did not know that before Beethoven decided on *Fidelio*, he had considered *Romeo and Juliet*, nor that the adagio of his Quartet, Opus 18, No. 1, was associated with Juliet's tomb scene. For nearly ten years Berlioz had been pondering the subject of Shakespeare's play. It was a drama designed for music, a musical condensation rather than an actual setting.

Free now for a time to devote himself to composition, Berlioz most meticulously planned and wrote his *Romeo and Juliet, Dramatic Symphony for Chorus, Solo Voices and Orchestra*. Instead of presenting disconnected scenes within the operatic format, he merged drama and symphony, in turn letting the solo voices, chorus and orchestra tell the essence of the story, again choosing only those situations suitable for music. The suggestion had come from Shakespeare himself: "Let music's rich tongue/ Unfold the imagined happiness . . ."

After an orchestral introduction, the prologue sung by a contralto and chorus tells the story of the feuding families and the tragic love of their children. Themes of sadness, revelry and love are heard. The second part depicts Romeo alone in his melancholy, then indifferent at the ball. The singing of the Capulets, as they leave the festivities, introduces an adagio, the passionate and touching love music. Instead of using words, Berlioz here preferred the richer and wider range which the orchestra permitted his musical imagination. Shakespeare had compared his lovers' talk to music: "How silver sweet sound lovers' tongues by night/ Like softest music to attending ears!" Berlioz translated the scene into pure, mellifluous sound. The somber atmosphere is broken by the light and fanciful Queen Mab scherzo, followed by a funeral march in which the Capulets sing the dirge. In the finale an instru-

mental section recapitulates earlier motives, then as in the prologue the chorus takes over as the families quarrel over the
corpses. The voice of Friar Laurence is heard—in contrast to the
contralto of the prologue singing about young love—admonishing the families and pleading for a reconciliation which they
finally accept, concluding the music drama.

The Dramatic Symphony was a novel work in every sense;
effort was required to grasp it. While Wagner somewhat later
insisted that in music drama the music must be joined to words
and staged action, Berlioz preferred to preserve music formally,
independently of stage business and text. He created the drama
within the music through inventive use of rhythm, melody, harmony and orchestration, adding words only if he deemed them
necessary or enhancing. Following the same principle employed
in the theatre, he composed discontinuous scenes, simply leaving
out those portions that did not lend themselves to imaginative,
dramatic, musical treatment.

The artistic, elite audience, including Chopin, Heine, Liszt,
Wagner, César Franck, Stephen Heller, Balzac and Théophile
Gautier, which attended the first performances of *Roméo et Juli-
ette* in November and December, 1839, welcomed the new work.
Berlioz was praised for his "unshakable will" and for not succumb-
ing to commercializing his art. The only important absentee, ill in
Nice, was Paganini to whom Berlioz had dedicated the score,
"for it owes its existence solely to him."

For many years Berlioz had hoped to visit Germany. Even at
the time of his *prix de Rome* he would have preferred a trip to
Germany, a country whose music was much more congenial to
him, where he could really study and learn about the "new
music." His first tour of Germany began in September, 1842, and
was followed by several others including stops at Vienna, Prague
and Budapest. Many years later Hanslick reported, "Whoever
heard and cheered (as I did) at the time of Berlioz' concerts in
Germany can bear witness that never was any dazzling musical
phenomenon ever greeted with such excitement and enthusiasm.
. . . His music came as a fiery meteor above our heads."

It was more than a realization of a cherished dream and the

opportunity of renewing old friendships, as with Mendelssohn and Ferdinand Hiller, or making new ones with artists such as Robert and Clara Schumann. Berlioz stepped beyond the physical and musical confines of France into Europe, for the present leaving French music behind. This break and subsequent profoundly felt experiences broadened his musical outlook and reaffirmed his beliefs. He visited Weimar, the center of the new music of Liszt and Wagner, but to the literary Berlioz also the city of Schiller and Goethe. In addition to his many stimulating cultural contacts, traveling through the German countryside reawakened his youthful fondness for *Faust*. Thus he was inspired to compose one of his finest scores, *La Damnation de Faust*. He wrote twelve scenes of the book himself, adding the eight fragments translated by Gérard de Nerval twenty years earlier, which he had set to music at that time.

"I am working strenuously," he informed his father in September, 1846, "on a large work which is nearly done and which I want to put on in Paris by the end of November. I have had to be poet and musician both, because my score, begun and pursued across country, in Bavaria, Austria, Hungary, Bohemia and Silesia, was going faster than my versifiers in Paris and I was thus compelled to do without them. It quite surprised me to be able to do so." In his *Memoirs* Berlioz mentioned where and how he had composed certain selections:

> One night, when I had lost my way in Pest, I wrote the choral refrain of the *Ronde des paysans* by the gaslight in a shop. At Prague I got up in the middle of the night to write down a melody I was afraid of forgetting, the angels' chorus in Marguerite's apotheosis. . . . At Breslau I wrote the words and music of the students' Latin song. . . . On my return to France I composed the grand trio. . . . The rest was written in Paris, but always improvised, either at my own house, or at the café, or in the Tuileries gardens, and even on a stone in the Boulevard du Temple. I did not search for ideas, I let them come, and they presented themselves in the most unforseen order. When at last the whole outline was sketched, I set to work to re-cast the whole, touch up the different parts, unite and blend them together with all the patience and pertinacity of which I am capable, and to

finish off the instrumentation, which had been only indicated here and there.

On October 19, 1846, the score was completed. Although *The Damnation of Faust* is usually described as a "concert opera," it is actually subtitled *A Dramatic Legend* and was composed according to Berlioz' principles of adapting a dramatic work to music. He aimed at being concise; the wealth and diversity of his material, grouped into four main sections, each connected by recitatives, are astonishing. The numerous tableaux, the complications of plot and character, the three solo voices and the ingenious use of choruses and orchestra are distinctly dramatic and musical without being visual. To understand the symbolic implications and philosophic nature of this work, the listener's full attention is required.

Because Berlioz shared Goethe's love of nature, pantheistic beliefs, respect for the aesthetics of Catholicism, and affirmation of moral responsibility and love as opposed to the potency of evil, he diverged only slightly from Goethe's original. Berlioz was chastized by one German critic to whom Goethe's drama was sacred for placing his Faust in Hungary at the beginning of the action so that he could include his popular Rákóczy March, written one night in Vienna. Another German critic objected to Berlioz' treatment of the students' song, asserting that German students were well mannered. Moreover, he accused Berlioz of vilifying Mephistopheles, explaining that the German devil was honest, carrying out every part of the contract with Faust. Berlioz' Mephistopheles pretended he was bringing Faust to Marguerite's prison cell, but actually conducted him into the abyss.

Such minor divergences were of no significance to Berlioz who molded the drama to suit his musical representation. He was concerned with the grand scheme of the work, its passion and philosophy. He opened the action with Faust, the philosopher, contemplating nature. Faust hears a peasant song and the call of military glory. Rejecting all power, he is, however, beset by doubts and tempted by fantasies of love. Marguerite, who represents and truly experiences the love of Faust's dreams, is ultimately destroyed by it. Tormented, Faust returns to nature, but is damned for failing to rescue Marguerite, who is saved. Berlioz mentioned the *Ciel* scene when he described the "prevailing characteristics" of his music as consisting of "passionate expression, intense ardor, rhythmical animation, and unexpected turns. When I say passionate expression, I mean an expression determined on enforcing the inner meaning of its subject, even when that subject is the contrary of passion, and when the feeling to be expressed is gentle and tender, or even profoundly calm."

For the premiere of the *Damnation* Berlioz had hired the Opéra Comique, the only hall available, for two Sunday evenings in December. The public stayed away, preferring the current lighter entertainments—Auber's *Diamants de la couronne* and Clapisson's *Gibby—la cornemuse*—to the ponderous, dramatic *Faust* of Goethe and Berlioz. "As a result the *Damnation* was performed twice to a half-empty room," lamented Berlioz, adding:

> The concert-going Parisian public, supposed to be fond of music, stayed quietly at home, caring as little about my new work as if I had been an obscure student at the Conservatoire and these two performances at the Opéra Comique were no better attended than if they had been the most wretched operas in the theatre's repertory.

Though his admirers organized a banquet in his honor and had a gold medal struck to commemorate the work, these demonstrations could not obliterate the fact that Berlioz was financially ruined. He was an outsider; both Opéra and Conservatoire were closed to him. Accustomed to abuse for his innovations and reforms, he admitted bitterly in the *Memoirs*, "Nothing in all my artistic career ever wounded me so deeply as the unexpected indifference." Having for some time considered a trip to Russia, Berlioz now turned this temporary escape into reality.

It was not until 1855, stimulated and encouraged by conversations and correspondence with Liszt and the Princess Sayn-Wittgenstein, that Berlioz once more began the composition of a music drama. He set himself an enormous literary and musical task which absorbed him for more than three years, although he was frequently interrupted by concerts, the publication of other

works, tours and illness. During this period he also suffered the
sudden death of his second wife, Marie Reccio. A belated honor
that came to him was his election to the French Academy.

With irrepressible zest and typical determination Berlioz fashioned an opera on a text of his own based on Virgil's *Aeneid,* a
subject he had cherished and nurtured within him all his life. He
chose Books Two and Four, comprising the fall of Troy, the
Trojans' arrival at Carthage, and Queen Dido's tragic love for
Aeneas.

Berlioz' music animates three main characters: Cassandra, the
prophetic, lamenting heroine of the first part; Dido, who dominates the second part in her anticipatory restlessness, love and
final despair; and the hero Aeneas, somewhat less striking in
stature, who moves through the entire music drama, unifying its
epic nature. It has been suggested that Berlioz in Aeneas' place
would have left for Italy, but ultimately would have managed to
return to Dido.

In keeping with his former procedure Berlioz dispensed with
lengthy explanatory sections and the usual operatic dialogues and
gesticulations. In April, 1856, he wrote to Liszt:

> I have started working out the main lines of the great dramatic busi-
> ness that the Princess takes so much interest in. It is beginning to
> take shape: but it's huge and therefore dangerous. I need plenty of
> peace of mind. . . .

About five weeks later he had finished the poem for the first part,
La Prise de Troie. "It will be the longest and it took me ten days
to write it," he informed the princess.

At heart Berlioz knew that it would be neither profitable nor
practical for him to write another opera, especially a large, serious
work on an antique subject that he would have trouble in getting
performed. His duties as a music critic were keeping him constantly occupied. Besides he had to overcome the psychological
resistance of creating a new major work which after many disil-
lusionments must have seemed to him utterly superfluous. While
it was merely an idea in the planning stage, the urge to discard
it recurred frequently: "I have been a dozen times on the point of

throwing everything into the fire," he explained to the princess, "and giving myself over to the contemplative life. But now I am sure not to lack the courage to reach the end. The work has got hold of me. Besides I reread your letter from time to time to spur myself on."

Toward the end of June he could report to the princess that the libretto was nearly finished:

> I grow more impassioned about the subject than I should, but I am resisting urgent appeals to attention from the music. I want to finish it all properly before I start the score. Yet last week it simply was not possible not to write the Shakespearean duet:
> In such a night as this
> When the sweet wind did gently kiss the trees . . .

Another month and he had chosen the provisional title *Les Troyens*. "Would you believe it," he wrote, "I have fallen in love, but utterly in love, with the queen of Carthage. I adore her, this beautiful Dido. . . ." In August he thanked the princess for her analysis of the libretto:

> You go so far as to credit me with the beauty of Virgil's poetry and praise me for my thefts from Shakespeare! Do not fear: I have the courage to carry on to the end: it was not necessary to try and lure me on with eulogies that I do not deserve—it is beautiful because it is Virgil: it is striking because it is Shakespeare. I know it. I am only an interloper: I have ransacked the gardens of two geniuses and cut a swathe of flowers to make a couch for music where God grant that she may not perish overcome by the fragrance.

He compared his efforts to those of Wagner, "I am for that kind of music which you yourself call 'free'—free, imperious, all-conquering. . . . Music is so powerful that in certain instances it can triumph alone. . . . To want to take music back to the old recitation of the antique chorus is surely the most incredible folly. . . ." He elaborated on his own problems of composition:

> To find the means of being expressive and truthful, without ceasing to be a musician: rather, to endow music with new means of action—

that is the problem. Another hurdle in my path is that the feelings to be expressed move me too much. That is bad. One must try to do coolly the things that are most fiery. This is what held me up so long in the *Romeo and Juliet* adagio and the finale of the reconciliation. I thought I should never see my way. Time! Time! He is the great master. . . .

In February, 1858, he was able to tell his son Louis, "I am working as hard as I can to finish my score and gradually it's getting done. At the moment I am at Dido's final monologue ('*Je vais mourir*'). I am more pleased with what I have just written than with anything I've done so far." At the end of the month the score was finished and Berlioz could say, "It no longer matters to me what happens to the work—whether it is produced or not produced. My musical and Virgilian passion has been sated."

Berlioz was not destined to see *Les Troyens* produced in its entirety. It was accepted by the Opéra but in the summer of 1863, after he had been kept on tenterhooks for three years, he took the score to the Théâtre Lyrique: "But I had to consent to letting the work be cut down to the last three acts only; they will be re-divided into five and preceded by a prologue which I have just written, the theatre being neither large enough nor rich enough to put on *The Taking of Troy.* . . ."

Before the opera was actually performed in November, it was further mutilated but the press received the work with respect and even praise. Some critics were profoundly moved and Berlioz' artistic integrity and superior ability were recognized. *Les Troyens* was given twenty-one performances with more and more cuts being made. Most of the younger musicians attended; Meyerbeer came nightly "for my pleasure and my instruction." Berlioz, too, was observed enjoying some moments of satisfaction. He might comment in a whisper, "It is beautiful," and at times wept silently.

But the public, as in the case of *Benvenuto Cellini*, was not ready for so imposing and complex a work. It was monumental in scope rather than in the performing forces required. At the *Benvenuto* premiere the audience had tittered at indelicate, realistic lines in the libretto such as "in early morn the roosters crowed." *Les Troyens* shocked Parisians with the idea that two sentries were indolently enjoying good food and women at Carthage. But these were minor objections of a public unable or unwilling to follow Berlioz's swiftly paced, vast, epic tale. It was a long, varied pageant, but subtly and tightly constructed musically and dramatically. Here Berlioz unfolded his Euripidean view of life. After the fall of Troy, Cassandra chooses death; after Aeneas' desertion Dido also commits suicide. The audience—exposed only to *Les Troyens à Carthage*—was puzzled by some of Berlioz' musical intentions. It could not grasp the point of the young sailor's plaintive song. Nor was the public, still used to conventional, set pieces such as arias, duets and choruses, ready for as effective a theme as the Trojan March, recurring in perpetual, colorful variation throughout the drama. As in *Romeo and Juliet,* a symphonic interlude, "The Royal Hunt and Storm," evoking a lovely, haunting, pastoral setting, depicted the love of Dido and Aeneas, without any stage action.

The Trojans required many hearings to be understood and appreciated. It was an all-encompassing exposition summarizing Berlioz' life-work, his conception of music drama. But such attention one could not expect of Parisians who were unused to making an effort at the opera; they wanted to be lulled and lightly entertained. They might venture to hear Offenbach at the Bouffes-Parisiens, where Parisian society was slyly and satirically mirrored in sprightly rhythms and lilting tunes. Froth and frivolity were the order of the day, more easily digestible than tragedy.

But again the connoisseurs recognized Berlioz' achievement, his progression from dramatic symphony and dramatic legend to a staged music drama of epic proportion. Donald J. Grout has described *Les Troyens* as "the most important French opera of the nineteenth century." Sir Donald Tovey called the opera, "One of the most gigantic and convincing masterpieces of music drama." Of Dido and Aeneas' love scene by the Mediterranean shore, Ernest Newman has written, "a man needs to have lived long and to have suffered much to compass a beauty so wistful and so touched with all the humanities." Their Shakespearean love duet reminded Newman of a wonderful passage in *Romeo and Juliet* where "Berlioz had sounded this note of a love so vast that the heart becomes almost still under the pressure of it; but here the note is at once more prolonged and more profound." It was the love of Berlioz' dreams—momentarily personified by the Estelle of his adolescence and the young, beautiful Harriet Smithson—but never truly found. He expressed it in his music written for Dido.

Upon the completion of *Les Troyens* Princess Sayn-Wittgenstein suggested that Berlioz compose an *Antony and Cleopatra*. He pondered this idea as well as others, including a commission from the director of the Baden-Baden theatre to write an opera on the Thirty Years' War. To the princess he explained how he felt about Cleopatra in November, 1859, "I think I would make an attractive creature out of that torpedo. It would be different from anything I have done." He finally did produce something quite different. Rejecting the Thirty Years' War, he substituted a choice of his own, *Much Ado about Nothing*, a comedy that he had considered in 1833. He had even sketched the situations in the Shakespeare play suitable for musical treatment. After some revisions of the original plan and versification, he was ready for its composition. In a happy, creative mood he wrote his son, "I can scarcely keep up with the music of my little opera so rapidly do the pieces come to me. Each wants precedence and sometimes I begin a fresh one before the previous is done."

The texture of the two-act opera is light and sparkling, the tone coquettish, mocking and gently melancholy. A series of disconnected brief episodes joined by spoken dialogue tells the story. In amusing and reflective scenes the reluctant lovers Beatrice and Benedict, both proud and cautious, are tricked by Hero and Claudio to confess their love for each other. The grotesquely comic conductor Somarone, a creation of Berlioz,' adds some broadly funny moments. An exquisite, touching simplicity and irresistible charm emanate from this work. It is a gem in its freshness and perfection of arias and ensembles. Gounod was overwhelmed by the nocturne concluding the first act:

Here is all that the silence of night and the serenity of nature may do to imbue the soul with tenderness and reverie. The orchestra utters divine murmurings that find a place in this admirable landscape without taking anything away from the delicious cantilena of the voices: it is absolutely beautiful and perfect; it is immortal like the sweetest and deepest things ever written by the great masters.

Having completed *Béatrice et Bénédict*, Berlioz informed his son, "I have done now everything I had to do." His efforts at music drama had begun with a reformed Italian opera, climaxed with a heroic classical tragedy, and concluded with a true *opéra comique*. Berlioz decided that this was to be his last work. He had expressed himself fully as a musician and dramatist. But he was also weary, disillusioned, ill and alone. Most of the audiences he had wanted to reach through his free, pure music had failed to understand him. To divert himself from the dreariness of much of his life and the difficulties of having *Les Troyens* performed, he had turned once more to his beloved Shakespeare. When asked in which romantic spot he had composed the lovely duet, *"Vous soupirez, madame,"* he replied, "I sketched it one day while listening to a speech by one of my colleagues at the Institute."

Berlioz conducted the premiere of *Béatrice et Bénédict* at Baden-Baden in August, 1862, where the work was welcomed with great acclaim. In his *Memoirs* he noted that it "produced a tremendous effect. Critics, some expressly from Paris, praised the music warmly, especially the song [Beatrice's] and the duet. Some thought that there was a great deal of rubbish in the rest of the score and that the spoken dialogue was stupid. It is copied almost word for word from Shakespeare. . . ."

Berlioz felt fatigued and defeated, but he knew that even at this low point at the end of his career as a composer, he had written one of his most spirited and original works. There still burned within him the conviction of his worth as in his historical hero Benvenuto Cellini, who had boldly stated to his patron that a fair appraisal of his Perseus statue was impossible because no one in Florence was able to judge its merits. During his last years of failing health, until his death in 1869, Berlioz had no more musical statements to make; but he knew he had remained loyal to his early loves—who, he reflected, "perhaps might have loved me"—Gluck, Beethoven, Virgil and Shakespeare. He had served them as faithfully and well as he had the entire cause of music.

IN WAGNER'S SHADOW

THE MUSICAL, AND PARTICULARLY OPERATIC, CLIMATE IN MID-NINE-teenth-century Germany was one of ferment and innovation. The center of musical activity was Weimar, the city that readily evoked the names of recent literary giants such as Schiller, Goethe, Herder and Wieland. Their memories were fresh and kept alive by those who had known them intimately, like Bettina von Arnim, older now and the mother of two charming daughters. Still spirited and inspiring, she welcomed the young avant-garde composers with equal enthusiasm.

If the city of musical happenings was Weimar, its leader and prime innovator naturally was the court *Kapellmeister* Franz Liszt. The court theatre came alive with performances of Gluck, Berlioz and Wagner operas, among others, including the premiere of *Lohengrin*. As the spokesman for the *neue Musik*, Liszt attracted numerous disciples to Weimar. They probed into new directions and tested novel ideas under the master's tutelage and guidance. However, for a contemporary of Richard Wagner to achieve success was no mean accomplishment.

One of these young composers was Peter Cornelius. Born in Mainz in 1824, the son of an actor and a relative of the painter of the same name, Peter Cornelius originally intended to follow in his father's footsteps. But his character was ill-suited for the stage. He was shy and reticent, an inconspicuous and inner-directed youth rather than a brash aggressive person who could attract and sustain the attention of an audience. The footlights intimidated him and his first appearance on stage was a failure. Because of his background and environment, however, he was thoroughly acquainted with literature and drama. He himself developed into a gifted writer who produced numerous delightful lyrics in the romantic vein.

After his theatrical fiasco, Cornelius decided to turn to composition. He went to Berlin where from 1845 to 1850 he studied with Siegfried Wilhelm Dehn. But for the hospitality of several friendly families and some mild harmless amorous adventures inspiring innumerable verses, his years of study were largely fraught with tedium.

By 1852 he had arrived in Weimar and joined Liszt's intimate circle. Here he became acquainted with Wagner's music and was immediately converted into an enthusiastic Wagnerite. In 1853 he met Hector Berlioz, whom he also admired. He continued to write poetry, inspired by and suitable for all kinds of occasions and people. His versatility as a writer proved a great asset. He contributed articles elucidating the new principles of musical composition to the *Neue Zeitschrift für Musik*. Since he was fluent in seven languages, mostly self-taught, he translated many of Liszt's French lectures for publication. He also prepared German translations of Berlioz' *Benvenuto Cellini, Lélio* and *L'Enfance du Christ;* Gluck's *Alceste* and both *Iphigénies;* and Pergolesi's *La serva padrona* for performances in Germany.

But his literary activities soon became secondary. Suddenly his Opus 1 was born. He had been a guest somewhere outside of Weimar. The young lady of the house was both an accomplished pianist and singer. In lieu of a thank-you note, he penned six songs, each just filling a sheet of note paper.

As early as 1858 Cornelius had completed the composition of his major work, a comic opera in two acts, entitled *Der Barbier von Bagdad*. Liszt produced it at Weimar's court theatre on December 15, 1858, with catastrophic results. The Liszt opposition forces were so strong that the opera had to be withdrawn after its first and only performance. This fiasco caused Liszt to relinquish his position at the court.

Cornelius' opera was perhaps too refined, its story too slight, its wit too delicate and intimate for audiences accustomed to massive compositions on a heroic scale of the Liszt, Wagner,

Berlioz and Meyerbeer order. *Der Barbier von Bagdad* relates a simple tale, freely drawn from *A Thousand and One Nights.* Nureddin, having recovered from an illness, is about to keep a rendez-vous with his beloved Margiana, the cadi's daughter, while her father is away praying at the mosque. Nureddin's barber, Abul Hassan, a loquacious fellow more interested in casting his master's horoscope than in shaving him, follows Nureddin to the cadi's house, where he overhears the cries of a slave being whipped. Mistakenly assuming that Nureddin is being murdered, Abul Hassan with a band of men rushes into the house. The lovers are interrupted and confused by all the commotion. Fearfully Bostana, Margiana's companion, hides Nureddin in a chest. The barber accuses the returning cadi of having killed his friend. But Nureddin, rescued from the chest, has only fainted. The caliph arrives on the scene and orders the cadi to present his daughter with the "treasure" discovered in the chest.

Cornelius of course had written the sparkling humorous text himself. The failure of the opera did not overly disconcert him, although in his lifetime it was never to be performed again. But with this work, unfortunately so poorly received, Cornelius' most original, individualistic and productive phase in the field of opera had come to an end. Though he composed a great number of impressive and beautiful songs and choruses, using his own texts as well as the lyrics of Heine, Rückert, Goethe and Johannes Scheffler, his later operatic ventures were mostly imitative.

In 1858 he had moved on to Vienna where he fell entirely under Wagner's spell. His choice of operatic subjects, for which he wrote his own librettos, in itself was telling. *Der Cid* was composed after Corneille, *Gunlöd,* which remained unfinished, after an episode from the *Edda.* Cornelius had surrendered to the taste for lengthy complicated heroic themes, which continued to prevail. Ironically, his grand opera *Der Cid,* when produced in Weimar in 1865, was received with much acclaim, while that small gem of subtle charm and bubbling humor, *Der Barbier von Bagdad,* which had been rejected, remained forgotten. *Der Cid* was presented several times, but it is hardly surprising that it did not impress sufficiently to become a repertory piece. For Cornelius was a true small master. For him poetry and music went hand in hand. He was not a symphonist or an operatic composer in the grand manner. Like his personality, his art was modest. It was powerful in a unique, unobtrusive way. He excelled at graceful and lyrical invention.

It has been said that Wagner's creative genius was greater, but that Cornelius was superior in breeding. Although the two composers were friendly, Cornelius could at times be critical of Wagner's character. Wagner's attraction proved so strong, however, that Cornelius followed him to Munich in 1865 as a reader to King Ludwig II. Later, after the conservatory had been transformed into the *Königliche Musikschule* with Hans von Bülow as director, Cornelius was appointed professor of harmony and rhetoric.

In 1865 Cornelius became engaged to Bertha Jung of Mainz, whose family he had known for many years. In a typical humorous poem to her he described how he had lived just around the corner, yet it had taken him forty years to find her. Their two-year engagement period inspired several delightful and moving songs, full of droll humor, fine perceptiveness and the warmest feelings. The range of emotion sustained in the *Brautlieder* is second only to Schumann's song-cycle. *Frauenliebe und Leben.*

Though obviously throughout his career Cornelius was influenced by Liszt and Wagner, there are indications that these dominating outside pressures caused him considerable inner conflicts. At the time of his marriage, when he had decided to settle down and raise a family, the question very seriously arose whether he should return to Munich, that is, re-enter Wagner's magnetic sphere. Though outwardly so mature and self-controlled, he was deeply troubled by his inner struggle.

Unlike other Liszt and Wagner followers, Cornelius had always retained his integrity, guarding his independence and freedom of judgment. Even in his early Weimar days he remained somewhat aloof. Admiration for—even friendship with—composers such as Liszt, Berlioz and Wagner did not necessarily presuppose that one must compose like them. *Der Barbier von Bagdad* stands as the best example of Cornelius' insistence on expressing himself in his own musical idiom. Only after the failure of this opera did he begin to imitate the more successful masters whose accomplishments easily eclipsed the efforts of the disciples struggling in their shadows.

Cornelius once dared to criticize a Liszt composition to the Princess Sayn-Wittgenstein who in response promptly praised the piece without reservation. When Cornelius spoke favorably of an opera by Anton Rubinstein, she emphatically expressed herself against it. Later Cornelius learned that the Princess had simply repeated Liszt's opinion. Cornelius avoided involvement in the various opposing musical factions and their animosities. Totally unprejudiced, in a poem praising Clara Schumann, he boldly linked her name to that of Liszt as well as Joseph Joachim, proclaiming the three as the ideal triumvirate.

Reaching a decision on whether or not to return to Munich was a little more difficult than pronouncing fair and forthright judgments. In spite of their friendship, Cornelius was aware of the vast gulf that separated him from Wagner. He himself knew the shortcomings of his *Cid*, realizing it contained too little melody. He understood that his music was basically and naturally cheerful, fresh, serene and humorous in contrast to the oppressive, sensuous and decadent atmosphere of a *Tristan*, which his nature could not abide. He felt the need to be free, not to be forced in a certain direction, and near Wagner such freedom seemed impossible.

Cornelius' sensitivity and conscientiousness intensified the conflict within him. Where he was modest and unassuming, Wagner was demanding and tyrannical. Ultimately, he capitulated to financial considerations and the sober advice of his family; he returned to Munich. The joyful period of his marriage was destined to endure for only seven years. He died in Mainz in 1874, a victim of diabetes, leaving his wife and four children, of whom the two youngest died soon afterwards.

Der Barbier von Bagdad received a performance in Hanover in 1877. In Karlsruhe it was presented in a revised version orchestrated by Felix Mottl in the Wagnerian tradition. Both performances passed into history without any significant repercussions.

But in 1885, when the opera was revived in Munich, Cornelius'
gift was at last fully appreciated. The work is one of the most
elegant German operas ever composed, appealing to the connoisseur rather than to the masses. It is often ranked second only to
Die Meistersinger on which it undoubtedly had a decided influence. It is certainly not impossible that sometimes Wagner learned
from his followers. The characterization of Abul Hassan, combined of robust, rollicking, grotesque, lyrical and philosophical
qualities, points to the later, more fully developed, romantic hero
Hans Sachs and the comical villain Beckmesser. The famed
second-act riot scene of *Meistersinger* surely derived from its
forerunner's climactic rousing mob scene and choruses.

Today *Der Barbier von Bagdad* with its delightful humor remains a warmly ingratiating work, an enduring testament to the
composer who wrote his own characteristically modest epitaph:

> *Ich war ein Hauch, ich war ein Ton*
> *Von Lust und Schmerz durchdrungen,*
> *Nun ist es still, nun bin ich schon*
> *Verklungen.*

> I was a breath, I was a tone
> Penetrated by joy and pain,
> Now it is still, now I have already
> Faded away.

GOTHIC SWAN SONG

AT THE AGE OF FIFTY-SEVEN, AFTER HE HAD WRITTEN SOME NINETY operettas, Jacques Offenbach began the composition of his most ambitious work, *The Tales of Hoffmann*.

In 1876 his world-wide fame was securely established for the *opéra bouffe* which bore his unique stamp. Acclaimed for the saucy, satiric music and subject matter of his pieces, worked into libretti by men superior in their art, he was applauded by Parisians of the Second Empire, Europeans in general and, last but not least, Americans, who became wildly enthused over his music. Upon his visit to the United States, admirers were disappointed when the slight composer, whom they probably had expected to dance a cancan on the podium, conducted his *Orphée aux enfers* as quietly as any other conductor might have done.

So this was the man who had made the world chuckle! He has been compared to Aristophanes, Molière, Cervantes, Heine, in our time Chaplin—vastly different men of different eras, nationalities, and temperaments, but gifted with the same talent of satire and parody. And in the mind of the people, the image of the man who made them laugh was himself a caricature.

This was Offenbach, who on the stage had dared to poke fun at the majestic Greek gods, who had moved them down from Olympus and the clouds to live, speak, and act like everyday human beings with common attributes. *Orphée aux enfers* was a parody of the legend but contained lyrical music as well. The gods were not above snoring or dancing the cancan. *La belle Hélène* sparkled with wit but also reflected a touch of realism. *Barbe-bleue,* a burlesque of medieval customs, mocked the adventure of marriage. His numerous other light operettas disclosed sharply etched satire, glowing humor, and destructive parody. The music itself was always rich in melodic inventiveness, simple in rapidly changing harmonies of tonic and dominant, clear in rhythm, easily singable.

Many of his contemporaries found much that was praiseworthy in this "musical brother of Heine" whose compositions had given birth to musical impudence. He was called a wish-dream of Nietzsche. Nietzsche himself felt that Offenbach was "the most intellectual and high-spirited satyr who, as a musician, abided by the great tradition and who—for the man who has something more than ears—is a real relief after the sentimental and at bottom degenerate musicians of German romanticism." He described Offenbach's art as "French music imbued with Voltaire's intellect, free, wanton, with a slight sardonic grin, but clear and intellectual almost to the point of banality and free from the *mignardise* of morbid or blond-Viennese sensuality. . . . If by artistic genius," Nietzsche continues, "we understand the most consummate freedom within the law, divine ease and facility in overcoming the greatest difficulties, then Offenbach has even more right to the title 'genius' than Wagner. Wagner is heavy and clumsy; nothing is more foreign to him than the moments of wanton perfection which this clown Offenbach achieves as many as five times, six times, in nearly every one of his buffooneries." Wagner, too, was impressed and wrote, "Look at Offenbach. He can do what the divine Mozart did. . . . Offenbach could have been a Mozart."

Yet the man who so ably contrasted sensibility and buffoonery in his works, whose coarseness was mitigated by engaging originality, was also attacked with violent criticism. He was accused of damaging the true interest of art by catering to the corrupt taste of his period and the base instincts of the masses by providing for their vulgar appetites. Showing utter disrespect for his subject matter, even when it touched on religion, he had profaned the noble art of music. The man who was a master of savage caricature himself became a favorite subject of attack by the press and by cartoonists. He was in turn called "Offen*bacchus*," "*Affe*nbach" (*Affe* = monkey), "*Orphen*bach." The critic Oskar von Blumenthal lucidly and objectively summed up the masses' reaction to the composer:

> You liked it well that he should dare
> Profane the stage without a care;
> But that he pleased you, it is true,
> Forgive him that you'd never do!

This, then, in 1876, was a picture of Offenbach, the originator of the Bouffes-Parisiens. It has been said that his operettas were commercial ventures but that his final composition, the *Tales,* was an expression of his ideals. It was his tribute to German romanticism, no longer his trifling French grace and humor. What made him abruptly turn away from the type of composition that had caused his success and fame? Why did the man who had made all the world laugh embark at this point upon a new form, attempting a serious opera? Had he a reason for choosing the *Tales* for his subject?

Although considered a clown by his audiences, Offenbach was in reality a sober man. Like many men he made the world laugh in order not to cry himself. His wife knew him at times to be despondent, afraid, and nervous, a person who could not bear to be alone. E. T. A. Hoffmann, too, had avoided solitude when working at night because he began to believe his grotesque creations were coming alive. Often *his* wife, knitting in hand, would sit up with him to keep away these hallucinations. It is not unlikely that Offenbach felt a kinship for this fellow-countryman who was a composer and musician as well as the author of many fantastic tales.

Among Hoffmann's most interesting, partly autobiographical characters was the figure of Johannes Kreisler, an eccentric musician, with whom Jacques Offenbach seems to have identified. The critic Theodor Reik finds other identifications in the composer's choice of subject. If the three heroines, Olympia, Giulietta, and Antonia, represent three typical women in a man's life—the child, the siren, and the artist—Offenbach may have found a further summary of his own career in their depiction. Freud tells us that in dreams there frequently occurs a figure reversal; thus Olympia may be the mother symbol, Hoffmann the child. Giulietta represents the years of a man's sensual desires and Antonia the symbol of death. Vacillating between love and art, while Dr. Miracle ominously clatters with his bottles, Antonia chooses her art, sings, and dies. The three women have thus become mother, mistress, and annihilator. Offenbach, identifying with his hero, Hoffmann, also a musician, chooses his art and, like Antonia, dies in his swan song.

The pattern recurs. Antonia, like her mother, was a singer. Offenbach's father had been a composer of Jewish music and cantor in a synagogue. The students in the tavern all ridicule the disillusioned Hoffmann, just as Offenbach had been derided by his critics. One commentator adds the suggestion that the morbid Dr. Miracle and his horrid medicines stem from the illness of Offenbach's son, who died soon after his father.

The same basic design appears in the composer's lighter works. Orpheus is a musician, a violinist like Offenbach. Euridice embodies three women in one: child, bacchante, and death, for whom Orpheus must descend to Hades. *Helen* repeats the theme of three women: the third and chosen one, Aphrodite, goddess of love and death, is silent. Later in Offenbach's life, the theme of frustration took on more sombre hues and *Les Contes d'Hoffmann* was conceived.

To those who watched the composer play his cello, he seemed an apparition from another sphere. His extreme pallor, narrow lean figure, unusually high forehead, pointed nose, flowing long hair and strange glittering eyes became exaggeratedly pronounced when he bowed his instrument. Alfred de Musset called him a harbinger of misfortune. A French critic maliciously suggested that Offenbach had looked in a mirror and been struck by his own evil eye.

As he began the composition of the *Tales*, Offenbach's illness befell him. In 1879, as though with the knowledge that it would be for the last time, he visited the city of his birth and childhood, Cologne. Upon a sad return to Paris, his adopted home, he desperately wrote to Carvalho, director of the Opéra Comique, "Please rush with the production of my piece [*Tales*]; I am in a hurry and have only the one wish of seeing its premiere. . . ."

Ill, impatient, with the constant ominous presentiment that he might not live to see a performance of his opera, Offenbach arranged to have excerpts of the score played at his home for a selected audience. Afterwards, *Minêstrel* enthusiastically prophesied,

"A descendant of Weber has been born among us, in the middle of Paris, on the Boulevard des Capucines." Offenbach had achieved a blend of Parisian charm and German romanticism, truly a tribute to Weber, whom he so admired.

Four months before the premiere, the composer was dead.

NO OPERA, NO WIFE

"HAVE I NEVER TOLD YOU OF MY FINE PRINCIPLES," JOHANNES BRAHMS wrote to the Swiss poet Josef Viktor Widmann in 1888, "of not trying an opera or a marriage. . . ? If you, dear friend, were truly broad-minded in your views and principles, you would realize how much money I am saving and shall have left for an Italian trip—if I don't marry toward the summer and don't buy an opera text!"

The superficial bantering tone could not altogether obliterate the statement's underlying seriousness and melancholy. Coming from the acknowledged master at the age of fifty-five, it coupled the two great regrets of his life. Because Brahms was truthful and forthright, his reasons should not be altogether discredited. He refrained from marriage, he told Widmann, because at the time when he should have liked to embark on a family life he was insufficiently established as a composer. When fame and financial success did come, it was too late. He failed to compose an opera because he never found a suitable text. These are the surface explanations of Brahms' clear, logical and highly disciplined mind. Yet the fact that he linked marriage and opera may be an indication that his negative attitude toward both subconsciously stemmed from the same source.

The key to the composer's inner life may well be contained in *Des jungen Kreislers Schatzkästlein,** a collection of favorite excerpts from a variety of contemporary and classical authors, copied by the youthful Brahms into small notebooks. *Kapellmeister*

---

* The Young Kreisler's Little Treasure Chest.

113

Johannes Kreisler was the eccentric and romantic fictitious character created by E. T. A. Hoffmann, with whom both Robert Schumann and Brahms identified. Brahms' formal education had ceased at age fifteen. From his earliest youth, however, he had been an avid reader, spending his modest allowance at a circulating library where accidentally and to his delight he discovered authors including Schiller and Tieck. While playing the piano at taverns, he would keep an open book in front of him. Finally, in Düsseldorf, in the early 1850's, he reveled in the Schumanns' extensive and diversified library of books and music. His little anthology grew, becoming more discriminating and self-revealing. Judging from the selections, his reticence, particularly in forming personal attachments, was most pronounced. "Much is too tender to be thought; still much more, to be discussed," he quoted from Novalis. He agreed with Friedrich von Sallet:

> Mostly one finds the highest degree of what is called openness in the most frivolous and thoughtless persons; of that which is called reserve in the deepest, richest and truest minds. . . . There is in the mind a holy of holies. I would not bring forth what shines there in the innermost hidden recesses to glimmer vainly and childishly in the universal light of day. Let it remain there in sacred night! I would not even tell of it to my friend, though he be the noblest man, not even to my beloved (if I had one). . . . What would man love in his fellow-man if not the unspoken, the unexplored? To analyze and describe the sacred within us is a shameless desecration. . . . I myself must not reveal any of it in words, except in poetry. There I may do so for there it happens in some divine way, incomprehensible to me. . . .

The great event of Brahms' life, whose memory he treasured until his death, was his meeting and unique friendship with Robert and Clara Schumann, whom he could love and respect as both artists and human beings. The shocking tragedy of Schumann's insanity and subsequent death deeply affected the young composer. He renounced his momentary, passionate love for the extraordinary Clara, transforming it into a faithful lifelong devotion and admiration. In words he might equally well have applied to himself, he wrote Clara in 1857, "Passions are not natural attributes of the human being . . . they are always exceptions and outgrowths. . . . The fine true human being is calm in joy and calm in sorrow. Passions will soon pass, or one must banish them." Yet almost forty years later, in 1896, after Clara had suffered a stroke, he could barely suppress his emotion as he wrote to her daughter Marie, "Should you expect the worst, please let me know so that I can come, once more to see the dear eyes open; when they close— how much closes with them for me!" To no one did he ever again reveal as much of himself as in his letters to Clara Schumann during the period of her husband's confinement to the sanatorium and directly afterwards. It marked the climax and end of his short *Sturm und Drang*. From then on he was utterly self-controlled and at least outwardly calm. He became increasingly mistrustful of his emotions. A little later, his brief love for Agathe von Siebold ended disastrously because of his hesitancy.

Brahms always enjoyed and was most affectionate with children; they were free of the artifice and conceit he abhorred. If on rare occasions his way of life exceeded his normally simple habits, he would remark that he was living like Wagner. The basic pattern of his mature life was established. The shy, modest composer, whose forbidding exterior and ofttimes sharp tongue tended to obscure his humility, extreme generosity and kindness of heart, remained faithful to his Muse: "Music is the saint, the Madonna among the arts," he quoted Jean Paul in his *Schatzkästlein*. His independence and integrity, his lyrical and poetic mind, the depth of his emotional being were channeled into orchestral, instrumental, vocal and choral compositions. The same inwardness and caution that kept him from marriage, obstructed his attempts at opera. Though diligent and inspired, he lacked the dynamic quality of Beethoven, while the dramatic, flamboyant characteristics of Wagner were distasteful to him.

When Brahms considered an opera, it was not at all with the Wagnerian aim of unifying text and music. He felt composition of the entire dramatic action was unnecessary, that only the high points and those parts where music could contribute something worthwhile should be composed. This would permit the librettist more freedom for dramatic development. It would not interfere with the composer's independence and need to speak musically wherever necessary. He thought it barbaric and demeaning to music if it merely served to accompany dramatic action throughout several acts. In form, Brahms' concept of opera reverted to Mozart's *Zauberflöte* and the early *Singspiel*.

Brahms actually came closest to dramatic composition with his *Rinaldo*, a cantata by Goethe, for tenor solo, men's chorus and orchestra, premiered in 1869. It is an interesting piece, if only to judge his accomplishments in this category, but it is not one of his strong works. Brahms' perceptive friend, the noted surgeon Theodor Billroth, perhaps stated the reason most succinctly: "He is enthusiastic about the text because it leaves so much to the composer."

At this time Brahms was also seriously considering the composition of an opera. He discussed such a project with the poet Paul Heyse at Munich and with Turgenev at Baden-Baden. The engraver Julius Allgeyer presented him with a completed libretto based on Calderòn's *El secreto a voces*. Through the poet Claus Groth he obtained an unused text written by Emanuel Geibel for Felix Mendelssohn.

To Heinrich Bulthaupt, a rising young writer, Brahms suggested as a possibility Schiller's dramatic fragment *Demetrius* of which he thought very highly. However, in the initial stages of mere theoretical discussion, it became apparent that Brahms could not take for granted any minor illogical or inexplicable details for the sake of stage requirements. Such difficulties would no doubt have disappeared in the course of actual composition. Bulthaupt, on the other hand, expressed the opinion that the music should contain Russian characteristics and feared that this would prove unacceptable to Brahms, whose music was so completely German. The suggestion of including a Slavic element was quite unwarranted but, added to Brahms' own reservations, it caused him to drop the project. It is interesting to note the subject of this proposed tragic opera which so appealed to Brahms. The action stems from the ambition of Demetrius, pretender to the throne; the female interest is centered in his mother, Marfa, a role of powerful conflicting emotions. It recalls Brahms' devotion to his mother as well as that to Clara Schumann who was many women to him: mother figure, beloved friend, admired artist—the "priestess of his Muse." His interest in *Demetrius* also reflects his friendship with the violinist Joseph Joachim, with whom he discussed the drama and who himself composed a *Demetrius* overture.

The second time Brahms approached opera came in the late 1870's, in conversations and correspondence with Widmann. Though he hesitated to become involved in a project of such magnitude, he indicated that he might be persuaded if the text were quite to his liking. Brahms was attracted to Gozzi's *Il re cervo* and *Il corvo* as well as his version of *El secreto a voces* (*Il pubblico segreto*). These choices confirm Brahms' predilection for fables and comedy in interpretations accenting a deeper meaning or moral, consistent with his classical ideas regarding opera in *Die Zauberflöte* tradition. This retrogression in the development of operatic composition was surely not exclusively formulated by Brahms without taking into consideration a significant outside influence. Both he and Wagner had reached a certain position and eminence in opposed areas of music activity. It would have been out of the question for Brahms to emulate Wagner, though at the time *Die Meistersinger* was produced in Vienna in 1870, he had written, "The thought of Wagner would not prevent me from setting to work at an opera with the greatest alacrity." Several years later, however, when nothing had come of his various operatic plans, he responded to the question of why he had written no opera, "Beside Wagner it is impossible."

Brahms certainly possessed sensitivity and understanding for the theatre. When Goethe's *Geschwister*, by no means a tragic play, was performed at the Burgtheater in his adopted hometown Vienna, he was moved to tears by its sheer beauty of human sentiments. He had a good knowledge and judgment of drama, and his criticism was lucid. However, his own basic earnestness was often camouflaged by humor or irony. This caused a major difficulty in his choice of a libretto. He recommended *Il re cervo* to Widmann especially for its strong comical aspects while its underlying serious current remained ever present. It is difficult to imagine that

Brahms, who habitually checked the passionate impulses hidden within him with sarcasm or even rudeness, would shed his characteristic caution and reserve, and let his emotions play freely on the operatic stage. This depth of feeling, arising from a protective philosophical and intellectual shell, was beautifully expressed in his affecting instrumental and vocal compositions which never transgressed the bounds of self-imposed limitations. One might mention the wedding of Robert and Clara Schumann's daughter Julie in 1869. Obviously upset by the news, Brahms, who had never divulged his deep feelings for the girl, composed the Alto Rhapsody as his "bridal song." "If only once he would speak thus from his heart in words!" Clara complained. In songs, symphonies or piano music, he could dream of ideals and speak with wisdom, sorrow and resignation, distilling his own personality. This was not the fabric of opera.

In his estimation of opera, Brahms never underrated Wagner. He was thoroughly acquainted with Wagner's music as well as his librettos. He found "fine things" in *Die Walküre* and *Siegfried*, liked some of the leitmotivs and admired the scene where Siegmund pulls the sword from the tree. But he felt that it would all be even more powerful if it concerned a recent historical hero, for example Napoleon. Some of Wagner's duets were simply too long and tedious and the language was too stilted and bombastic for his taste. Understandably, he appreciated *Der fliegende Holländer* but could not abide *Tristan und Isolde*. Although he never attended the Bayreuth festival, Brahms heartily approved of it. He respected the magnitude of Wagner's intentions and his ability and energy in carrying them out.

Brahms never cared much for Italian opera, too alien to his reserved German nature, but he considered Verdi's *Requiem* a work of genius. Of French operas his favorite was Bizet's *Carmen*. He also enjoyed Boieldieu's *Dame blanche* and Auber's *Domino noir*. A Johann Strauss enthusiast, he tried to attend performances of his operettas in Vienna whenever possible. He was quick to point out the vaudeville characteristics of the first act of Beethoven's *Fidelio*. The first opera he saw as an adolescent in Hamburg was Mozart's *Nozze di Figaro*, which remained a lifelong favorite.

"I simply cannot understand how anyone can create something so absolutely complete. It has never been done so again, not even by Beethoven," he told Billroth. Once he was so delighted with a performance of *Don Giovanni* that he rushed to embrace Gustav Mahler who had conducted it.

During the last twenty years of his life Brahms rarely attended opera performances, although he continued to visit the theatre frequently. Creating the music that truly reflected what was in his heart, he was resigned to a simple, solitary life in which there was to be no wife and no opera. When Widmann visited him in 1881 at his summer home at Pressbaum near Vienna, he found Brahms stocky, heavily bearded and decidedly set in his way of life. During their conversation the composer spoke rather agitatedly of what might have been. "But," he concluded, his calm and confidence restored, "it was good this way too!"

TCHAIKOVSKY AND HIS OPERAS

TCHAIKOVSKY, THE MASTER OF ORCHESTRAL MUSIC, IS BARELY KNOWN as the composer of ten operas. Although hardly successful with his dramatic stage works, excepting *Eugene Onegin* and *The Queen of Spades,* he again and again tried his hand at operatic subjects.

Possibly his attempts failed because these works were less inspired by an inner need for personal expression than were his orchestral compositions in which, abstractly, without live scenes and personages, he could freely project whatever moved him toward creative urges. At one time he, himself, wrote Madame Nadejda von Meck, "Words often are disturbing, and always pull music down from its heights. . . . In this perhaps lies the reason that my instrumental compositions are comparatively more successful than my vocal works." When he explains, ". . . I always describe what I should or shall experience, not what I have experienced already," it is apparent that he speaks in terms of his orchestral music. Here, broadly, without limitation or restraint, he reveals himself, his experiences, emotions, ordeals, and longings. In this constant subjective musical self-portrayal, where the entire outside world is drowned out by groping or soaring orchestral outpouring, consisting entirely and only of the man, Tchaikovsky, lies the composer's enduring appeal to his admirers. Only here his music is significant and profound. His adverse critics, understandably, are repelled by "too much Tchaikovsky"—the repetitive, long-winded, emotional outbursts.

He applies his talent and skills as a masterful orchestral technician to his operas as well, but in these rather than project himself, he attempts to depict characters and situations objectively. Subsequently, although effort and workmanship exist, the soul is missing. Since Tchaikovsky does not identify with any aspects of these creations, there is no personal rapport, and the audience, in turn, finds nothing to which it can relate. He describes without emotion, but in opera, as in the theatre, the listener or spectator wants to be moved, immerse himself into and experience the action and events on the stage. Therefore Tchaikovsky essentially is not a dramatist. Although his subjects arouse interest, the plots are not always in good taste or easy to stomach, and the dramatic action is rambling rather than tightly interlaced.

When Tchaikovsky turned to opera, he may have reasoned that while an orchestral work, if successful, might at most enjoy a performance here and there, an opera that has won acclaim would be repeated any number of times. Through opera—always of wider appeal to the masses than symphonic or chamber music—the composer had more of an opportunity to become known and, eventually, to gain financially. Moreover, Tchaikovsky's publisher, Jurgenson, had excellent connections with the directors of the Petersburg and Moscow theatres. Thus all the circumstantial factors toward writing operas were in Tchaikovsky's favor. Only the prime prerequisite, the true, profounder, immaterial spirit of inspiration was lacking. This realization Tchaikovsky never acknowledged until it was too late, after the premiere performances of his operas when, with this subconscious knowledge, he hurriedly fled from the scene.

One of Tchaikovsky's biographers has classified his operas in three categories of which the first comprises the three forgotten operas, *The Voyevode, Undine,* and *The Oprichnik.* The next four works, *Vakoula the Smith, Joan of Arc, Mazeppa,* and *The Sorceress,* are bracketed as having a chance for survival. Finally, the remaining group of three works, *Eugene Onegin, The Queen of Spades,* and *Iolanthe,* is termed as the three successful operas.

Tchaikovsky composed his first opera, *The Voyevode,* at approximately the same time he wrote his First Symphony, in 1867. As a dramatic basis for his libretto of three acts, he used Ostrovsky's five-act play, *The Dream on the Volga.* The premiere in 1869 was a huge success: Tchaikovsky was called to the stage fifteen times.

Yet the fire of enthusiasm was quickly extinguished after five performances. Tchaikovsky, himself, destroyed most of the score. One
reason for the opera's failure, claimed Tchaikovsky's brother, Modeste, was that the composer neglected to retain the colorful true-
to-life folk scenes of Ostrovsky's play. Twelve years later, Tchaikovsky was able to comment objectively on the work to Madame
von Meck: "*The Voyevode* is without doubt a very bad opera. I
am not speaking alone of the value of the music, but especially of
the sum of all the conditions which bear an influence on the quality
of an opera. First of all, the subject is quite unsuitable, that is, it
lacks dramatic interest and action. Secondly, the opera is too
haphazardly and carelessly worked out; as a result its form received
no real operatic character and is not fair toward the requirements
of the stage. The third reason for failure is due to the massive orchestra which dominates over the solo voices. All these are mistakes
resulting from inexperience. One must have had a number of unsuccessful trials before one can reach a high rung of perfection."

Tchaikovsky's second opera, *Undine*, composed in 1868, did not
even fare as well as its predecessor. On a text by Count Sollogub,
Tchaikovsky completed the score within six months and submitted
it to the Imperial Theatre in St. Petersburg. After evading the issue
for some time, the theatre rejected the work. When Tchaikovsky
demanded a return of the score, the music could not be found. Since
he feared his insistence might cause the loss of a job to an employee,
the composer remained silent. When several years later the manuscript was found and returned to the composer, he flung it unopened into the fire.

In 1869 Tchaikovsky composed the ever popular *Romeo and
Juliet* Fantasy Overture. During the same year, he wrote a "Chorus
of Insects" for a projected but abandoned opera, *Mandragora*, and
began his next opera, *The Oprichnik*. This work in four acts, for
which he salvaged some of his musical ideas from *The Voyevode*,
was completed in 1872. Tchaikovsky had neither qualms about destroying his inferior works, nor hesitated to preserve from them and
incorporate elsewhere such material as he deemed worthwhile.

The Oprichnik was taken from a tragedy by Lashetchnikov
which, as the title implies, dealt with the soldiers forming the body-

guard of Ivan the Terrible. Although the action of the play is powerful, Tchaikovsky, as his own librettist, failed artistically to make a
success of it. To his own inadequacy in this respect was added the
censor's preventive hand which would not condone any profane
delineation of the tsar. The story of the opera in brief concerns a
young nobleman, Morosov, who loves Natalie, the daughter of a
prince, but is rejected by the father in favor of another suitor. The
nobleman becomes an *Oprichnik* and receives permission from the
tsar to revenge himself upon the prince. During a celebration, he
abducts Natalie, who refuses to follow an *Oprichnik*. His mother,
too, is horrified to see Morosov a bodyguard of Ivan the Terrible.
He, himself, attempts to sever his connection with this notorious
regiment. While he is being married to Natalie, a messenger appears stating that the tsar desires to convince himself of the bride's
beauty by her presence before him, alone. Enraged, the bridegroom
follows and both he and Natalie are killed.

The role of the tsar, because of the censor, had to be omitted entirely. The horror of the ending was intensified by having Morosov
executed on stage while his mother, forced to watch from a window,
dies of shock and grief.

The opera was accepted by the St. Petersburg theatre and first
performed there in 1874. It won much applause by the audience.
Cui was not impressed, while Laroche was enthused. Tchaikovsky,
himself, again admitted that this was by far no masterpiece. Long
before the premiere he had written his favorite pupil, Taneieff,
"There is nothing good about this opera." After the performance
he judged, "This opera is so bad that I could not stand it during the
rehearsals and ran away not to hear another note; at the performance I felt as though I must sink into the ground for shame. . . .
No action, no style, no inspiration. The curtain calls and applause at
the first performance mean nothing, because, first of all, many of
my friends and acquaintances were in the theatre and, secondly,
because my better reputation had preceded me."

Tchaikovsky was so concerned with the inferiority of this work
and the achievement it might have been, that shortly before his
death, he had intentions of remodeling it completely, but his plans
came to naught.

In contrast to *The Oprichnik,* Tchaikovsky often referred to his following opera, *Vakoula the Smith,* as the "favorite of my children." Based on a fairy-tale by Gogol, and translated into a sensitive and clever libretto consisting of three acts and seven scenes by Y. P. Polonsky, *Vakoula* was composed in 1874. The libretto had been prepared originally for the composer, Alexander Serov, who died before he could set it to music. Consequently, a contest was announced for the best composition using the libretto. Tchaikovsky, who considered it very beautiful, immediately commenced to work on it. Having made an error in the entry date, he rushed to complete the opera within three months. Actually, the contest was to close one year later. Now Tchaikovsky was concerned that his work be produced as quickly as possible. He approached the St. Petersburg opera house requesting whether it might not be performed before the winner was announced. This action set a number of the judges against him; he had to convince them that he had no dishonest motives. The incident was smoothed over and the score copied in a handwriting not likely to be recognized. However, Tchaikovsky, in his own characteristic hand known to the judges, had written on both score and envelope the motto, *"Ars longa, vita brevis."* Moreover, he had circulated the news in Moscow that he was participating in the contest; even before entering it, he had ascertained for his own peace of mind that his three most serious competitors, Anton Rubinstein, Rimsky-Korsakoff, and Balakireff, would not submit scores. Finally, through all his efforts, he was certain of five votes out of eight in his favor: his two friends, Nikolai Rubinstein and Laroche, as well as Davidov, Rimsky-Korsakoff, and Napravnik. All five insisted that Tchaikovsky truly deserved the prize.

Vakoula the Smith stands apart from all of Tchaikovsky's other operas. It is gay and humorous; the composer seemed to enjoy writing it; it is musically far more interesting and distinctive than the preceding operas. There are comic situations and attractive dance episodes. At the beginning a witch cavorts with the devil. The witch's son, Vakoula, is in love with Oxana, the daughter of one of her several suitors. Oxana claims she will marry Vakoula only if he brings her the tsarina's shoes, which Vakoula does with the devil's assistance. Oxana then admits that she really did not want the shoes at all, but only her beloved Vakoula.

Tchaikovsky's contest competitors exerted their utmost influence to condemn his work by publishing adverse criticism. Tchaikovsky wrote Taneieff about the premiere. "*Vakoula* was a grand failure. The first two acts were received by an auditorium as silent as the grave. After the third and fourth acts I was called out several times but simultaneously repelled by hissing." Later performances were accepted with more warmth. After several years the composer made extensive changes in the work, entitling it *The Shoes;* it was performed under his own direction in 1887 and won generous but short-lived praise.

Tchaikovsky's next opera, in the order of composition, was to be his most successful one. It served to widen his local as well as world-wide reputation as a dramatic composer. Pushkin's verse novel, *Eugene Onegin,* which was suggested to him as an operatic subject in 1877, immediately caught his fancy. He fashioned it into an opera within the following year. The significant aspect of this opera is, in Tchaikovsky's words, "that this music literally flowed out of my being, that I did not invent it." Many times he wrote with how much dedication and fervor he worked on the opera. He knew it lacked drama and would not be much of a success. Nevertheless, it did possess "a great wealth of poetry" and "life's truth."

Composition tellingly falls into the period of Tchaikovsky's brief unhappy marriage. No doubt, for once, he identified with an operatic character of his creation, Onegin, who replies to Tatiana's love letter with the words: "You wrote me, why deny it, you admitted with impatience, truthfully and openly, the longings of your soul. I respect this honesty which aroused in me a feeling long dead, but I shall not flatter you, rather be frank as you are. You shall know everything, but do not condemn me entirely before you have heard my side. . . . I was not born for happiness; my heart is in conflict with itself. All your love and kindness would be wasted on me for, as much as I could love you, our union would be torment. . . ." Tchaikovsky's wife, Antonina, too, had originally written him an impassioned letter; whereas he had his hero wisely retain his freedom, the composer, himself, became unfortunately entangled in matrimonial ties with a girl he could not love.

The story of *Eugene Onegin* concerns four major characters. The sisters Olga and Tatiana are visited by their neighbor, Lensky, in love with Olga, and his friend, Eugene Onegin. Tatiana falls in love with Onegin. Although first torn by feelings of maidenly modesty, despair, misgivings, and the ecstasy of first love, she finally writes him a love letter. Onegin cannot appreciate her simplicity and innocent sweetness. Coldly he thanks her for her letter, tells her he can only love her as a brother, and advises her to act with more maidenly reserve in the future. Tatiana, of course, is heartbroken. At a ball given in honor of her birthday, Onegin is bored and flirts with Olga. Lensky challenges him to a duel and is killed. Many years later Onegin again meets Tatiana, now the Princess Gremin, a beautiful worldly woman. Too late, Onegin falls passionately in love with her. He implores her to come with him. She wavers momentarily, but ultimately leaves him in despair, alone.

The first performance took place, as Tchaikovsky wished, by a group of young students of the Moscow Conservatory in 1879. In 1881 the work received its "official" Moscow premiere and three years later was given in St. Petersburg. No one was overly enthusiastic about it; neither was it harshly criticized. Although the reception was lukewarm, it eventually won the distinction of being the most successful Russian opera.

The year of composition of *Eugene Onegin* had been very productive; it included the creation of the Violin Concerto and the Fourth Symphony. The following year, 1878, Tchaikovsky concentrated chiefly on *Joan of Arc,* an opera in four acts based on Schiller's drama. Tchaikovsky strove for a simple monumental style, but as a result his music emerged uneven and lacking in originality. Schiller's long monologues as arias proved tedious. Once again, Tchaikovsky seemed to realize that this was not one of his major achievements. A year after its completion, he wrote Madame von Meck, "I do not believe that *Joan of Arc* is my most beautiful and warmest work." The opera could hardly be termed an artistic success, but possessed rousing mass appeal, if judged by the ovation accorded to it after its St. Petersburg premiere in 1881. The press, however, almost unanimously turned against the composer, called the work reactionary, a poor mixture of Meyerbeer and the Italians. Cui considered it the weakest of Tchaikovsky's compositions.

Mazeppa, a three-act opera, composed from 1882 to 1883, similarly exhibited Italian influences which had a strange, incongruous effect on the basically Russian theme. Tchaikovsky was not exceptionally inspired by his subject but used it because he had nothing better available at the moment. A problem arose about performing rights in Moscow where the premiere took place in 1884. A lower figure than customary was offered to Tchaikovsky because the opera consisted of three acts instead of the usual four. If that was the case, Tchaikovsky pointed out, he could equally well have divided it into ten acts, but since it adequately filled the evening's program, he could not see why the number of acts should make any difference at all in the sum paid to him. The reception of this opera, too, proved a disappointment.

The plot of *Mazeppa*, based on a Pushkin poem, treats the hero's feud with Kochoubey, who has refused to give his daughter Maria in marriage to Mazeppa. Mazeppa elopes with the girl, then captures Kochoubey, has him tortured and executed (all on stage!), causing Maria to go insane.

Mazeppa was followed in 1886 by the composition of *The Sorceress*, an opera in four acts, which was produced in St. Petersburg in 1887. Drawn from a drama by Shpashinsky, the subject matter did not appeal to the taste of St. Petersburg society. A nobleman falls in love with a bar mistress, is rivaled by his son whom he kills out of jealousy, while his wife poisons the bar mistress. Although Tchaikovsky's musical intentions are sincere, the libretto fails in helping to carry them out.

Twelve years after the creation of *Eugene Onegin*, in 1890, Tchaikovsky composed *The Queen of Spades*, which was destined to be his second successful opera. Based on the Pushkin story, the libretto was written by Modeste Tchaikovsky. Herman, a poor officer, with a craving for wealth, learns that an old countess, whose niece he loves, possesses the secret of three lucky cards. If she divulges it, she will die. Herman succeeds in obtaining entrance into the house and confronts the old lady, who immediately dies of shock and fright.

Her spirit appears to him later, disclosing which are the three favorable cards. With this knowledge, he begins to win a fortune, but suddenly the third card, the ace of hearts, turns into the queen of spades. Driven out of his mind by the spirit of the old countess, he commits suicide.

Musically, this opera bears some similarities to *Eugene Onegin*. Tchaikovsky's characterizations are more pronounced than in his former operas; there are moments of dramatic excitement and intensity. *The Queen of Spades,* which received its premiere in St. Petersburg in 1890, seems to have caused the composer fewer misgivings than his earlier dramatic creations.

Tchaikovsky's final opera, *Iolanthe,* in one act, based on Hendrik Hertz's drama, *King René's Daughter,* was again set to a libretto by brother Modeste. It was composed in 1891 and first performed the following year, the evening also of the *Nutcracker* Suite premiere. Critical opinion of the ballet was divided and of the opera unfavorable, in spite of which *Iolanthe* enjoyed a number of performances in Germany and Denmark.

Tchaikovsky did not foresee a bright future for *Iolanthe*. Again faith in his own ability wavered. The story of the opera is a sentimentally charming tale of a blind girl with indefinable longings. She wonders if those who have their eyesight can see the song of the birds, the smell of flowers, the rolling of thunder, and the babbling of the brook. Iolanthe is cured of her blindness and marries her knight.

With *Iolanthe* ended Tchaikovsky's endeavors into the operatic field in which, unfortunately, he could never rise to the heights he hoped to scale. Apart from the better known *Eugene Onegin* and *The Queen of Spades,* it is of interest to hear recorded portions of Tchaikovsky's lesser dramatic attempts. But his fame, no doubt, will continue to rest quite securely on his orchestral achievements.

Agathe (Arlene Saunders) at prayer in Act II of Weber's *Freischütz* at the Hamburg State Opera. *German Information Center*

A bust of Gioacchino Rossini (1792–1868). *Metropolitan Opera Archives*

Scene from Weber's *Oberon* at the Cologne Opera. *German Information Center*

Scene from Act II of Rossini's *Barbiere di Siviglia. Metropolitan Opera Archives*

Scene from Act I of Rossini's *Barbiere di Siviglia* at the Paris Opéra Comique. *French Cultural Services*

Countess Adèle (Mady Mesplé) is wooed by Count Ory (Anastasios Vrenios), disguised as a nun, in Act II of Rossini's *Comte Ory* in The Opera Society of Washington production. *Christian Steiner*

Count Ory's men, disguised as nuns, secretly drink a toast to Adèle's brother, their absent host, in Act II of Rossini's *Comte Ory* in The Opera Society of Washington production. *Christian Steiner*

The opening scene of Meyerbeer's *Prophète. Metropolitan Opera Archives*

The council chamber scene from Meyerbeer's *Africaine. Bavarian State Opera, Munich*

The prison scene from Meyerbeer's *Africaine. Bavarian State Opera, Munich*

Giacomo Meyerbeer (1791–1864). *German Information Center*

Hector Berlioz (1803–1869) conducting an orchestra. *French Cultural Services*

Benvenuto Cellini's statue of Perseus in Florence.

Somarone (Richard Clark) rehearses his bridal song in Act I of Berlioz' *Béatrice et Bénédict. The Manhattan School of Music*

The drinking song from Act II of Berlioz' *Béatrice et Bénédict. The Manhattan School of Music*

Franz Liszt (1811–1886). *Austrian National Library Picture Archive, Vienna*

Johannes Brahms (1833–1897). *Austrian National Library Picture Archive, Vienna*

Clara Schumann (1819–1896). *R. Berges*

Brahms' house at Bad Ischl. *Austrian Information Service*

Johann Strauss (1825–1899) and Brahms at Strauss' villa in Bad Ischl in 1895. *Votava, Vienna*

Brahms' grave in Vienna. *Austrian Information Service*

Part Three
A Look at Others:
Librettist and Cataloguer

ARABELLA'S FATHERS

THE COMPOSITION OF *Arabella* REFLECTS THE FINAL ACHIEVEMENT OF collaboration between Hugo von Hofmannsthal and Richard Strauss. During their association of more than twenty years they had created five other operatic masterpieces, in a librettist-composer relationship that stands as unique in the history of opera. It was never disturbed by serious disagreements but only strengthened through occasional minor differences of opinion—which were debatable from an artistic point of view and always culminated in harmonious agreement. The common work on *Elektra, Der Rosenkavalier, Ariadne auf Naxos, Die Frau ohne Schatten,* and *Die ägyptische Helena* had thoroughly acquainted composer and poet with their respective arts, their working habits, their demands, and their shortcomings.

Ever since the completion and success of *Rosenkavalier*, whose inspiration came to Hofmannsthal "in his sleep" and which proved a joy for Strauss to set to music, both men hoped to create someday a second work with similar facility and enthusiasm. A thread expressing this wish weaves through their entire association, in spite of their being continuously at work on other projects. Finally in 1923, fourteen years after the conception of *Rosenkavalier*, Hofmannsthal seriously discusses such a second work, which should be entertaining on a bourgeois level. In 1927 Strauss becomes more insistent; musically he is ready for a second *Rosenkavalier*, but he lacks an idea, a libretto. Hofmannsthal momentarily suggests a substitute comedy, *Der Fiaker als Graf,* for which he has made notes, but a little later he dismisses the plot as too conversational and not colorful enough for an opera. He has been able, however, to use

131

some of its mood and setting and combines it with his original story, *Lucidor*. At the end of 1927, he is convinced that this material will yield a libretto which will be "no less gay than *Die Fledermaus* and related to *Rosenkavalier*."

Hofmannsthal's prime concern is four main parts: two sisters (sopranos), whom as characters he compares to Carmen and Micaela, one (Arabella) proud and brilliant, the other (Zdenka) gentle and humble; and two male figures opposite them, a tenor (Matteo) and a baritone (Mandryka). The baritone has captured and fired the poet's imagination and enthusiasm, although Arabella is to be the heroine. The baritone will be a "wonderful" person, a wealthy Slavic landowner who comes from the country and with his native customs and tunes invades that "strange world" which is Vienna of the 1860's. Strauss construes Hofmannsthal's enthusiasm to mean that the baritone is the main character, but Hofmannsthal reassures him that it is to be the female figure who holds the center of attraction. He also tries to dispel the composer's fear that Mandryka will be just another Ochs von Lerchenau. But Mandryka, like Ochs, will be the character through whose arrival the plot is set into motion. "The principal character," explains Hofmannsthal, "is a woman . . . in this instance [in contrast to the Marschallin] a young girl. But a mature, knowing girl, aware of her power and dangers, who has the situation completely in hand . . . an altogether modern figure. This type of young woman is of special interest these days—one must not stay behind with the old fashions, but create new ones." Eloquently Hofmannsthal begs Strauss to have faith in his ability to create such a heroine by judging from his past performance, and he cites Elektra, the Marschallin, Ariadne, the dyer's wife, and Helen. He elucidates how "all the characters and the plot revolve about [Arabella]. She is the favorite of the parents; the tenor, Matteo, loves her; the younger sister is her humble rival; the counts are her admirers; she is queen of the ball and the entire piece and, at the end, as in a fairy tale, she marries the wealthy stranger. But what she is and who she is, only the action can reveal."

As a form for the opera Strauss suggests a loosely woven frame, a succession of scenes, to which Hofmannsthal is decidedly opposed. Through the growth of importance of motion pictures this form has become popular; still the poet feels that operas carried out in the strict, conventional form—such as *Meistersinger, The Marriage of Figaro, Carmen* or *Rosenkavalier*—will outlive the loose form that is merely a rushing from scene to scene, a climactic and anti-climactic succession. When Strauss toys with the idea of injecting into the ball scene a big ballet based on Slavic melodies, the thoroughly accurate Hofmannsthal is horrified. "Everything must be right!" in this Vienna-of-1860 setting; at a Viennese *Fiakerball* a Serbian dance would be quite out of place. "Actually, in 1860," he writes Strauss, "one would have danced the waltz. . . ."

In spite of Strauss' occasional blind acceptance of his text, which led him to set such directions as *Diskret vertraulich* (*Der Rosenkavalier*, Act I) and *Leise, sie ist es!* (*Arabella*, Act I) to music, the composer continues to question various aspects of the libretto so that Hofmannsthal defends himself: he is not "blindly in love" with his material. Furthermore, Franz Werfel and Jakob Wassermann have expressed approval of his planned text. The composer's criticism, as usual, stimulates him and spurs him on to be especially attentive and self-critical. With confidence and clarity he expounds the original main theme, taken directly from *Lucidor*: that of the girl whose love for her older sister's suitor increases the more her sister maltreats him. At last, in order to comfort her unsuspecting beloved, she grants him a rendezvous, in the older sister's name, in a dark room at night. Hofmannsthal recalls that some years ago Max Reinhardt found this theme well suited for a musical comedy because of its sentimentality. This, like the entire plot, Hofmannsthal admits is insufficient.

Momentarily, like lightning, a situation for Arabella occurs to him. "This mature, beautiful young girl, who has glimpsed too deeply certain problems of life, has become somewhat bitter, cynical, and resigned; she is ready to go into a dull, sensible marriage (with someone who does not even appear in the opera)." Suddenly she is confronted by the "most unlikely suitor." Inspiration for the abrupt appearance of this picturesque figure has kindled Hofmannsthal's imagination; consequently this second motif replaces the original, which in turn presents a logical reason for the development and acceleration of action as well as a touch of mystery, satisfactorily solved in the last act.

When Hofmannsthal submitted his manuscript to Strauss in May of 1928, the composer was on the whole satisfied with Act I. He liked the characters, in particular Mandryka. His immediate instinctive reaction was, however, that the act weakened toward the end; there were too many important themes treated too casually. Strauss pointed out that for a play the act in its present form might be satisfactory, but for an opera, where so much of the text is lost, the outline must be "stronger and clearer"; the sequence of the "rising action does not follow harmoniously." There is not enough brilliance; Arabella herself does not emerge strongly enough from the frame of surrounding characters. Since these others are interesting and sympathetic themselves, it is difficult to make Arabella more unusual and sparkling without robbing her of her realistic, true-to-life personality. The irresponsible and frivolous suitors, the doubtful financial situation of Waldner, a Vienna that is dangerous and somewhat decadent, are in sharp contrast to the figure of the touching, unstable Zdenka. They actually set off the character of Mandryka who, in Hofmannsthal's words, "is surrounded by the purity of his villages, his oak forests, untouched by an axe, his old folk songs— here the breadth of that big, half-Slavic Austria enters into a Viennese comedy and brings with it a completely different air." But Mandryka must not overshadow Arabella, who with her "courage and sense of responsibility" also rises far above the ordinary, pleasure-loving Vienna.

Strauss' sharp theatrical sense felt again and again that as the heroine Arabella did not project strongly enough. Compared to the Matteo-Zdenka theme, the Arabella-Mandryka action remained secondary, the character of Arabella colorless, Mandryka too good-natured, both altogether "harmless." There were no conflicts to arouse interest, sympathy, or condemnation on the part of the audience. Strauss was groping for a situation in the course of the second act where visual evidence would cause Mandryka to doubt Arabella. Further, he was not entirely happy about the "1860 Viennese atmosphere," too reminiscent of *Die Fledermaus*. Hofmannsthal reminded Strauss that he was not the librettist of *Fledermaus*

but of *Rosenkavalier*. The commonplace, frivolous, French-influ-
enced atmosphere of Vienna which was the prime factor of *Fledermaus* would only be secondary to the realistic, serious characterizations in *Arabella*. The librettist reassured the composer that the
music would instil the necessary mixture of lightness and nobility to
make the opera rise above the level of *Fledermaus*. After all, was it
not Strauss himself who had said, "Write like him [Lehár] I cannot,
because in a few measures of mine lies more music than in an entire
Lehár operetta."

Hofmannsthal was content with Strauss' suggestion to breathe
more action and personality into the principal characters, and thus
into the plot itself. At the same time he did not forget to keep the
action natural, compatible with the characters—"lifelike and breathing." Strauss had been somewhat skeptical about the symbolic glass
of water. After all the magic potions of *The Egyptian Helen*, some
of the adverse critics might exploit the joke that "Hofmannsthal has
become quite watery." The poet was not afraid of such censure; the
ceremony was an actual Slavic custom and consequently the scene
was retained.

Never before in their association had the composer exhibited such
pronounced hesitation in setting to music one of Hofmannsthal's
librettos as in the case of *Arabella*. In November, 1928, he was overcome by the feeling that "the characters are not interesting—all like
a bit of old-fashioned theatre. . . . I find it difficult to become enthusiastic about them. As a result I have not yet been able to find a
musical beginning. I shall have to have the whole [libretto] before
me in order to get into the first act." How about giving the final act
a tragic ending? Strauss suggests recklessly, after complaining once
more that Arabella experiences no "spiritual conflict," and that the
"most beautiful poetic raspberry syrup poured into the 'glass of
water' will not overcome the piece's inherent weaknesses and con-
ventionality."

Hofmannsthal remained confident and, with numerous trials, re-
jections, and changes made both on his own initiative and as a result of the composer's suggestions, work on the libretto continued.
Gradually Strauss began to like Acts II and III while Hofmannsthal

almost completely remodeled Act I, especially to expose Arabella as the dominant character.

On the tenth of July, 1929, Hofmannsthal submitted a rewritten Act I to the composer. For the first time, Strauss expressed unreserved enthusiasm for this libretto in a brief telegram. The congratulatory message, however, remained unopened by the poet. On the day of its arrival, Hofmannsthal died of a stroke. Strauss, deeply mourning his "dear poet," completed in solitude the score of what remains their final masterpiece of collaboration, the brilliant, warm, and vibrant *Arabella*.

KOECHEL LISTING . . . .

INSTEAD OF THE USUAL OPUS NUMBER, THE LETTER "K." (FOR KOECHEL) and a number follow each listing of a Mozart work. This identification originates from a chronological catalogue to the composer's works, made possible by one man's painstaking labor in ploughing through the maze of more than 600 unnumbered compositions.

Ludwig Alois Friedrich Koechel, one of the "divine Mozart's" greatest admirers, was born at Stein on the Danube on January 14, 1800. His father, a government official, as well as his mother, brothers, and sister, died while Ludwig was small, so that the boy spent a lonely youth without companionship or cause for joy. In his solitude, he turned all his attention and concentration to his studies and proved a brilliant student. After a thorough education at the Gymnasium at Krems and high school in Vienna, he achieved his doctorate in law.

Because he was intelligent, well-bred, and widely cultured, he was favored to become tutor to the Archduke Carl's sons from 1827 to 1842. With one of his charges, young Friedrich, he visited England and found that he as well as his pupil profited from this trip by being able to further his own academic interests and meeting famous men everywhere.

In 1832 Koechel was elected imperial councillor; in recognition of services to the court, he received the cross of the Leopold Order of Knighthood in 1842. At the age of forty-three—now Ritter von Koechel—he retired from the royal service and settled in Vienna. Five years later, however, when his friend Franz von Scharschmid became president of assizes in Teschen, Koechel followed him there and later to Salzburg. In 1850 Koechel accepted the position of imperial and royal councillor for education but did not retain it for long, since his theories and views were considered far too liberal. After this final official position, he devoted himself exclusively to his own studies of musicology, botany, and mineralogy.

In 1863 we find him back in Vienna with Scharschmid, until on June 3, 1877, he died at the home of his former pupil, Fieldmarshal Grand Duke Albrecht, where he had been granted permission to reside for life.

By nature a studious, quiet, and methodical person, it is not surprising that Koechel was shocked at the disorganized state in which he found the works of his beloved Mozart, who had died so young— nine years before he himself was born. Neither is it surprising that with utmost confidence this orderly-minded man, trained as a lawyer and teacher, set himself to the tremendous task of dating all Mozart's compositions. Koechel did not spare time, effort, or money; he followed each clue, left no stone unturned, and plodded through every detail. Manuscripts had to be located and examined, people interviewed, records carefully checked.

The basis for Koechel's work was a catalogue, started by Mozart himself and kept up to date until shortly before the composer's death, entitled *Verzeichnis aller meiner Werke vom Monath Februarius 1784, bis Monath*—(Catalogue of all my works from the month of February, 1784, until the month of—). Koechel's labor required diligence, enthusiasm, and idealism. He possessed all three, as well as a reverential admiration for Mozart. When the serious, scholarly, and retiring man let his profound love of music and adoration for Mozart shine through the stiff and rather cool exterior of his personality, his learnedness reflected an infectious sparkle and his reserve was softened by an appealing charm.

Koechel's dignity, sureness, and intellectual superiority, resulting from his seriousness and early maturity, were often misunderstood as snobbery in circles which could not penetrate the surface of his reserve. Although he was witty and socially at ease, people believed him to be proud and aloof. Only those who were more intimate with him knew Koechel to be kindly, generous, sympathetic, a true friend in need and deed.

Koechel's varied interests and thorough schooling are best illustrated by his publications on many subjects. First printed in 1856 was the study *Die Litterarische Thaetigkeit des Carl Ehrenbrecht, Freiherrn von Moll* (The Literary Activities of Carl Ehrenbrecht, Baron Moll). His diverse scientific projects took him on long trips to Italy, Sicily, France, Switzerland, the northern tip of Scandinavia, and Russia. A man of means, he was able to make these voyages to substantiate his research. Various contributions to scientific literature resulted from this work. He published books on minerals and meteorology, as well as historical and biographical volumes. The first of these dealt with an account of music at the Austrian court (*Musik am Oesterreichischen Hofe,* Vienna, 1856). In 1862 Koechel produced his first Mozart essay, entitled "On the Extent of Mozart's Musical Productivity." Three years later he edited *Eighty-three Newly Discovered Original Letters of Ludwig van Beethoven to Archduke Rudolf,* Vienna, 1865. Next he discussed music at the Imperial Court in the middle of the sixteenth century: *Die kaiserliche Hofmusikkapelle von 1543–1567,* Vienna, 1869. His final contribution to musical literature, a treatise on the composer and court conductor Johann Joseph Fux, was published in Vienna in 1872.

Through all these works, however, in addition to a volume of poetry discovered after his death, Koechel would never have attained a fraction of the fame he did achieve through his comprehensive Mozart catalogue.

For twenty years of his life he traveled to gather the valuable, systematically ordered information contained in his *Chronological-Thematic Catalogue of all Compositions by W. A. Mozart.* He was familiar with the exactitude demanded by scientific classification and applied his knowledge and experience to the confused state of Mozart's compositions. He even followed Mozart's journeys, travelling extensively in Germany, France, England, and Italy. The atmosphere of the years spent in Mozart's Salzburg with his friend von Scharschmid provided additional incentive to his project. Because he revered the master, he expected no credit for his work, enjoying it as a good deed to the composer's memory. He had to infuse a sense of orderliness into everything he particularly loved and esteemed.

His earlier work on Mozart's productivity was only a forerunner to the great *Catalogue,* published by Breitkopf and Haertel in Leipzig in 1862 with an introduction eulogizing Mozart's famed biographer, Otto Jahn, and dedicating the work to him. The fact that somewhat later (1876–1886) Breitkopf and Haertel published the first complete edition of Mozart's works is also credited in part to Koechel's efforts. After publication of the *Catalogue* itself, Koechel continued his research and in later years contributed additions to his book in the *Allgemeine Musikzeitung*.

A long illness slowly shattered the unusual vigor of Koechel's body and mind. He had been a man of pious nature. His picture shows him to have been a handsome man with bright eyes and a high forehead. Only after his death, through bequests to many institutions, the extent of his philanthropic acts became known. His herbarium and large collection of minerals went to the K. K. Obergymnasium at Krems. Other schools and cultural organizations became the beneficiaries of large sums of money.

It was a fitting tribute that Mozart's Requiem was performed at the funeral of the man whose name was to remain linked with his master's.

Three Italian comedy figures, porcelain of Kloster-Veilsdorf, 18th century.
S. Berges

Gaetano Donizetti (1797–1848).
Opera News

The Donizetti monument in Bergamo, his birthplace. *Opera News*

Heinrich Heine (1797–1856), engraving by Weber. S. *Berges*

Vincenzo Bellini (1801–1835). *Ballerini & Fratini*

Bellini's birthplace, Catania. *Italian State Tourist Office*

The Beethoven monument in Vienna. *Austrian Information Service*

Johann Wolfgang von Goethe (1749–1832), engraving by Mueller. *S. Berges*

Leonore shields and saves Florestan from Pizarro, in a scene from Beethoven's *Fidelio*. *Austrian Information Service*

A room in the Brentano country home where Goethe often visited. Bettina Brentano was a friend of both Beethoven and Goethe. *German Tourist Information Office*

Jacques Offenbach (1819–1880), as seen with his cello by Laemlein in 1850. *French Embassy Press & Information Division*

E. T. A. Hoffmann (1776–1822). *Opera News*

Scene from Offenbach's *La belle Hélène*. *French Embassy Press & Information Division*

Onegin (George London) tells Tatiana (Lucine Amara) that he cannot share her affection for him, in a scene from Tchaikovsky's *Eugene Onegin*. *Metropolitan Opera Assn., Inc.*

Onegin (George London) meets Tatiana (Lucine Amara), now Princess Gremin, for the last time, in a scene from Tchaikovsky's *Eugene Onegin*. *Metropolitan Opera Assn., Inc.*

Part Four
The Play's the Thing

GENOVEVA—A FORGOTTEN OPERA

IT WAS A NATURAL PART OF HIS DEVELOPMENT AS A COMPOSER THAT Robert Schumann should venture into the operatic field. He had become successful as a composer of piano music, songs, orchestral and chamber music, and even a secular oratorio. At the height of his creative power, in the early 1840's, he became seriously engrossed in searching for a suitable operatic subject. Like Beethoven, Schumann had no especial passion for opera, but was obsessed with the idea of composing for the stage. Both composers probably felt with equal conviction that without having been creative in this important dramatic musical form, their lifework would be incomplete. Because their abilities were more pronounced in other areas of musical composition, they made conscious and conscientious efforts to meet the challenge of opera. They worked with characteristic fervor and intensity, unlike Wagner or Verdi, whose very temperaments breathed drama and who, once naturally drawn to the magic and passion of the stage, were never again to withdraw from it.

On September 1, 1842, Schumann wrote to the composer, Carl Kossmaly, "Do you know my artist's prayer for morning and night? It is called 'German Opera.' Here one can be active." At this time he was attracted to a number of varied subjects of romantic, historic, or fantastic nature and literary merit. Among other ideas, he considered stories by E. T. A. Hoffmann and H. C. Andersen, "The False Prophet" from *Lalla Rookh* by Thomas Moore, Byron's *Corsair* and *Sardanapalus, Faust, Till Eulenspiegel, The Nibelungenlied, The Song Contest in the Wartburg,* Calderón's *El Galán fantasmo, Abélard and Héloïse,* and *Maria Stuart.* Inevitably, the dominating spirit of German romanticism led him to consider subjects similarly

143

chosen by Richard Wagner. Thus after Wagner had read his *Lohengrin* text at one of the weekly meetings held at Eduard Bendemann's, Schumann rejected his own thoughts about the Arthur legends.

In 1847 he began to keep a *Theaterbüchlein* in which he recorded his ideas and impressions of operas he had seen. He observed with a constructively critical mind as his own desire to compose an opera grew more urgent. On March 15, 1847, he noted in his *Haushaltbuch* simply, "Desire to compose an opera. Plans." He was enthusiastically reading in the *Odyssey*, discussing opera plans for Slowacky's *Mazeppa* with the poet Robert Reinick, and composing scenes for *Faust*. Then, within two weeks, he had spontaneously chosen a text not previously considered. For April 1st the *Haushaltbuch* reads, "*Genoveva* by Hebbel. Ideas for the overture and decision to use this text." During the month of April he expressed several times his happiness over having discovered Friedrich Hebbel's tragedy. Within four days he sketched the overture. With Reinick he worked on the libretto. For relaxation he continued to read in the *Odyssey* and played the Beethoven C Minor Quartet.

Soon, however, differences arose between him and Reinick concerning the book. Reinick was "terribly sentimental," although "he has such an exceptionally strong example in Hebbel," Schumann complained to Ferdinand Hiller. To solve the problem of the libretto, Schumann ultimately approached the greatly admired and respected author himself. Modestly and parenthetically he introduced himself: "After having read your *Genoveva* (I am a musician), I became not only absorbed with the poem itself but also with the thought of what marvelous material it would be for music. The more often I read your tragedy . . . the more musically alive did its poetry become within me." He related his problem of deriving a suitable libretto from the play: "At last, in some desperation over its success, it occurred to me whether the straight path might not be the best, if I might not turn directly to the true poet to request his assistance." Hebbel's reply was cordial, he even visited the Schumanns on his next trip through Dresden, but he left the adaptation of a libretto from his tragedy entirely to Schumann. That Schumann's esteem was reciprocated by Hebbel is evidenced by the fact that six years later the poet dedicated and sent to the composer the manuscript of his *Michel Angelo*. Schumann, in turn, acknowledged the gift with a musical setting of the poet's *Nachtlied* with which he surprised Hebbel on his birthday.

Schumann might have consulted with Wagner who had offered advice about the *Genoveva* text. He hesitated, then went ahead to work on it alone, relying entirely upon his own limited operatic observations. Enthusiastically he became engrossed in the composition of the music. He worked with such excitement and intensity that he was taken ill during the time of the opera's creation. In August, 1848, *Genoveva* was finished. To his friend Johannes Verhulst, Schumann wrote in the fall: "I completed *Genoveva* last August and, coming in sight of the end, I felt joyfully convinced that much of it had been successfully accomplished. Now I want to see and hear it. . . ." He considered 1848 his most fruitful year and named *Genoveva* and *Album for the Young* with particular satisfaction as products of that year.

Schumann sent the *Genoveva* score to the Leipzig opera conductor, Julius Rietz, with a request indicating a vague uncertainty about the dramatic aspect of the work: "Wherever the dramatic effect is held up through too much music or otherwise, everything must be sacrificed, and I would be grateful to you for pointing this out to me."

The opera was to be premiered in Leipzig but the first performance was postponed several times. Finally after two years of disappointments and waiting, on June 25, 1850, *Genoveva* was produced. Among the celebrities present at this event were Franz Liszt, Nils Gade, Hiller, Ludwig Spohr, Ignaz Moscheles, Carl Reinecke, and Moritz Hauptmann. The first two performances were conducted by the composer, the third was taken over by Rietz.

On the surface the opera was a grand success. Clara Schumann noted in her diary after the premiere that, "The singers took all sorts of pains. The first two acts went very well; but in the third, Wiedemann (Golo) had the bad luck to forget the letter for Siegfried. Both ran desperately about, and this scene went quite for nothing. The singers themselves were so upset by this that the last two acts went less well. And another handicap lay in the poor furnishing of the magic chamber. Still, the public was very attentive, and at the end loud applause twice made the singers and Robert appear." Although each of the following two performances proved more successful than the preceding, there seemed to be no further interest in the opera. Schumann, who at first had believed in the work's success, soon had to realize that *Genoveva* did not quite match his earlier masterpieces in other forms of composition. He comforted himself with the thought that the public was easily carried away by momentary operatic fashions, such as the flamboyant works of Meyerbeer, which he detested. He believed that *Genoveva*, if "fostered with some love cannot miss a lively effect. To come close to nature and truth was my highest aspiration; whoever expected something else will of course be disappointed in the opera." On August 2, 1851, he wrote to his publisher, Peters, who had printed the opera in advance of its premiere, "I begin to worry whether you are going to get back your large investment in the opera. But it will not be the fault of my work if it does not become so quickly profitable to you. That would assuredly be owing to the terribly degenerated taste of the theatrical public."

As soon as he had completed *Genoveva*, Schumann again had "several plans, namely dramatic ones, going through [his] head." In the future he intended to devote his entire strength to opera. After realizing that *Genoveva* was not the overwhelming success he had expected it to be, he still hoped in 1850 that "with time my aspirations in this, the dramatic field, will receive their true appreciation." But his health and his creative activity were on the decline; *Genoveva* remained his only opera. Five years later, on April 9, 1855, Liszt produced the work in Weimar. Since that performance, *Genoveva* has been dismissed as one of Schumann's lesser compositions and, except for the overture, seems to have been utterly forgotten.

Such neglect was and is not justified. If Schumann's strength did not lie in operatic drama, this does not mean that his only opera is without merit. The work must be heard and judged as a product of its particular composer and of its time. Schumann's operatic style can hardly be considered less advanced than Wagner's of this period. Parts of the score employ chromatic progressions which Wagner was later to use in his *Tristan und Isolde*. The fact that Wagner's strong and unique dramatic genius devoted exclusively to opera overpowered other, lesser voices in this field, was merely an unfortunate stroke of fate for Schumann. Since he was of minor importance on the operatic scene, his innovations over the conventional romantic works of Weber, Spohr, and Marschner went unnoticed. He used themes, or leitmotivs, throughout the opera to express psychological associations. He dispensed with recitatives so that the opera is of a fluent texture throughout. This novel method had its disadvantages since moments that should be highly dramatic were simply woven into the overall song-like fabric.

That Schumann slightly by-passed dramatic forcefulness in his opera obviously stemmed from his own character. He was a poet rather than a dramatist. His work was romantic-lyric. The endearing honesty and sincerity of his nature were reflected in his music. To such simplicity and straightforwardness in self-expression the exaggerated histrionics of emotional and melodramatic climaxes were foreign. He abhorred artificiality and effects; his artistry expressed truth. He felt that every dramatic piece of fiction should represent a slice of life. In his efforts to keep characters and situations true to life, he weakened the drama of the story. He tried to avoid sentimentality in the character of Genoveva. Because of his fear of triteness and exaggeration his message on the stage became an understatement. His character outlines tended to blur instead of retaining the sharply etched reality and complexity they possessed in Hebbel's tragedy.

What Schumann's artistic integrity did achieve was a sensitive lyric delineation of character and situation instead of a powerful dramatic work. He imbued his opera with the intimate poetic qualities of his songs and piano music. Similarly, he created moments of vigor and freshness as we know them from the symphonies or the piano concerto. Schumann is not a "popular" composer in the sense as are Puccini or Tchaikovsky, or even Beethoven of his early and middle periods. Neither could *Genoveva* ever be measured against the popular *Aida* or *Carmen*. The well-made overture with its exposition of themes which become meaningful as the opera unfolds is a fine concert piece as well as introduction to the opera. Its summarizing nature adds to *Genoveva*'s unity. The opera itself offers much music of outstanding quality, such as Genoveva's touching arias and the bright choruses.

Schumann has been criticized for excessive tampering with Hebbel's text, for simplifying characters and situations, for entirely omitting the moving epilogue of the drama. I know of no opera taken from a play that has not somehow suffered through its transformation into a libretto. Schumann's text, if not highly dramatic, certainly has poetic and literary value. If, as adverse criticism has stated, events occur too quickly one upon the other in the opera, those who disapprove of long operas and operatic tirades should become staunch supporters of *Genoveva*. It has been said that the opera simply becomes a message of virtue triumphing over evil, that the psychological complexities of Hebbel's characters are lost. However, it cannot be gainsaid that Genoveva remains a poignant figure in her virtue as in her plight and that the traits of her antagonists are properly expressed. The predicament of the young wife (Genoveva), left in the care of her warring husband's favorite (Golo), who himself loves and desires her and who, when she refuses to yield to him, accuses her of infidelity, presents an affecting situation. The credulous husband (Siegfried) does not much arouse our sympathy either in Hebbel's tragedy or Schumann's opera, regardless of his contrition at the end. Golo's complex characterization loses some effectiveness in the opera. On the other hand, Genoveva's stature remains impressive; she glows with the composer's understanding and sensitivity.

One might tie Schumann's success in musical portraiture of women to his happily realized relationships with women in real life. Both his mother and Clara favorably influenced his attitude toward the female sex. The heroine of *Frauenliebe und Leben,* the Peri, and Genoveva bespeak this admiration. Beethoven, too, in *Fidelio,* praised womanly virtue, but in his case it was an idealization of what he could not find in real life, rather than Schumann's appreciation of what he had experienced. Nevertheless, it is interesting to note that both composers searched extensively for a suitable libretto before they embarked on their operatic ventures. Both stressed their heroines, neglecting other important operatic aspects. Both were eminently successful in expressing themselves and their aims in the orchestral overtures to their operas. Both thought highly of their single endeavors into the musical-dramatic field.

In Schumann's case, however, it was not only the saintly heroine who attracted him to Hebbel's subject. Schumann was drawn to the poet whose words regarding his own work might also be applied to that of the composer: "I want only to contend against the widely spread misconception that the poet can give something else but himself, his own process of life." Schumann, too, might have said, "History for the poet is a vehicle toward the embodiment of his views and ideas, but not in reverse is the poet the resurrection angel of history."

Genoveva should not be compared to the operas of Wagner or of anyone else, consequently to be judged as undramatic and inferior. It should be considered rather as an individual independent work. As the sole effort in its genre by a prominent acknowledged composer acclaimed for many forms of musical expression, *Genoveva* has lain forgotten far too long. It is high time that the opera is produced on the stage or in concert form so that it can be evaluated on its own merits as a work representative of its composer and his place in the history of music.

THE DEVIL'S DOMAIN

THE FINAL ACT OF GOUNOD'S *Faust* OPENS WITH THE WALPURGIS Night, or Witches' Sabbath, a brief but eerie and effective ballet through which flit fantastic creatures veiled in semi-darkness. A light flickers here and there, penetrating the hazy atmosphere under a shrouded moon. There is ceaseless movement and activity in the scene depicting the underworld. Mephistopheles and a bewildered Faust ask "Where are we?" in this unearthly world. Immediately the witches surround the stranger, offering him nectar and caresses. Visions of courtesans of ancient times, as well as Helen of Troy and Cleopatra, arise before him and momentarily dispel his memories of former events. But then a haggard, disheveled white figure, tortured and cringing in anguish and despair, wildly dances in upon the scene. Faust, recognizing her as Marguerite, notices a red ribbon like the cut of an axe around her neck and, when she falls lifeless to the ground, commands Mephistopheles to take him to her.

Like the rest of the opera, this scene is based on Goethe's drama *Faust* (Part I); but the German poet is more explicit than the librettist in his description of the Walpurgis Night, so that there may be no mistake as to its amoral and lowly setting. Here is his chance to contrast Mephistopheles' abode with the noble dignity of the Prologue in Heaven, with which the play opens. (The Prologue was not used in the opera.) The Lord allows the devil a certain amount of freedom in causing the evil which is an important element in life. But the devil's actual effectiveness is negligible; "evil is only ridiculous; it is not dangerous." Here then is the extent of Mephistopheles' activity in his own sphere.

In Goethe's Walpurgis Night a demonic will-o'-the-wisp—known to lead men astray and corrupt them—guides the way for Faust and Mephistopheles to the Brocken in the Harz Mountains. As they approach they hear trees groaning and roots creaking and yawning, accompanying the choruses of the witches. Faust, still the passive onlooker, the doctor and scholar searching for knowledge, hopes that in all this evil some riddles may be solved. He asks Mephistopheles if he is going to appear as a magician or the devil, but Mephistopheles replies that he is so at home here that no matter how he disguises himself he will be found out—"smelled out." He calls Faust's attention to Lilith, the seducer of young men. One witch offers her wares to attract customers. Everything she sells has an appropriately evil past: cups that contained poison, jewels that led beautiful women astray, swords that broke vows. To the accompaniment of ribald conversation, Faust dances with a beautiful young witch while Mephistopheles capers about with an old one. Faust leaves his partner when a red mouse jumps out of her mouth— a common occurrence with witches, but one that usually happens when they are asleep. Mephistopheles cannot understand why this should make any difference to Faust.

But our hero's attention has been taken up elsewhere. He is shaken by an apparition of Gretchen standing alone in the distance in chains. Her eyes are like those of a dead person, not closed by a loving hand. Mephistopheles attempts to assure him lightly that she is lifeless, a vision conjured up by magic, an idol. To meet it bodes no good; it might turn him into stone. But Mephistopheles' words arouse Faust's feelings more strongly. The evil one does not take Faust's absorption seriously and is quite unwilling when the despairing lover endeavors to return to Gretchen. This time Faust's will prevails, however.

Faust, who after Gretchen's (Marguerite's) seduction and Valentin's death let himself be guided into Mephistopheles' domain, feels the pangs of conscience. In this scene his inner conflict becomes apparent. His love for Gretchen is the weapon that helps him conquer the difficulties with which Mephistopheles confronts him and obstructs her path toward salvation. In addition, Gretchen's case has fallen under godly jurisdiction, thus paralyzing the power of Mephistopheles, the true murderer of her brother. The police, a human invention, cannot harm the devil, but crimes like murder and manslaughter are punished through heavenly judgment in whose execution the devil is powerless to intervene.

Gretchen, on the other hand, pure and innocent, has been seduced by the Mephistophelian side of Faust; a demoniacal hand has gripped her life. It follows that her brother is killed. She herself is beset with a mounting sense of guilt and harassed at church by the Evil Spirit. Devilish forces have struck with full impact and intensity into her orderly bourgeois life. The Walpurgis Night accentuates the contrast between Gretchen's former bright existence and her dark present by plunging us into the totally enveloping atmosphere of the devil's world. Her lonely, touching figure at church left the impression of her wavering in the mist that is to be the deciding factor between sanity and madness. The penetrating dissonance increases in the subsequent scene where Valentin is slain and dies cursing her. The Walpurgis Night serves as the tense *cadenza* sustaining the tone that leads to the tragic prison-scene finale.

As for Mephistopheles' part in the Walpurgis Night scene, his motive is to draw Faust away from Gretchen—mentally and physically—and divert him with other pleasures from the sequence of events which has already occurred. Thus he leads Faust into his world of degradation and depravity. The sensual pleasures awaiting Mephistopheles there will surely entice Faust as well. Mephistopheles knows only such pleasures; his straightforward uncomplicated mind and active nature have no alternative. His action merely affirms the legitimacy of every wish. He does not divine the "two souls" that are harbored in Faust's breast, the good and evil, or the conflicting active and passive forces contending within a man. How could he, the simple devil, guess that the godlier Faust, seeing Gretchen's suffering figure among all this base, lewd, meaningless, and almost ridiculous revelry, would forget his surroundings on the spot and command the devil to help him save her immediately? The night of the witches' celebration only accents the wronged Gretchen's helplessness and misery, arousing in Faust the first signs of noble human instincts.

Although the Walpurgis Night is often omitted at performances of Gounod's opera, and similarly is accorded a secondary place in

Goethe's drama, the scene is a significant part of the play. One commentator goes so far as to suggest that "in spite of grandiose descriptions of nature and other magnificent details [the Walpurgis Night] is best excluded from performances and without hesitation may be skipped in reading."[*]

The seemingly superfluous Walpurgis Night serves as the necessary transition giving unity to the whole, climaxed by Gretchen's madness and death in prison. While Faust tastes the shallow pleasures of hell in company of the witches, the significant moment occurs when immersed in sinfulness he is confronted by purity. Simultaneously the thought hovers that during the course of this scene, although not present, Gretchen is going through a purgatory which her gentle nature cannot withstand. Hope or sanity yields to utter despair or madness. Faust escapes from the hell of Walpurgis Night to find himself at the gates of another more horrible damnation which has his beloved Gretchen in its grasp. It is ultimately her goodness, her faith that save her.

* * * * * *

In the interest and development of the three main characters concerned there was ample reason for Goethe to include the Walpurgis Night in his drama. In 1777 the poet visited the Brocken in the Harz Mountains, obviously with the intention of studying the background for the writing of this scene. The idea to utilize it in his *Faust* may have stemmed from a poem by J. F. Loewen, written in 1756, which for the first time associated Faust and the Walpurgis Night. The poem mentioned "immortal great Faust" and "to the left of Beelzebub sat Dr. Faust."

The Walpurgis Night events which furnish such an appropriate setting to activate the passive Faust originate in an old folk superstition. The night takes its name from the historical St. Walpurgis, or Walburga, who followed her brothers Willibald and Wunnibald from their native England to Germany to help spread Christianity. After Wunnibald's death she assumed and until her death held the

---

[*] Karl Alt in *"Einleitung des Herausgebers," Goethes Werke, Fünfter Teil, Faust,* Goldene Klassiker Bibliothek, Berlin.

direction of the cloister of Heidenheim, which he had founded in 763. Her earliest biography, written by the monk Wolfhart at the cloister of Hasenfried near the end of the ninth century, states that from her bones flowed a miraculous healing fluid. In the middle of the ninth century her body was removed to Eichstätt where a cloister was erected in her honor. Her attributes are a flask of balm and three ears of grain. Wolfhart's biography contains numerous legends about her which spread and became quite popular. She was canonized on the first of May, the date which bears her name. Other harvest days are also dedicated to her. The nine nights preceding May 1st are called Walpurgis Nights. Of these, most important is the eve of May Day.

According to common belief, at this time of the year Walpurgis, as a woman in white with fiery shoes on her feet and a golden crown on her head, is pursued by evil spirits in valleys and fields. Whoever offers her protection and assistance in her need is rewarded generously with gold. The legends that sprang up identify her with tree spirits and other legendary figures, so that as a spirit she received her name from the calendar. Since this time of the year was considered holy by the barbaric Germans, the Walpurgis Day, too, was holy. The day and preceding night are rich with magic, favorable for predicting the future and known for certain cures.

During Walpurgis Night all the witches ride on broomsticks or he-goats into the mountains and have their yearly tryst with their master, the devil. After applying the witch ointment and reciting a secret formula, they are able to ride up through chimneys and hurry through the air. In the company of the devil, whom they honor with their evil practices, they dance away the snow from the mountain tops and perform crude diversion for their master. Then they fly about and cause what havoc they can. It's a big night for the devil and his witch associates! High mountain tops (*Blocksberge*) are their meeting places, in particular the highest summit of the Harz Mountains, the Brocken.

The folk superstitions take their origin in the sacrificial May Day feasts of the heathen Germans, who gathered on the mountain tops for frolicking, dancing, drinking, and mass meetings. Female magicians were usually present at these affairs and came to be associated with witches who might be of a friendly or hostile disposition. According to superstitious belief, they continued to meet clandestinely with their disciples, even in Christian times when such gatherings had been prohibited. When Christian priests taught that the cult could claim the devil himself as its originator and master, tales of spooks, ghosts, apparitions, and haunted places flourished in the susceptible minds of the sixteenth and seventeenth centuries.

These superstitions, nourished with the darkness of ignorance, inspired many German poets but especially Goethe, who used them effectively to shape the transition scene which resolves in Gretchen's death and salvation, and Faust's first glimpse of the realization of life.

DUMAS, SON OF DUVAL

IN NINETEENTH-CENTURY PARIS, WHERE INTRIGUES WERE AS TURBU-
lent in private as in public life, Alexandre Dumas, *fils*, developed
under his reckless father's influence from a handsome young dandy
into a severe bourgeois moralist.

Alexandre had suffered an unhappy childhood and adolescence
through his irregular birth. When the elder Dumas, having gained
renown and popularity, finally decided to acknowledge his son, he
told him to enjoy life. Alexandre obeyed. Thus, at twenty, he was a
fashionable lion of the Parisian boulevards, an expert in foils and
fancies, hurrying from loge to salon.

Courtesans reigned like queens. Lola Montez, who later attached
herself to Franz Liszt, in turn to become the mistress of King Ludwig I of Bavaria, frequented the boudoir of Marie Duplessis, known
in opera as Violetta Valery. Liszt himself, who for a time had chosen
to live an idyllic life in Switzerland with Countess Marie d'Agoult
after she had left her husband and child for his sake, became one of
Marie Duplessis' lovers. Five years had elapsed since Georges
Sand's association with Alfred de Musset, when she embarked upon
her celebrated affair with Frédéric Chopin. Through intrigue as
well as talent, Rachel, who had rejected the elder Dumas' love,
achieved supreme heights as the outstanding actress of the period,
ruthlessly leaving behind her such shadows as Mademoiselle
George, another favorite of the elder Dumas.

Intense feelings of competition and subsequent revenge drove
courtesans, actresses, and female literary figures alike into scandal-
ous situations, liaisons, feuds, and jealousies. These became the
themes of the novels of Georges Sand, Marie d'Agoult, and Honoré
de Balzac.

Into this period of wild extravagance falls the younger Dumas'
affair with Marie Duplessis. From it emerged his first literary successes, the novel *La Dame aux camélias* and the play he adapted
from it in 1849. For three years the play was barred by the censors
as immoral. Dumas, who was to be remembered as one of the century's reformers as much as a great dramatist, was criticized in three
confidential puritanical reports prepared by the censors of the Second Empire. These reports, which he did not see until a few years
before his death, stated that his choice of characters and their
crudeness went beyond the most advanced limits of theatrical tol-
erance. The liberal-minded Gustave Flaubert, in agreement with
the censors, observed that Dumas would conciliate *à perpétuité
toute la lorettanerie,* while Horace de Viel-Castel remarked bitterly
that "this piece is a shame for the period it supports, for the government which tolerates it, for the public which applauds it. . . ."

Yet this youthful play, idealistically painting free love in a romantic setting and totally disregarding the outside world, is also a
product of the author's realistic and moral sense. A casual reading
shows the dramatist carried away by passionate love. Impulsively
he translates its memory into a play. Subjectively he reflects the
period in which he lives and immortalizes his personal tragic adventure. Boldly he takes a well known courtesan from contemporary
life, still alive in memory to those who knew her personally and by
repute, and idealizes her as she rises above her situation, capable
of pure selfless love. This was certainly without precedent.

At the same time the playwright serves as a spectator, pointing at
the hollow life of the courtesan, and satirizing foolish fops who are
the mainstay of her life. It is an idle existence without vigor or ambition. There is Prudence, most realistically drawn, whose lovers have
disappeared together with her youthful beauty and charm. She becomes the laughing stock of the others and lives a drab existence
by endless borrowing and procuring. Such an honest lifelike characterization can hardly serve to spread or support immorality. As a
final touch, two of the minor characters, Gustave and Nichette,
legalize their love affair by marriage.

But it is in the figure of the father, M. Duval (Verdi's Giorgio
Germont), that Dumas first projects his moral views. It is he who im-

troduces wisdom, sensibility, and dignity into the play. He remains adamant in his demand of Marguerite that she break off her association with his son, Armand. In the final act he relents enough to write her in sympathy and admiration because "she has kept her word beyond her strength." In the *Traviata* libretto, however, the unbending moralist loses his inflexibility by two superfluous appearances. At the end of the third act he appears briefly to upbraid his son for mistreating a woman who *did* love him truly and faithfully. In the final act he remorsefully admits his error in separating the lovers. The respectable Germont, bowed with contrition, begs forgiveness of the courtesan.

Although the libretto remains essentially faithful to the play— except for the elimination of several minor characters—this self-accusing old man is too meek to be compared to the decorous, sensibly conventional father of the original. When the play was first performed in 1852, M. Duval removed his hat when he spoke to Marguerite. In 1884, however, when the play enjoyed another long run, Dumas gave instructions to Lafontaine, who was playing M. Duval, to keep his hat on throughout the scene. In his later years he also stressed the fact that Marguerite Gautier was not a symbol, but a momentary experience in his own life. He cited her as an example of self-sacrifice carried out by an unlikely character. In his maturity Dumas was able to reason in this manner, but as a passionate young man, his nature was torn between romantic desire and common sense. As a result he created and projected himself into two characters, father and son, the man he wished to be and later became, and the man he was. The implication of the father-son relationship depicted is obvious. Dumas, whose father served as a companion in easy living rather than a guiding spirit, longed for the type of father he created in the play, a man who extricates his son from impossible situations, instead of setting a lusty example and noisily plunging into them. But M. Duval is also Dumas, the moralist, not entirely developed because his own love for Marie Duplessis is still too recent to permit other important aspects of his character to emerge.

More obvious at this early period of the author's life is the direct reflection which M. Duval offers of his actual wish for an idealized understanding father. Although the elder Dumas was more than generous, and elated at his son's success, the son could never quite forgive him for abandoning his mother, and thus making her life and his own childhood so miserable. He was able at the same time to admire his father tremendously, not only because of his success, but also because he lacked altogether the moral scruples which made his son's life so difficult. In 1861, after an illness in Naples where his father was living at that time, he was suddenly over-come during an attack of delirium by an urgent desire to murder his father, sleeping in the adjoining room. He was found on his knees absorbed in fervent prayer and fearing he might be struck with insanity. This moment exaggerated his unforgiving, moral sense so that it outweighed his balanced reasoning power and his actual affection for his father.

His moral sense, springing from his own experience, expanded itself in later years upon the social dangers of prostitution, adultery, desertion, and illegitimacy. M. Duval's moral sermonizing, his realistic reasoning to which Marguerite can find no answer but submission, continues with heightened significance in Dumas' later plays. Never again, however, is he inspired to write so passionately and fluently of romantic love as he did in *La Dame aux camélias* so that here, when M. Duval appears on the scene, the immediate contrast between the immoral courtesan and the stern moralist is especially pronounced.

In *Diane de Lys* (1853), Dumas again recorded a personal experience. After a love affair with Madame de Nesselrode, interrupted when she was recalled to her native Russia, Dumas decided to follow her. Either passport difficulties in East Prussia prevented his traveling farther, or her husband had Dumas expelled from Russia; in any event, he did not see her again. Consequently, he wrote *Diane de Lys*, letting his moral scruples create a denouement in which the adulterous lover is killed by the husband. As Dumas explains in the preface to the play, "It is the counterpart of a personal experience to which art has given a logical development and conclusion which, luckily, were missing in reality."

From middle age onward his moral sense gained such momentum that he tended to create characters as antitheses of "right" and "wrong." They became symbols of a type, destroying the atmosphere of reality he had achieved in the early *Dame aux camélias*. Here, although he was young and loose in his habits, Dumas was able to preach morality in opposition to sincere passionate feelings; yet his M. Duval was human and sympathetic despite his stern moral aspect.

Little is known of Dumas' marriage and family. With maturity he became more reticent about his inner and family life. His daughter called it a typical bourgeois existence with regular hours and filled with work. Although such an agitator for moral reform, he was not entirely faithful to his wife, but on the whole proved to be a good, loving husband and father.

It is ironic that the popular author of *La Dame aux camélias*, from whom the public expected more plays in a similar vein, should in subsequent creations stand firmly as a relentless moralist, since he, himself, had planted a major obstacle in his own path. The success of his early play had provoked such torrents of literature extolling the courtesan that prostitution spread and flourished. It remained unnoticed that the earnest voice of respectability was most persuasively expressed by M. Duval in the "immoral" *La Dame aux camélias*.

THE MARRIAGE OF
NORTH AND SOUTH

A NUMBER OF RENOWNED POETS—FRIEDRICH VON SCHILLER, VICTOR Hugo, Alexandre Dumas—furnished Verdi with books for his operas. Yet all his life the one poet who most fascinated, challenged, eluded, and was conquered by his creative spirit was Shakespeare. In Verdi's operas based on Shakespeare's plays there emerged a unique fusion of northern dramatic and southern musical genius. It was not an easy meeting, nor was it totally successful; it was a singular artistic interaction between two creative giants, each best representing his particular art and region.

The attraction between North and South is old, appearing throughout history. Civilization and culture had their origins in southern climes, gradually growing northward; the Renaissance flourished for a long time in Italy before it reached out to touch and spread into forbiddingly dark northern countries. And in the North artists were ever longing for the sunny southern regions, for warmth, color, lightness, and joy to soften and enrich their own rugged, ponderous, distantly cool and reserved natures, especially during the romantic movement.

Verdi, on the other hand, was a true, full-blooded Italian as well as a romantic composer. He was characteristically earthy and straightforward; his melodies simply flowed, exuding warmth and optimism, even in tragic subjects. Although the psychological and philosophical aspects of Shakespeare's art no doubt fascinated him as part of the strange and only vaguely understood northern artistic temperament, it was the terse dramatic situations, the outright

161

horror, and unfettered passions that stimulated his creativeness. These were closely akin to the Italian character and Verdi's period.

Lessing had stated that "Shakespeare will be studied but not plundered." Verdi, who claimed that he had devoted much time to the study of the poet, defended himself against his critics after the Paris failure of *Macbeth*, in 1865: "I may not have been successful in *Macbeth*, but to say I do not know, I do not understand Shakespeare —no, by heaven, no! He is one of my very special poets; I have had him in my hands from my earliest youth and read and reread him continually."

No doubt Verdi did understand Shakespeare—with the interpretation of a southerner who is able to create a diabolically villainous Iago out of a psychologically complex character, but who in the case of an enigmatic Hamlet, poetically pondering eternal questions, wisely desists from transforming him into an Italian operatic hero. Verdi remains at all times a realist. The range of his creativeness would never have comprehended characters who are idealistic bearers of ideas and missions, such as Wagner's Parsifal. He could be concerned only with elementary human emotions that affect all people, that cause suffering, joy, misery, and tragedy. His ceaseless attempts to present life and truth dramatically and musically find their focal point in Shakespeare's characters and situations. Several times Verdi was inspired by the English poet's overwhelming, sweeping dramas, with their strangely haunting Nordic flavor and frequently bleak settings, their searching characters often in conflict with the basic elements of existence, their complex thought-processes and actions contrasted with the atmosphere of a barbarian era not long past. But the composer's natural dramatic instinct ultimately chose from Shakespeare's plays only what he could handle; certain plots and actions adapted themselves ideally to operatic treatment. Naturally, even what he selected had to be transformed to suit his purpose and comprehension, so that since the fiasco of *Macbeth* in Paris he has been much criticized for mutilating rather than enhancing Shakespearean perfection.

Verdi was thirty-three when he approached *Macbeth*, his first Shakespearean subject. A conflict other than a love plot attracted him to the tragedy, but from the beginning he admitted that this would not be an easy opera to write. Unquestionably much of Shakespeare's distinction escaped Verdi. He chose the Shakespeare play because it possessed reality of action, even in its fantastic or supernatural scenes, and lent itself to theatrical presentation in the grand-opera tradition. Thus the murder, the appearance of Banquo's ghost, and the atmospheric night scenes generate the proper excitement and terror, while Lady Macbeth's sleepwalking scene is completely convincing and moving. The characterizations tend to become more drastic and simplified. The witches assume greater importance and increase in number so that they can be employed in effective choruses. Lady Macbeth is transformed into a real demon, the unsexed woman she aspires to be in Shakespeare's drama; similarly there remains in Macbeth none of the original's early nobility. Absolved of his conscience through Verdi, he turns into a weakling and becomes a tool of his wife's self-centered ambitions. Verdi's Lady Macbeth seeks her own gain rather than her husband's.

In his second attempt to fashion an opera out of a Shakespearean subject, essentially through simplification of character and action, Verdi was confronted by many obstacles. Certainly the choice of *King Lear*, one of the most complex and poetic of Shakespeare's plays, was a huge challenge; perhaps the fact that he had experienced difficulties in composing *Macbeth*, and gained more insight into Shakespeare's art, cautioned him to proceed with special care. In any case, when Andrea Maffei suggested *King Lear* to him as an operatic subject, soon after he had completed *Macbeth*, Verdi rejected the idea with the words "Where there is no love, there can be no music." Possibly there was a lack of desire to understand the powerful and demanding drama, and an instinctive knowledge that this was a play completely unapproachable by Italian opera. But the subject continued to fascinate Verdi.

When Giulio Carcano offered him a libretto for *Hamlet*, Verdi declined it: if a *Lear* was difficult, a *Hamlet* would prove even more so. This was not intended to mean, however, that he might not be interested in *Hamlet* at a later date. But like *Hamlet*, *King Lear* was not to materialize. The structure of Italian operatic music, which draws a distinct line between human emotions and the effects of nature, does not encompass the poetic simile between the agonies of a man's soul and the raging of unleashed elements. Verdi's storm music in *Macbeth* or *Otello* is colorfully descriptive and atmospheric, aptly setting the mood.

It was not until he was past seventy that Verdi turned once more to his favorite dramatist for an operatic subject. Through the machinations of Giulio Ricordi, his publisher, and Franco Faccio, the conductor-composer, Verdi met Arrigo Boito, who consequently wrote for him the libretto of *Otello*. In this play the difficulties were not insurmountable, as they had been in the case of *King Lear*. Here was no necessity of portraying complicated characters whose self-aggrandizement causes horrible murders and the protagonist's eventual downfall, brought on from within rather than by outward circumstance. Nor was there need of depicting the even more intricate inner development and grandeur of a Job-like, universal theme. Although the stature of Othello's character, too, diminished in the operatic treatment through oversimplification, and Iago was transformed from a pathological miscreant into a black operatic villain, Verdi was able to salvage from the drama the basic love story of Othello and Desdemona, who are unwittingly caught and destroyed in the net of Iago's devising. Verdi's music hardly enhances Shakespeare's masterful tragedy; he rather borrows from Shakespeare to create an effective operatic drama. Certainly the composer had gained a profounder understanding of Shakespearean characters since his youthful *Macbeth*. Without altogether sacrificing his Italian operatic style, but by imbuing it with more freedom of form, distinction, and nobility, Verdi drew his delineations more strongly, if with some distortion, and achieved a blend of his own realism and that of Shakespeare.

As has often been noted, Verdi, like Wagner, turned in his old age to comic opera. For forty years he had wanted to write a lyric comedy; its subject, *Falstaff*, had been suggested to him long ago by Carcano. Finally the libretto, drawn from *The Merry Wives of Windsor* and *Henry IV*, was written by Boito, and Verdi at seventy-seven composed what was to be his last operatic masterpiece, the comic counterpart balancing all of his earlier tragedies. In this work he came closest to understanding a character created by the poet he had loved so well all his life. "Falstaff is a wicked fellow," Verdi commented, "who plays nasty pranks of all sorts, but in an engaging fashion. He is a type. They are so rare, such types! The opera is purely comical. Amen."

After Verdi had at last decided on his subject for a comic opera, which had been even harder to find than good dramas, he explained that he was writing it "only for my own amusement." His reputation secure and well earned, he was completely justified in composing with lightness and abandon—without a care for his public—his farewell to the operatic stage. This relaxed, joyful mood after a long and arduous life enabled him to capture in his musical characterization the spirit, irony, and sparkle of the great English clown and his companions. He is loath to take leave of Falstaff, judging from his words of farewell on the original score: "All is ended! Go your way, as long as you can, amusing type of a rogue, forever true, though under different masks, at every time and every place. . . . Go . . . go, away with you. Farewell!"

Comedy had become the closing segment in his completed cycle of creativeness. Age, experience, and wisdom ultimately had brought the appreciation of subtlety and grandeur, and consequent success in treating a comic situation. Though never discarding his basic tradition of Italian opera, he grew in *Falstaff* both musically and dramatically beyond his national boundaries, justly claiming universality. In unconsciously breaking through the barrier, he had also taken a giant step northward—toward Shakespeare.

NO NAME FOR IAGO

THE CHARACTER OF IAGO WAS BORN AS A NAMELESS ENSIGN IN A TALE
from the *Hecatommithi* by Giovanni Battista Giraldi Cinthio, published in 1565. From this original, Shakespeare forty years later
created his drama, on which Verdi in turn based his opera in 1879.
Cinthio's work is a plain, straightforward narrative, without much
artistry in its structure or consideration for sequence and arrange-
ment; the characters merely carry out their respective actions. Consequently, the development of the ensign is not so complex as in
Shakespeare's masterful tragedy. Cinthio describes him as "a man
of handsome figure, but of the most depraved nature in the world.
This man was in great favor with the Moor, who had not the slightest
idea of his wickedness; for despite the malice lurking in his heart, he
cloaked with proud and valorous speech and with a specious presence the villainy of his soul with such art, that he was to all outward
show another Hector or Achilles."

Although he has pledged fidelity to his wife and loyalty and
friendship to the Moor, this "wicked ensign" falls in love with Disdemona. When his devious but passionate advances remain unsuccessful, he imagines she loves the captain of the troop (Cassio); as
a result, his love turns to hatred. He decides to eliminate the captain
and at the same time divert the Moor's affection from Disdemona by
convincing him of her infidelity. He awaits an opportunity for action. When the captain is deprived of his rank for having struck a
soldier, and Disdemona pleads with her husband to become recon-
ciled to him, the ensign lays his plot and accuses her of being unfaith-
ful; for proof there is the handkerchief, which the ensign snatches
from the sash of the unsuspecting Disdemona when, on a visit with

his wife, she picks up their little daughter. The ensign attempts to assassinate the captain but succeeds only in wounding him. Subsequently he beats Disdemona to death with a sandbag and helps the Moor pull down part of the ceiling upon her so that death seems accidental. As time passes, the Moor mourns the loss of his wife; he grows to hate the ensign and strips him of his commission. In revenge the ensign, together with the captain, accuses the Moor of murder. The Moor, in spite of torture, refuses to confess to the crime, is banished, and eventually slain by Disdemona's family. The ensign is tortured for another crime and dies in misery. Only after his death does his wife reveal the entire story.

To give wider dramatic scope to this rambling story, Shakespeare tightens the plot and vividly brings the characters to life. In the case of the ensign he takes a more or less habitual criminal and builds him into a destructive personality who, by nature, is a Machiavellian villain. Where the original character simply acted out his own thoughts and intentions, Iago becomes a forceful agent who directs the actions of others. In Cinthio's novel the ensign's motives arise from his thwarted passion for Disdemona. In Shakespeare this cause remains but is sublimated; the more obvious promotion of Cassio over him incites his murderous deeds. Iago, having been denied a command, now delights in dominating the lives of those around him, whom he hates for one reason or another.

Here begins the great difference between the ensign, who acts upon impulse and leaves things to chance, and Iago, whose every move is premeditated. While the ensign himself steals the handkerchief from Disdemona, Iago waits for Emilia to pick it up and then wrests it from her. Shakespeare invents the character of Roderigo as a tool for Iago's machinations. Cinthio's ensign attacks and wounds the captain; Shakespeare's Iago induces Roderigo to do so. Where Cinthio merely tells us that the ensign gave a great deal of time to wicked plotting against the Moor, at the opening of Shakespeare's play Iago seizes upon the recriminations voiced by Roderigo to reveal and explain his hatred of Othello.

The motives of Iago's actions have been the source of much speculation. He has been called a downright villain—which might apply to the *alfiero* of Cinthio's novel but hardly to Shakespeare's subtle characterization. Hazlitt seconds Coleridge in reflecting that some critics thought "this whole character unnatural, because his villainy is without a sufficient motive." He claims that Shakespeare was wise enough to know that "love of power," like the "love of mischief, is natural to man." Iago is an extreme example, he continues, "of diseased intellectual activity, with the most perfect indifference to moral good or evil or rather with a decided preference of the latter" which "gives greater zest to his thoughts and scope to his actions." Since Iago is indifferent to his own fate, he is daring and shows no fear of running risks. A. C. Bradley comments that "Iago's motives appear and disappear in the most extraordinary manner," and that his reasons for his actions are no more the true ones than Hamlet's reasons for his delay. "Each is moved by forces he does not understand," Bradley points out; "Iago's thwarted sense of superiority wants satisfaction."

According to Lytton Strachey, "Shakespeare determined that Iago should have no motive at all. He conceived of a monster whose wickedness should lie far deeper than anything that could be explained by a motive—the very essence of whose being should express itself in the machinations of malignity." Because of the character's monstrosity, "when the moment of revelation came, the horror that burst upon the hero would be as inexplicably awful as evil itself."

George Lyman Kittredge, on the other hand, would find it strange if Iago, of all Shakespeare's heroes, in whom motives are distinctly defined, were left without one, especially since this particular play is of rare construction: it is the hero who is passive, acted upon and swayed by the opposing negative power, the villain. Thus it might be explained that Iago is motivated by injustice, which is natural rather than maniacal. The victim of Cinthio's ensign is Disdemona, but Iago's hatred is directed primarily against the Moor, even if his sweeping vengeance expands to include others as well. Perhaps Iago, because of his meritorious record as a soldier, did have a sounder claim to promotion than Cassio, an inexperienced foreigner (he was Florentine). When to this exaggerated resentment is added his jealousy of Othello, because of his own love for Desdemona, and his suspicion that Othello is the lover of his wife, Emilia, his torments become sufficient motivation.

It may even be that Iago's suspicions arise from feelings of inferiority, that actually he is not so self-assured or clever as he seems. Granville-Barker has pointed out that Iago's best stratagems are the result of sudden inspiration rather than a process of reasoning; Bradley adds that because Iago lacks real intelligence, he becomes enmeshed in his own conniving and eventually causes his own downfall.

All must agree that Iago is an actor, "an amateur of tragedy in real life," who instead of manipulating imaginary characters divides the roles among his best friends, rehearsing the parts with unflagging resolution and brazen nerve. Because his plans and treachery succeed, he is in a buoyant mood and able to pose as a good-natured friend—"honest Iago." He is expert at adapting to every character: he entertains Desdemona, is comradely with Cassio, cleverly advises and goads Roderigo. He affects candor, reticence, remorse, or boldness as the situation demands, particularly in his masterful scenes with Othello, whom he persuades to believe the most incredible falsehoods.

Whether motiveless, driven by motives, or simply unaware of them himself, Iago is a flagrant malcontent, and Boito in his libretto continues the tradition of picturing him as a ruthless villain. The operatic Iago may lack Shakespearean subtlety, but he motivates the action and dominates the scene. Accordingly Boito suggested that the opera be called *Iago;* Verdi however hesitated. Boito dispensed entirely with Shakespeare's first act, thus eliminating the depiction of gradual growth and the emergence of Iago's plan resulting from his gnawing hatred of the Moor. The Boito-Verdi Iago, in contrast to Shakespeare's, plunges into action immediately without much preliminary exposition of his character. Upon his initial triumph over Cassio, he is given an opportunity to lay bare his twisted Mephistophelean soul in the second-act *"Credo,"* an interpolation of the librettist.

Paul Dukas writes that this "monologue is full of philosophical-satirical pretensions whose declamatory childishness is beyond all comment." Although Verdi has set it suitably to music, with a great deal of expression, Dukas finds the character himself so antimusical that all of Verdi's efforts are in vain.

Whether Iago's great aria is successful or not musically is a matter of opinion. In any event, because of the one-sidedness of the monologue Iago is stripped of the many stimulating aspects of the personality which he possesses as a Shakespearean character. He loses the human and dramatic touches with which the poet endowed him and enters the realm of purely inhuman, diabolic evil. In this manner Cinthio's uncouth and wicked ensign has turned into Shakespeare's enigmatic, psychologically complex villain, finally to emerge as Verdi's completely negative and destructive operatic miscreant, who triumphantly proclaims that heaven is an "ancient lie" and that he believes in nothing—*nulla!*

THE ABYSS OF REALITY

AMONG THE POSTHUMOUS MANUSCRIPTS OF THE GERMAN POET GEORG Büchner, who died in 1837 at the age of twenty-four, was found nearly fifty years later the soldier-drama *Woyzeck*. The gradual unfolding of a promising career in the natural sciences and as a poet had already been evident in Büchner at the time of his premature death. He had received permission to lecture in Zurich; his first dramatic effort, *Danton's Death*, had been accepted for publication. The influence of the French Revolution had contributed also to his political orientation. His participation in the Hessian revolt, and his pamphlet *Der Hessische Landbote* (The Hessian Country-Messenger) bearing the motto "Peace to the lowly huts! War on the palaces!" forced him to seek asylum in Strasbourg and Zurich. When he was criticized by more conservative republican elements as being perhaps too outspoken, the young author replied, "It is not difficult to be an honest man when one has enough soup, vegetables, and meat to eat." In another instance he pointed out, "I hope I have always turned upon suffering, downtrodden creatures more glances of compassion than I have expended bitter words on the cold hearts of those in authority."

Woyzeck, spectral, unadorned, and heartbreaking, stands as the testament of this hopeful expression: a casually constructed drama of twenty-six brief scenes in which the poet departs from the smoldering embers of late romanticism and anticipates naturalism by candidly, cynically, compassionately picturing the oppressed in the abyss of reality. It was in Vienna, in 1914, that twenty-nine-year-old Alban Berg first attended a performance of *Woyzeck*. The serious young composer, never one to condone anything trifling or un-

171

worthy, was overwhelmed by the misfit soldier's tragedy. He had found a perfect and powerful subject for an opera. His admiration for Büchner was hardly surprising; like the poet, Berg was intensely concerned with social problems. Both men were earnest and liberal in their thoughts and tastes, especially in their choice of literature. The poet, like the composer, had grown from a sensitive boy into a mature creative artist of logical, precise mind. While Büchner applied this gift for objective reasoning to his scientific research, lecturing, and political writings, as well as to his poetic output, Berg employed his technical ability above all in adapting Schönberg's revolutionary theories of musical composition to his own needs and purposes.

Like the well-matched team of Weill and Brecht, there emerged the historically anachronistic but perfect team of Berg and Büchner. Both occupied their creative energies with vast human problems and succeeded in expressing them. Although they portrayed characters who, as individuals, command our interest, contempt, or sympathy and situations that arouse our indignation or sense of justice, it is ultimately the humane aspect, the universality of their theme, that affects us. It is a spiritual affinity—a kind of *Wahlverwandschaft*—bridging a span of nearly a century, that drew together a living composer and a poet long dead to create an opera. The work's dimensions encompass the common ideals of Büchner and Berg by depicting their roles as reformers and artistic innovators.

The drama by the early transition poet points directly to our own time, where its form and theme are tightened and polished by the modern composer, expert in the new idiom of atonality. Berg, ruled by painstaking exactitude in his art although totally liberated from conventional methods of composition, restricts himself to severe classic forms and superimposes upon the drama his modern score, resounding in pain, horror, grief, and compassion. Yet this music is characterized at the same time by a touch of romantic lyricism. The result is *Wozzeck*, a balanced fusion of psychological drama and bold, structural music.

It is interesting that a court decision served Büchner as the immediate inspiration to express, in the framework of a drama, his sympathy for those pitiful, oppressed human beings who are unable to voice their misery and anguish. A brief stay in the army enabled Berg to underscore with authenticity the range of emotions and sense of righteousness aroused by the drama. In Leipzig in 1821, a soldier-barber by the name of Johann Christian Woyzeck had been tried for the murder of a widow. Throughout the court proceedings he maintained that he had been instructed by supernatural powers to kill her with his dagger; since a medical analysis declared the defendant to be of sound mind, he was sentenced to death. This report became the basis for Büchner's play.

Soon after he had seen *Woyzeck*, Berg began to adapt it for an opera. The advent of World War I partially interrupted his work. Never robust and now suffering from asthma, he nevertheless volunteered to serve in the army, where he expected to be assigned to an office position. Instead he was placed on guard duty and often had to accompany transports on foot, sometimes serving up to thirty-six-hour periods without rest. Because of his honesty and utter lack of wordliness, he knew no special protection. Injustice, favoritism, senseless discipline and regimentation, the ineptitude of those in authority—these things upset him. In 1915 he suffered a breakdown and was confined to the military hospital. Here, as letters indicate, he met in person an army physician like the one created by Büchner, who goaded the soldiers and threatened to send them to the front. The close atmosphere of the hospital and snoring of the soldiers inspired the opera's second-act scene in the barracks at night. Other details, too, are translated from personal experience: Berg's soldiers eat beans (Austrian rations) instead of Büchner's peas.

Autobiographical elements undoubtedly helped Berg to crystallize and synthesize his artistic conception of soldiering. Once he was engrossed in the creative process, of course, his personal experiences receded into the background, reappearing only in the vivid portrayals of characters who emerge as types as well as individuals. His leading character especially rises to a symbolic plane reminiscent of Kafka, whose bureaucratic nightmare of inexplicable persecution is translated into army life. When Wozzeck utters his mechanical reply, "*Jawohl, Herr Hauptmann*," or exclaims his pitiful "*Wir arme Leut!*" Berg does not speak for one passive inarticulate soldier but convinces us through his music that these pathetic words are the echo of anonymous multitudes. Wozzeck's pinnacle of eloquence, his shattering outcry *"An was soll man sich da halten?"* (What is one to hold on to?), wins every crusading spirit. Finally, the orphaned child's innocent "Hop, Hop!" ringing through the charged atmosphere of tragedy becomes a moment to haunt all human conscience.

These brief instances best exemplify Berg's mastery of lucidity and restraint. His expertness as a dramatist is further apparent from the way he chose fifteen scenes from Büchner's loose sequence, dividing them into three strictly cohesive acts that unfold as exposition, development, and denouement. The dissonance and complexity of the music are in harmony with the sordidness and suffering of the subject, interspersed by moments of sheer lyric beauty. Throughout the opera Berg retains an appealing simplicity, presenting his theme almost as an understatement. Although the composer becomes increasingly concerned with the main character and his psychological problems, this concentration never deflects Berg from his primary purpose:

> No matter how cognizant any particular individual may be of the musical forms contained in the framework of this opera, of the precision and logic with which everything is worked out, and the skill manifested in every detail, from the moment the curtain parts until it closes for the last time, there is no one in the audience who pays any attention to the various fugues, inventions, suites, sonata movements, variations, and passacaglias . . . no one who heeds anything but the social problems of this opera, which by far transcend the personal destiny of Wozzeck. This I believe to be my achievement.

Hugo von Hofmannsthal (1874–1929). *Austrian Information Service*

Richard Strauss (1864–1949). *Austrian Information Service*

The final scene from Strauss's *Arabella:* the heroine offers Mandryka the symbolic glass of water. *German Tourist Information Office*

Ludwig Alois von Koechel (1800–1877). *Opera News*

Wolfgang Amadeus Mozart (1756–1791). *The Roy Bernard Co., Inc.*

Robert Schumann (1810–1856). *The Roy Bernard Co., Inc.*

Friedrich Hebbel (1813–1863), after a painting by Karl Rahl. *Roy Bernard–Archiv*

Scene of the Walpurgis Night: the Brocken in the Harz Mountains. *German Tourist Information Office*

Charles Gounod (1818–1893), portrait by L. Nauer

Gustaf Gruendgens as Mephistopheles in Goethe's *Faust. The Roy Bernard Co., Inc.*

St. Richard with his sons, Willibald and Wunnibald, from *Caractéristiques des saints dans l'art populaire*, Cahier, Paris, 1867. *Opera News*

St. Walburga, with her phial of miraculous balm, from *Caractéristiques des saints dans l'art populaire*, Cahier, Paris, 1867. *Opera News*

Alexandre Dumas *fils* (1824–1895). *French Embassy Press & Information Division*

Marie Alphonsine Duplessis, prototype of Camille and Violetta, after a painting by Viénot. *Opera News*

Mlle. George, a popular 19th-century French actress, beloved by Dumas *Père*. *Opera News*

The house in Roncole where Verdi was born. *G. Ricordi & Co.*

The house in Stratford-on-Avo
where Shakespeare was born. *F
Berges*

below. Scene from the third act o
Verdi's *Otello. G. Ricordi & Co.*

Verdi (right) and his librettist, Arrigo Boito (1842–1918), admiring Milan from the Casa Verdi balcony, during construction. *G. Ricordi & Co.*

Giuseppe Verdi (1813–1901). *Ballerini & Fratini*

His suspicions regarding Cassio confirmed, Otello (Mario Del Monaco) promotes Iago (Leonard Warren) in rank, in the third act of Verdi's *Otello. Metropolitan Opera Assn., Inc.*

Franz Kafka (1883–1924). *Schock-en Books*

above. Georg Büchner (1813–1837), engraving by Aimbach after A. Hoffmann. *Roy Bernard-Archiv*

Alban Berg (1885–1935). *BMI Archives*

Part Five
History and Legend

THE THREE RIDDLES

THE ESSENCE OF THE TURANDOT FABLE IS CONTAINED IN THREE riddles. They form the story's plot and climax. When Turandot asks the riddles of her unknown suitor, his life is at stake. Solving the enigmas will mean marriage with the princess while the price for admitting ignorance will be death.

Contrary to the common assumption that riddles are simply a pastime to liven up a dull party, their history will prove that they have often served a more earnest purpose. They were posed in serious situations, frequently crises. The Turandot story is only one example.

Riddles rank with folktales, myths, fables, and proverbs as an ancient and widespread form of thought and literary expression. An endless source for the matching of wits, they were tests and tortures to the minds of sages. They brought fame and happiness to some, shame, frustration and downfall to others.

Riddles probably grew out of man's primary need of describing likenesses and differences in terms of metaphors. More than once, Aristotle pointed out the similarities between metaphors and riddles. Only as civilizations expanded and forms of literature became increasingly complex did riddles lose their early importance. Their original, often crude, humor and outspoken direct tone disappeared. Transposed from real-life situations into literature, the functional simplicity of riddles was supplanted by highly intellectual and poetic forms or degenerated into mere pun-like word games.

The earliest riddles extant are Babylonian school texts. Lessons taught through riddles easily held a child's attention. Rain-making, grain-growing, and harvesting festivals as well as weddings, circumcisions, and funerals were occasions where riddles were put forth. These were the most significant life situations. Perhaps because they were in themselves wondrous and enigmatic to the ignorant, the guessing of riddles became a part of the events.

When the riddle infiltrated Greek civilization, it became a dramatic adjunct to mythology and tragedy. It is said that a riddle caused Homer's death. A legend which existed about 500 B.C. relates that the poet once consulted an oracle about the place of his birth. The oracle's reply was in itself characteristically enigmatic. He was told that the island Ios was his mother's home; there he would be gathered in death. "But," warned the oracle, "beware of the riddles of the youths." As an old man Homer arrived on the island. Coming upon a group of fishermen, he asked them if they had caught anything. The young men, ill-tempered because they had not met with any success, replied, "What we caught is gone, what isn't we carry home." Homer misunderstood the answer, assuming the men were speaking of fish, when actually they were referring to lice. Grieved over his inability to solve the puzzling response, he died.

Most famous of Greek riddles, though probably of Egyptian origin, is that of the Sphinx. It belongs to the "guess or die" category. The Sphinx, a female monster sent to Thebes as a scourge, posed a riddle to every passer-by. Inability to solve it was punished with death. The riddle described a being with four feet having two feet and three feet and only one voice; but its feet varied and when it had most, it was weakest. After Oedipus had correctly identified this being as man, in infancy crawling on all fours, in manhood walking on two feet, and in old age using a staff to support his two feet, the Sphinx hurled itself down from a cliff.

The Bible makes use of riddles in various instances. Samson proposes a wager to the Philistines, its outcome to depend on their ability to guess his riddle. In Ezekiel, the prophet is commanded by God to put a riddle to the people of Israel in which the King of Babylon is likened to an eagle.

Riddles based on the Bible are sometimes propounded to demonstrate the wisdom of a hero in an entertaining manner. When the Queen of Sheba came to Solomon, she put this riddle to the monarch: "A woman said to her son: your father is my father and your grandfather is my husband; you are my son, and I am your sister." It did not require extraordinary wisdom on the part of Solomon to know that Sheba was referring to Lot's daughter. In trying to outwit the queen, according to the Koran, King Solomon overlaid his audience hall with glass. The Queen of Sheba, mistaking the glass for water, lifted her skirt in order to wade through it.

The riddle easily found its way into intricate Talmudic reasoning and dissertation. One has never been definitely settled:

> High from heav'n her eye looks down,
> Constant strife excites her frown;
> Winged beings shun her sight,
> She puts the youth to instant flight.
> The aged, too, her looks do scout,
> Oh, oh! the fugitive cries out.
> And by her snares whoe'er is lured
> Can never of his sin be cured.

Another Talmudic riddle questions, "What animal has one voice living and seven voices dead?" The answer is the ibis, from whose carcass seven different instruments are made. The Talmud also contains a version of the riddle of the Sphinx.

Norse mythology claims its share of riddles, often stressing the supernatural. Odin in disguise puts a number of riddles to King Heidrick, who is famed for solving them. "Who are the two that have ten feet, three eyes, and one tail?" Heidrick guesses the two to be one-eyed Odin riding Sleipnir, his eight-legged steed. At another time Odin questions, "Who are the maidens who go at their father's bidding, white-hooded, with shining locks?" And Heidrick is quick to reply, "The waves, or Aegir's daughters."

During the Middle Ages riddles were commonly posed among the people as well as by the poets or *Minnesänger*. One riddle, well known in varying Italian, French, and German versions, speaks of black seeds on a white field. It is interpreted as black lettering on white paper. Knowledge, which revealed itself through reading and writing, was impressive and mysterious to the unenlightened and illiterate masses. Comparing writing to seeds growing in a field was an ingenious way of explaining a miracle.

In the *Wartburgkrieg*, when all the knights meet, Klingsor of Ungerland and Wolfram von Eschenbach vie in guessing riddles. A fourteenth-century song of the world wanderer Traugemund recounts that he knows seventy-two countries and their languages. He is questioned, "Master Traugemund, which tree without blossoms bears fruit? Which bird has no tongue? Which bird has no stomach? Which bird nurses its young? If you can answer these questions, you are a goodly knight." And Master Traugemund replies, "The tree bearing fruit without blossoms is the juniper, the bird without tongue is the stork (according to a legend), the bird without stomach is the swallow, and the bat nurses its young."

In Spain, the great Jewish lyric poet of the twelfth century, Judah Halevi, posed the riddle of the needle:

> What is it that's blind with an eye in its head,
> But the race of mankind its use cannot spare;
> Spends all its life in clothing the dead,
> But always itself is naked and bare.

Circumstances under which riddles are asked may vary among different peoples and cultures. Yet in every civilization, whether in legend or reality, the contemplation of a marriage is one of the most popular occasions where riddles figure prominently. It is a custom among Central Asian Turkish girls to ask riddles of their prospective husbands. If the men are unable to give correct answers, they are punished. This would seem to be an elementary but also practical marriage test.

In some legends the girl's father, in others the daughter herself will pose the questions. Appollonius of Tyre, the hero of a Greek story which probably originated in the third century of our era, is tested with riddles by King Antiochus of Syria, whose daughter he desires to marry. Through a correctly guessed riddle, reminiscent of the Biblical Lot's daughter, he learns that Antiochus is having an incestuous relationship with his daughter. Because of many interpolated riddles the story became particularly popular during the Middle Ages, when it was translated into several European languages. Shakespeare treats the theme in his *Pericles*, where the princess herself expounds the riddle:

I am no viper, yet I feed
On mother's flesh which did me breed.
I sought a husband, in which labor
I found that kindness in a father.
He's father, son and husband mild;
I mother, wife and yet his child.
How they may be, and yet in two,
As you will live, resolve it you.

Where a father craftily outwits a suitor by means of riddles is exemplified in the *Edda*. Knowing that sunlight is lethal to the dwarf Alviss who wants to marry his daughter Thrud, Thor keeps him above ground throughout the night by putting riddles to him. Daylight and the rising sun creep upon them, turning Alviss into stone.

In the more modern literary or dramatic accounts where inability to solve riddles proves fatal to the suitor, there is often a reason why the heroine wants to avoid marriage and insists on the extreme alternative—the death penalty. Without a credible excuse to support her drastic action, she would arouse contempt rather than sympathy.

In the original Oriental Turandot tale, of which there exist several variations, the princess' examination of the prince and his answers are completely acted out in pantomime. At the end, Turandot capitulates and their symbolic actions are explained. When the Persian fairy-tale collection by François Pétis de la Croix, *Mille et un jour*, from which Carlo Gozzi drew his inspiration, was published in 1710, distinctly worded riddles had evolved.

The princess in Gozzi's *Turandot* of 1762, whose fantastic characters are more like marionettes than breathing human beings, simply nurses a profound unexplained hatred for men. She experiences a moment of pity upon seeing the young prince, then urges him to desist from trying her pride and only weapon which the heavens bestowed on her—her mind. While the prince insists on hearing the riddles, the princess remains cruelly firm with her terms.

When in 1802 Schiller wrote his tragicomic fairy-tale, modeling it after the F.A.C. Werthes translations of Gozzi's comedy, he hoped to replace its "pedantic stiffness" with some "poetic humaneness." Proof of his success is the character of the princess herself. She is no longer coldly beautiful, distant, and unfeeling. She is a pioneer for women's rights in Asia. She demands to be won by an intelligent man worthy of her. She will not simply consent to being a slave to and the object of any man's desire. Setting an example for all women on how to deal with man's raw treatment of her sex, she justifies her behavior by telling Prince Calaf:

> I see that throughout Asia womankind
> Is shamed and damned to serve in slavery,
> And my insulted sex I shall avenge
> Against this proud society of men which
> Over frail womankind has no advantage
> But that of crude strength.

In the early 1920's Puccini composed his opera on Gozzi's play. Like Schiller, the composer and his librettists Giuseppe Adami and Renato Simoni equipped their heroine with a reason for despising the opposite sex. Her story, *"In questa reggia,"* effectively told through Puccini's powerful music, is more melodramatic than Schiller's idealistic declamation. Her very first words in the opera, addressed to the challenging unknown prince, are her alibi:

> From this palace thousands of years ago went out a cry of despair, and that cry, uttered by the flower of my race, within my soul took refuge. Princess Lu-o-ling, ancestor serene and tender, who didst rule in silence enshrouded and in joys so pure, inexorably and steadfastly the dominion of men defying, thou livest in me today!

Then came war, Turandot continues, and her ancestor was "ruthlessly dragged forth by a man, a stranger. . . . In the cruel night, her voice so soft was stilled forever! . . . No, never shall man possess me! Hatred of him that slew her encompasses my heart! . . . Reincarnated in me is the pride of so much purity."

The riddles themselves posed by Turandot differ in the treatments by Gozzi, his translators and adapters, Schiller, and Puccini. One exception is Schiller's first riddle, taken from Gozzi. Picturing the year with its nights and days as a tree, this enigma, like the Turandot tale, apparently originated in Persia. The poet Firdusi in his *Book of the King* (*Shahnahmah*), dated 1011, describes the months comprising a year as twelve trees with thirty branches each. Gozzi and

Schiller speak of an ancient tree which remains ever young and tells the age of all things. Puccini's first riddle pictures hope, a phantom "born each night anew that fades away at daylight."

Gozzi's second enigma envisages the sun, known from east to north and dear to everyone. Schiller composes his own, a beautifully conceived poetic image of the human eye: "No gem is equal to it in value; it shines without ever burning; it absorbs all of the world; the sky itself is reflected in its wonderful ring; and yet, what shines forth from it is often more beautiful than what it absorbs."

In contrast to the optimism of his first riddle, Puccini's second represents a fearful image of blood, spurting "like a flame . . . delirious . . . always a fever," growing cold or ardently flowing, with the vivid coloring of the setting sun.

The "Adriatic lion" is the subject of Gozzi's final riddle, of restricted interest, chosen perhaps because the play was first produced in Venice. Schiller again prefers to write an original riddle, deciding on an unusual and little appreciated object, related to the sword but shedding no blood. It is the plough which "takes from no one but makes wealthy."

The operatic Turandot's final riddle, dramatically describing herself, results in an astute self-analysis: "Ice which gives fire! And from thy fire ice begets. Candid and obscure! If freedom she grants thee, into greater slavery thou fallest! If as slave she accepts thee, a king thou shalt be!"

A lesser known opera based on Gozzi's comedy was composed by Ferruccio Busoni (1917). Unlike Puccini, Busoni left Turandot's cruelty unmotivated, thus closely following Gozzi's text. His riddles, however, diverge from his source. Of all the Turandot riddles, these are the most intellectual and intangible. The first describes human understanding, which gropes in the dark yet kindles lights; the second is custom, which is changeable and steady, praised and punished; the last is art, a gift from heaven. Although these riddles are of a lofty and philosophical nature, they lack the poetry and profundity of Schiller and the compelling excitement of Puccini.

Solving the three riddles in both plays and operas is not the end of the prince's troubles. Turandot refuses to keep her word. He responds by testing her: She must guess his name by the following morning. If she does his life is forfeited; if not, she must marry him. This turn of events and Turandot's quest to learn the stranger's name is an entertaining yet anti-climactic continuation of the tale. The most exciting and decisive moment remains the princess' appearance to pose the riddles. Schiller was so well aware of the impact and spell-binding effect of this scene that every time the play was performed, he would insert new riddles to heighten its audience appeal. In this manner he accumulated a collection of *Parables and Riddles*, to which even Goethe made a contribution. As an experienced dramatist Schiller knew that whether a riddle is posed by the Sphinx, the Queen of Sheba, a Norse god, or the beautiful Princess Turandot, it will always captivate an audience.

ORPHEUS AND HIS LYRE

BEFORE THE BIRTH OF APOLLO ON DELOS, SEVEN BEAUTIFUL SINGING swans sailed seven times around the storm-tossed island. For this reason the sun god, when he constructed his lyre, gave it seven strings. Apollo subsequently presented the lyre to his son, Orpheus, who became its most renowned and eloquent player; through his entrancing music he calmed the raging Furies and won back to life and earth his beloved wife, Euridice.

The lyre was a common and popular instrument among the ancients, serving as musical accompaniment to the related arts of poetry and dance. As an attribute of Apollo—leader of the Muses, protector and champion of purity, godly representative of everything cultural, ethical, and spiritual—the oldest string instrument became a favorite in poetic and legendary allusions. Consequently, descriptions of the lyre and accounts of its invention vary widely.

It was said in ancient Greece that Apollo rivaled Hermes in inventing the lyre. At Olympia both Hermes and Apollo were honored with an altar, Hermes as inventor of the lyre, Apollo of the slightly different cithara. According to a Homeric hymn, Hermes stole a herd of cattle from Apollo; when the theft was discovered and he had to make amends, he presented the sun god with his lyre, newly invented. Since the roaring or whistling of winds and breezes was likened to the sounds produced by string and wind instruments, it seems logical to attribute the lyre's origin, as well as the simple flute's, to Hermes, the wind god. But because in musical terms the wind was imperfect—merely an intimation of music that might be created through the use of proper instruments—Hermes had to leave the lyre's development and refinement to Apollo.

185

Although the lyre is commonly known as a Greek instrument, its historical origins stem rather from Sumeria, Babylonia, and Assyria. Lyres may have been introduced into Greece through Thrace or Lydia; since musical instruments were trade items, they were in all likelihood played everywhere. Similarity exists even in the names for the lyre—for example, the Greek *cinyra* and Hebrew *kinnor* (in the Old Testament, usually translated simply as "harp"). An Egyptian painting at the rock tombs of Beni Hasan (XII Dynasty, about 1700 B.C.) pictures a Hebrew lyre-player of the time of Joseph, supposedly recreating the arrival of Jacob's family in Egypt. In Sumeria the instrument is reputed to have existed as early as 3000 B.C., in a larger primitive shape with carved bulls' heads and the like projecting at the far end. Sumerian lyres were richly decorated with gold and lapis lazuli and inlaid with shell mosaic, and they pictured heroes and mythical beasts.

Illustrations of the *kinnor* found on Hebrew coins authenticate the instrument's likeness to the Greek lyre and cithara. On one of the coins there appears under the strings a curious sounding-board shaped like a kettledrum, which later is mentioned by the Church Fathers in describing the instrument. Abraham ben Meir ibn Ezra in his commentary on the book of Daniel (twelfth century) likens the lyre to a candelabrum. Its frame consisted of a hollow body or sound chest from which two arms—sometimes hollow—bent outward and then forward, like the horns of an animal, connected close to the top by a yoke or crossbar. The deeper notes were farther from the player; since the strings hardly differed in length, more weight may have been gained for these by thicker and possibly slacker strings, as with bowed instruments today. The number of strings varied; most common were four, seven, or ten. Bowing was not possible because of the flat soundboard. A plectrum in the player's right hand set the upper strings in vibration, while the fingers of the left hand touched the lower strings. The early lyre was a more primitive instrument, with a bowl-shaped back over which a skin or parchment was stretched; it is considered the precursor of the lute family. From the cithara, with its box-shaped soundchest, the violin is said to have developed.

The lyre in Greece seems to have been in fashion—for artistic

purposes and literary inspiration as well as actual musical performance—for about 1,200 years (800 B.C. to 400 A.D.). During the
Golden Age it was carved out of ivory and decorated with precious
stones; poets sang the instrument's praises in their songs. The first
Biblical reference to the *kinnor*, made in Genesis, names Jubal as
"the father of all such as handle the harp and pipe." The *kinnor* that
"David and all the house of Israel played before the Lord" was made
of cypress wood. Among the many splendid gifts the Queen of Sheba
brought to Solomon was unequaled sandalwood from which, in addition to the pillars for the Lord's sanctuary and his own house, the
king made "harps also and psalteries for the singers." The *nebel*
(psaltery) had twelve strings and was played with the fingers only.
A midrash relates that Nebuchadnezzar commanded the Children
of Israel, "And you shall in my presence strike the cithara," suggest-
ing the use of a plectrum. David, however, before troubled King
Saul, "took the *kinnor* and played it with his hand."

In Biblical as well as mythological references, the music produced
by the lyre or the closely related cithara and harp falls into distinct
categories. The psaltery was reserved exclusively for religious purposes, whereas the lyre was more popular, played by noble and
lowly alike. The instrument of the sweet tone accompanied the
human voice at banquets and in festive processions. In numerous
instances of songs of praise and thanksgiving, the lyre (or harp) is
employed to heighten festivity. It is never used for mourning.
Isaiah laments that "the joy of the harp ceaseth"; Job, in his afflic-
tion, bewails, "Therefore is my harp turned to mourning"; the
Psalmist relates, "By the rivers of Babylon . . . upon the willows in
the midst thereof we hanged up our harps." To the Greeks, string
music was of a sobering, harmonious effect, as opposed to the
Dionysiac inebriation and ecstasy caused by flute music. Pindar,
speaking of the lyre, says that all things hateful to Zeus on earth and
in the sea trembled at the sound of its music. Horace called his lyre
"pain's sweet alleviator."

With famed musicians whose skill at the lyre reached legendary
proportions, the instrument assumed almost supernatural powers.
The Talmud relates that "a cithara used to hang above David's bed;
as soon as midnight approached, a north wind would come and blow

on it, whereupon it played of its own accord." Orpheus, who is comparable to David, charmed the beasts much as the Biblical hero exorcised evil spirits from Saul. The scene is similar to that in the prophetic Bible vision of messianic times, when wolf and lion, dog and rabbit will lie peacefully together. When Orpheus' music is heard, the winds stop blowing so as not to disturb him; hail and snow cease falling; the roaring of the oceans is silenced; rivers flow upstream instead of following their natural course. His playing had power to move trees and stones, not to mention the heart of Pluto. To some legendary extent, the gift of prophecy is attributed to Orpheus. Here, too, a parallel can be found in the Scriptures, where prophetic inspiration is associated with music.

After Orpheus, protesting against the orgiastic cults of Dionysos, was killed by the furious Bacchantes, his head and lyre were said to have floated to the island of Lesbos, later a noted seat of lyric poetry and music. Another version of the idealized instrument's perpetuation has Zeus take the lyre after Orpheus' death and place it as a constellation in the heavens, Lyra. Both endings seem appropriate. It is only fitting that the instrument which enjoyed historical, Biblical, and mythological fame and glory should both become an inspiring symbol to poets and musicians through the ages and be fixed in the skies for eternity.

CARMEN'S ANCESTORS

"IN THE BEGINNING WE ALL WERE BIRDS," RELATES A GYPSY LEGEND. "We flew high over mountains and trees. Once, half-starved, after a long flight, we feasted on rich, yellow, ripe grain in a vast field. We became so heavy with food that we could not rise into the air. The season began to change; worms and other creatures of the earth dug holes to provide for the coming winter. We, too, began to shake the grain from the blade and shove it into holes—all with our wings which were beginning to assume the shape of arms and hands. But we shall get our wings back, learn to use them again, and fly over mountains and trees. . . ."

As in the legend, Carmen's body and soul are free as a bird. She is a cigar-factory girl one day, the next a member of a band of thieves and smugglers whom in turn she abandons to join her new lover, the toreador. Wild and unbound, she follows her instincts and desires; there is no thought of duty or obligation. She is a true gypsy, here today, there tomorrow.

But who really are her ancestors? Where do they come from?

Mohammedan chronicles speak of a wandering tribe called Zotts who lived at the mouth of the Indus river. Roaming cattle breeders, they settled briefly, raising their tents wherever their black water buffaloes grazed. In the ninth century, after they were conquered by the Arabs, 27,000 prisoners were deported to Ainzarba, which soon afterwards was captured by the Byzantines. At about the same time, the records state, the first gypsies appeared on Byzantine territory.

The gypsies' fame for music dates back to the year 1000, when the Persian epic poet Firdusi reports that King Bahram Gur of Per-

189

sia wished to improve the situation of the poor. From India the king imported "10,000 Luris, men and women, who knew how to play the lute." They were to entertain the poor in his land with their artistry. The Luris, however, wasted their wheat and sold their cows so that soon they were without means. Bahram Gur became angry and ordered them to travel with their donkeys through the country, and make a living by song and instrumental music.

India has been accepted as the gypsies' country of origin. The key to their mysteriously unknown past was their language. A study of their tongue revealed it to have much similarity to Sanksrit and neo-Hindu dialects, and their affinity to various Indian tribes was established. From India the gypsies wandered to Persia and on to Armenia, where they remained for a longer period of time. Then their way led them westward through Asia Minor to Greece and especially Crete. Many Greek words in the gypsy tongue give evidence of a long stay in Greece. From Greece they moved their tents through Albania, Rumania, and Hungary, and thence to western Europe.

The tribes remained essentially pure throughout their centuries of wandering. They spoke their own language but with ease learned the tongue of the country where they happened to be staying. At their head was a count and the father of each family was ruler of that group. The "gypsy grandmother," oldest woman of the band, was treated with the greatest respect and esteem. Girls married in their early teens; men were not much older. Families were large, children numerous, and marriages could be dissolved easily. Weddings were occasions for great joy, with excess in eating, drinking, and wild merrymaking. The death of a member of the tribe produced noisy and profound mourning. Suicides were rare, for nothing in life could be serious enough to make one want to die. Death was the only feared and hated enemy. Asked if he believed in God, a gypsy replied that he did, but hated God because God caused death. The gypsy had no real religion and instead of living by faith, he constantly fought for his life and freedom.

There was not much else to fight for, certainly not in material goods. The gypsy home was a tent; sometimes he owned a silver cup which was prized highly and handed down in the family as an heirloom. In appearance, the gypsy still retains something of his Indian heritage. He is of medium height, well built, thin, with strong muscular limbs. His skin is yellowish-brown, his hair thick and black. The women in their youth are usually of pleasant and even beautiful appearance but age very quickly. Both men and women have perfect white teeth. Their most distinguishing features are their big, beautiful eyes with long black lashes. Gypsy clothing—when it consists of more than rags—has always been bright in color. While green and red are favorites, Spanish gypsies have tended to assume the costumes of the Andalusian horsetraders with whom they often do business.

When, in 1417, the gypsies made their first appearance in western Europe, they claimed they came from Lower Egypt. Dutch documents of the fifteenth century repeatedly name kings and counts from Lower Egypt. Even the gypsies' names in the various countries seemed to point to Egypt as their country of origin. In Spain they were called Egypcianos, later *gitanos;* in England, Egypcions, now gypsies; in the Netherlands, Egyptiërs, Egyptenaren, Egiptenaers, Giptenaers, also Heidenen, Heidens, as now; in France, Egyptiens, now *bohémiens.* But in the face of scientific research, tales of Egyptian origin can be discredited.

Upon their arrival in various cities, they claimed to have letters from emperors permitting them to pass unhindered through cities and provinces. The story was that their ancestors in Lower Egypt had once upon a time renounced Christianity to return to paganism. When they had reembraced Christianity and done the required penance of seven years' wandering, it was again commanded that each of their family must in turn wander for a like number of years. But since that time their period of penance had expired and, as one chronicle states, "they still do not cease to wander, to steal, to lie and to tell fortunes. . . ." In the beginning they had been received with kindness and sympathy in many cities. But soon they became known as thieves and frauds; many were caught and hanged.

In Italy the gypsies arrived in 1422 and upset the populace by shattering the teachings of the church. Then, in 1427, they reached Paris, where, as the description of a French theologian reads, they caused hardly less than a tumult: "Most of the men had their ears pierced and in each ear a silver earring or even two. The men were very dark with curly hair, and their women had harassed faces, and hair as black and coarse as that of a horse's tail. The clothing of these women consisted of a strip of cloth hanging from their shoulders by a cord. They were half-naked, immodest, bare-legged, bare-footed. . . ." They immediately busied themselves with fortune telling and magic among the pious Christians.

In 1447 the first gypsies were seen in Barcelona, and from there they quickly spread in small groups all over Spain. Each group was ruled by a duke or count who claimed that he received his orders from others higher than he. They began to associate with the Spanish kettle-menders and coppersmiths who wandered through the country.

Almost from the time of their arrival in Spain, the *gitanos* were accused of every conceivable crime. They had desecrated holy images; they had sold stolen children into African slavery; they were enemies of the state in the pay of the Moors. Although humble and persecuted, justly or unjustly, the *gitanos* learned to introduce and ingratiate themselves in prominent Spanish families and took every advantage of these acquaintances. The women tantalized the sensuous Spaniards with wild, seductive dances but withdrew as soon as the purity of their race was in danger. Their hatred for the Spaniards was more violent than for the Moors. Although they had no scruples about spying for either side, they preferred serving the Moors, to whom they felt more allied in temperament and character, sharing their taste for dancing and rhythmical expression. Many gypsy girls found a place in Moorish harems.

At the fall of the Alhambra and the Moorish retreat near the end of the fifteenth century, enough of the Moors' blood flowed in the *gitanos* who remained in Christian Spain to form a type of gypsy different in appearance and character from the others. They were more handsome, graceful, and proud, even disdainful. Along with Moorish blood they inherited a hatred for their Christian oppressors. They feigned to accept Catholicism but had no real understanding or love for religion. No gypsies died through the Inquisition; they would not sacrifice themselves for something not concerning them. Like the bird in the fable of his ancestry, the gypsy refused to surrender his freedom. Without duties or possessions, his life contained more joy, greater happiness, and profounder emotion: music and dance without end. And it seemed that the mournful Spaniards resented the gaiety and wild exuberance of the *gitanos* as much as the colorful brightness and splendor of the Moors.

The Spanish government more than any other tried to solve the gypsy problem. "To do something about it" became a pet subject of each successive ruler, so that over the passage of years many contradictory edicts were issued. At one time it was forbidden to call the gypsies "*gitanos*." Any Spaniard heard using the name would be imprisoned. Vagabonding would be prohibited, but subsequently gypsies were forbidden to live in cities and towns. Banishment was ordered. They were compelled to become agriculturists. They were barred from admission to churches but ordered to become good Christians. Last but not least, they were prohibited the trade at which they were most skilled—blacksmithing. In spite of using primitive tools, they had been adept at making knives, nails, rings, and needles.

Continually hunted and persecuted, Carmen's ancestors forged their own laws. They preyed on non-*gitanos* everywhere, robbed them on the highways, destroyed fields and villages, and poisoned their cattle. They practised sorcery; their women, who had pretended to possess occult powers since prehistoric times, by exercise of wit learned to read character or even thought, but truth and deception became indistinguishable. They disregarded human life and property completely outside the *leis prala*, the law of the brotherhood, and turned into cruel avengers. Even children grew up wild, artful, sly, and with murderous instincts. The story of the town of Logrono tells that after the gypsies had poisoned its wells and the inhabitants lay dying, men, women, and children armed with knives ravaged and plundered the city. There is no need to marvel at the evil in Carmen's soul. It does not take much imagination to think up what she may have been or done as a child. She is a typical product of heredity and environment.

At one time when vagabonding was outlawed, anyone catching a *gitano* in that state could claim him as his slave. Immediately the peasants set out gypsy hunting. The *gitanos*, growing reckless when their precious and only possession, their freedom, was threatened, withdrew to the mountains and mercilessly killed everyone who would rob them of it.

At the end of the eighteenth century Charles III passed more humane laws. Although death was the penalty for recalcitrants, waywardness would be forgiven. The *gitanos* decided to become Spaniards and settled in villages and towns. *Gitanerias,* or gypsy quarters, were formed because the Spaniards wished to have no intercourse with the former outcasts. But over the passage of many years, hostility diminished and eventually it even became an accomplishment for a Spaniard to speak *Calo,* the gypsy language.

Franz Liszt in Hungary tried to prove that Hungarian national music had its origin in gypsy music; in spite of indignant protests his theory has held ground. As the violin is indispensable to the Hungarian gypsy, the Spanish *gitano* is known for his extraordinary dancing. Much Spanish music and many Spanish dances are of *gitano* origin. Here, then, is the reason for Carmen's tantalizing airs and dances. Her forefathers' history is rich with musical rhythms, but it is also full of misery. There is much evil, and Carmen, as a true child of gypsy tradition, continues to perpetuate it. Yet the *gitanos,* as Carmen herself proves with song and dance, are primarily a happy people as long as they possess their freedom and can roam the wide world, unfettered like the birds.

ANTECEDENTS OF THE
MANTUAN COURT

THE DUKE OF MANTUA WHO HEEDLESSLY PRANCES THROUGH *Rigoletto* as a seducer of women, then sings about their fickleness, presents a curious paradox to the listener. One of the principal actors in the tragedy, he seems one of the least interesting, although he is actually the central character who molds the destinies of the others.

This profligate Duke of Mantua is, of course, Francis I, King of France, who, like other characters in the opera, was camouflaged in *Rigoletto* with a fictitious name and dukedom to appease angry censors. The action was conveniently transposed from the throne of France to the Court of Mantua. This same Francis, the French Renaissance King, and hero of Victor Hugo's *Le Roi s'amuse*, figures in the tragedy of the nineteenth-century English actress-playwright Fanny Kemble, *Francis the First*, and, more recently, in Samuel Shellabarger's historical novel, *The King's Cavalier* (1950).

Victor Hugo, and later Piave and Verdi, hardly exaggerated when they presented Francis as a reckless libertine. History tells us that although he lacked any outstanding talents or characteristics, he was self-confident and of a royal appearance, tall and good looking. His ability to speak well and to charm his listeners added to his matter-of-fact self-asurance; soon he displayed an unpleasant superiority over others, a vain self-complacency. Although ambitious and courageous, he lacked perseverance. Spoiled by his mother, Louise of Savoy, and his sister, Marguerite of Navarre, he remained untrustworthy, fickle, irresolute, and prodigal. Perhaps the devotion of these women led Francis to believe that all other women should

195

love him with equal fervor; out of his fear that they might not, he set out to conquer them all to preserve his own self-esteem. Certainly the operatic Duke of Mantua has no scruples about seducing women of every kind: a countess, an innocent young girl, and a common girl, the sister and accomplice of a professional assassin.

Francis is considered the king of the political and spiritual Renaissance in France. He was a patron of the arts, a lover of the gay easy life, the elegance and luxury of the Renaissance. For fifteen years (1523–1538) he employed 1,800 laborers to convert his *"maison de plaisance et rendez-vous de chasse"* near Blois on the Loire into the magnificent Château de Chambord. *"Souvent femme varie, bien fol est qui s'y fie,"* wrote the king on one of the window panes; the couplet has been passed on to us, through Victor Hugo and Verdi, as *La donna è mobile.*

Francis I had his share of mistresses, among them the beautiful Madame d'Etampes, of whom the poet Clément Marot, known to us in *Rigoletto* as Marullo, wrote:

> *Sans préjudice à personne*
> *Je vous donne*
> *La pomme d'or de beauté*
> *Et de ferme loyauté*
> *La couronne.* *

Mistresses were kept at the court under Francis' son Henry II as well. Although he remained married to Catherine de Medici, niece of the Pope, until his death in 1559, he was constantly influenced by the famed beauty, Diane de Poitiers, daughter of M. de Saint Vallier, the Count Monterone of the opera.

Clément Marot began his career with the king as his *valet de chambre. Le Temple de Cupidon,* one of his allegorical poems, won the king's favor.

Although the arts flourished during his reign, Francis' military venture into Italy also indicated his success as a warrior. Whether he undertook the march across the Alps to follow in the steps of his predecessor and father-in-law, Louis XII; whether he looked for

---

* Without prejudice to anyone, I present you with the golden apple of beauty and the crown of firm loyalty.

honor and laurels to enhance his vanity; whether he was merely interested in seeing Italy and its beautiful women, we may never
know. Perhaps all these reasons moved him to invade Italy. In any
case, Francis crossed the Alps, defeated a reputedly invincible
Swiss army defending the Sforzas at Marignano (1515), and claimed
the dukedom of Milan. The king's subsequent attacks proved fruit-
less and, later, disastrous. Having lost the battle of Pavia in 1525, he
was taken to Madrid as captive by the Emperor Charles V; into cap-
tivity with him for a year went Clément Marot. Characteristically,
Francis wrote to his mother: "Madame, to inform you how fares the
rest of my misfortune, all that has been saved and remains to me is
my honor and my life."

He was able to regain his freedom only by submitting to the
harshest terms (which he had no intention of keeping) and was required to leave his two sons as hostages. More war years followed,
but the cultural Renaissance continued to flourish.

Francis was concerned with the pleasures of living, a fact which
Rigoletto confirms. He brought the greatest Italian artists to the
French court. Leonardo da Vinci spent the last few years of his life
there and died at Cloux, near Amboise, in 1519. For a few months
in 1518, Andrea del Sarto lived at court, and several years later, in
1540, Benvenuto Cellini entered the king's service for five years.
Francis called him *amico*, Benvenuto writes in his memoirs, stressing how the king admired him. Later, however, the beautiful and influential Madame d'Etampes procured a royal commission for Francesco Primaticcio to design a fountain, thus supplanting Cellini, who
considered himself betrayed. He admired Primaticcio as an artist,
but could not forgive the insult to himself. According to Benvenuto,
hostilities between him and Madame d'Etampes caused his return
to Florence.

Cellini was a perfect companion for the king when he sought
pleasure, but it was the poet Marot who was concerned with the
more serious aspects of life—religion and ethics. At a time when
clashes were frequent between Reformers and Catholics, Marot had
accepted the new Reformist doctrines and was prosecuted for eating
meat in Lent (1532). Marot fled, first to the court of Marguerite of

Navarre, then on to the Duchess of Ferrara. He finally died a Protestant in Turin.

This is the shallow Marullo, courtier to the Duke of Mantua, seemingly insignificant in *Rigoletto* but actually a prime mover in the events which lead to the final tragedy. His discovery of Gilda and his mistaken assumption that Rigoletto has *"un'amante"* provide two of the drama's most significant moments. But in *Rigoletto*, the noble Marot, serious and thoughtful in history, becomes a tawdry prankster, a panderer who fits neatly into the company of assassins, profligates, abductors, and prostitutes whom Victor Hugo assembled for *Le Roi s'amuse.* Only if we look into history can we see these figures in their proper perspective, painted in their true colors. For the dramatist and librettist deprive them of their Renaissance glory and transform these historical figures into a sorry lot indeed, a company perfectly suited to the nineteenth-century melodrama which survives today only through its music.

THE FALSE DIMITRI:
HERO OR VILLAIN?

THERE ARE AT LEAST THREE CONFLICTING STORIES OF HOW DIMITRI, the youngest son of Ivan the Terrible and heir to the throne, met his death. A small child, he was living in Uglitch with his mother, the Tsarina Marfa, when he may have perished in a fire during an uprising in the village, was foully murdered by Boris Godunov's henchmen, or died from an accidentally self-inflicted injury while suffering an epileptic attack.

Even more puzzling and fascinating than the uncertain manner of the tsarevitch's death are the origins of the False Dimitri. Was he simply a dissatisfied and querulous monk who had escaped from his order? Or was he the true tsarevitch who had been saved from Boris Godunov's plot of assassination? Had he fled in the confusion of the fire in Uglitch and the body of another child been interred instead? Or, upon the widowed tsarina's orders because she feared Boris, had another child, a playmate, been substituted nightly for Dimitri in his bed and consequently been murdered?

Suppositions are manifold and without conclusive evidence and proof have continuously given cause for conjecture to historians. Similarly, the unknown factors, the tragedy arising out of the mysterious death of the tsarevitch and the appearance of a pretender during the reign of Boris have stirred the imagination of creative genius.

Historically, Ivan's youngest son Dimitri, born in 1583, was in immediate succession to the throne when his older brother Feodor became tsar. Since Feodor was sickly, Boris Godunov, his brother-

199

in-law (through his sister Irene's marriage to Feodor), was the actual ruler of Russia. In 1591, during Feodor's reign, Dimitri was murdered at Uglitch. Boris ascended the throne in 1598 upon Feodor's death. About two years later arose the first rumors of a pseudo-Dimitri. After having been "discovered" in the service of a Lithuanian prince, his cause was taken up by an impoverished Polish magnate, Yuri Mnishek, whose daughter Marina he later married. Mnishek was able, though unofficially, to enlist the aid of King Sigismund III of Poland. Having entered the Church of Rome, the pretender at the head of an army of Cossacks, Muscovite fugitives, and Lithuanian and Polish volunteers crossed the Russian frontier.

After the sudden death of Boris Godunov on April 13, 1605, the Russian army, under Basmanov, threw its support to the False Dimitri. Boris's son Feodor and his mother were killed, while his daughter Xenia was forcefully kept by the pretender as his mistress for several months before, upon Mnishek's reprimands, he sent her to a convent. Following his triumphal entry into Moscow on June 20th, he was crowned tsar. The Tsarina Marfa was released from her imprisonment in a convent and, possibly fearing for her life, acknowledged the pretender as her son although later she retracted her endorsement.

The False Dimitri immediately introduced a number of political and economic reforms. Not only did he create a senate, relieve the burdens of the peasants, and improve Russia's relations with Western Europe, but he also planned a mammoth crusade against the sultan of Turkey, enemy of Russia and Christianity. Although popular with the people at first, who had never wanted to believe that Ivan's royal line had completely died out, Dimitri soon aroused the wrath of the conservative boyars by assuming the title of emperor, ridiculing their ignorance, and favoring foreigners, of whom he employed 300 as guards. He disregarded time-honored traditions, such as eating forbidden meat and neglecting to bathe as custom demanded. The name Dimitri completely lost its magic charm when Marina Mnishek, who arrived with 2,000 Poles, mocked and ignored ancient Russian customs. The boyars rose in revolt, led by Basil Shuisky, a prime mover in making and breaking tsars.

After the murder of the tsarevitch, it had been Shuisky who, at the head of a commission appointed by Boris Godunov, had investigated the circumstances and determined that the child had died during an epileptic fit. After Boris' death, Shuisky supported the False Dimitri, claiming that a substitute child had been killed and the true tsarevitch been saved. Early in Dimitri's eleven-month reign, Shuisky conspired against him, was arrested, but subsequently pardoned by the tsar. Later, after Dimitri's downfall and violent death, Shuisky, who was responsible, asserted that the tsar had been an impostor, that he, Shuisky, had been present when Ivan's son, the true Dimitri, was buried. He now agreed with Boris Godunov's contention that the pretender had been one Otrepiev, an escaped monk, and even succeeded in having the monk's family corroborate his statement.

The False Dimitri was given a pauper's burial. Soon there were rumors that lights issued from his grave. The body was disinterred and burned. The ashes, mixed with gunpowder, were shot from a cannon into the direction whence he had come. Shuisky was proclaimed tsar.

These are the generally accepted facts. But it is inevitable that questions should arise. Was the False Dimitri a conscious impostor or was he the victim of scheming opportunists? How did he prove his claim? What kind of a man was he? How was his conquest of Russia possible? What caused his downfall?

There are varying opinions concerning the pretender's awareness of his origin and fraudulent claim to the throne. Some say that he was a clever adventurer, a monk who, longing to escape the tedium of the monastery, saw here his opportunity because he possessed certain physical resemblances to the murdered child at Uglitch, among them a shorter left arm and a wart under his left eye. Those who profess that he was an unconscious pretender believe that a man of his intelligence, knowing the tremendous obstacles and national prejudices opposing him, never would have challenged them so forcefully had he not been convinced that he was justified in his action. Neither would he so confidently have confronted the Tsarina Marfa. Perhaps it was his honest and disarming manner as well as her mixed feelings of vengeance and fear that led her at first to acknowledge him as her son. A willful usurper, fatally wounded, being tortured by Shuisky to tell who he really was, would hardly have continued to insist that he was Dimitri.

If this Dimitri was an unconscious pretender, those intrigants who fabricated the tales of his escape from Uglitch, planned the moment of public recognition, and agitated for him among the people were extremely shrewd and successful.

The two versions of how the False Dimitri made himself known would suit both the sympathetic believers in his innocence and the critical observers who consider him a villainous pretender. While in the service of the Lithuanian prince, according to one story, the False Dimitri fell seriously ill. Either he told the attending priest who he was or, the priest, discovering a precious cross worn by the youth, recognized it or had it identified as that having been given to the tsarevitch as a baptismal gift. The other account relates that the False Dimitri, on one occasion humbled and possibly struck by his employer, showed him the cross.

Whatever the means of discovery, the Jesuits, eager to win Russia for the Church of Rome, found here an instrument to promote their designs. Otrepiev, by some believed to have been a fellow-monk of the pretender, agitated for him. At one time secretary to Job, patriarch during the reign of Boris, Otrepiev prophesied the coming of Dimitri and was banished. The young monk who believed himself to be or impersonated Ivan's son is generally known as Gregory. The Polish nobility readily supported the False Dimitri since it was hardly adverse to gaining influence, power, and wealth in Russia.

In addition to Polish and clerical sympathies, rumors of Dimitri's survival and coming had paved his way to Moscow. The mere mention of his name stirred memories in the people's minds. When Boris suddenly died—some said in agony over his guilt; others claimed he swallowed poison—they were certain this was a sign from heaven.

The pretender himself possessed characteristics favorable to his undertaking. He was open-minded and of a cheerful, friendly disposition. There was little resemblance in him to his so-called forebears who were cold, hard, cruel, and suspicious men. They were shrewd and tough, economical and stingy, whereas the False Dimitri was trusting, forgiving, and generous to the point of being wasteful. What he did have in common with Ivan the Terrible were his sexual excesses.

Although the pretender was clever and able to speak well in Russian and Polish, he regretted not having had a better education. He requested that two Jesuits who accompanied him to Moscow instruct him in several subjects including Latin. In the near future he hoped to found a university in Moscow. He expressed himself: "For a nobleman, the most important knowledge is the art of war and a mastery of the sciences as the sources of true wisdom." Once upon the throne, however, he suffered from megalomaniac tendencies and led a dissolute life.

The False Dimitri's lucky star dimmed when the Tsarina Marfa ultimately was unable to accept him as her son. Apparently he had requested that she permit the body of the child murdered at Uglitch to be removed from the royal family's burial place. The tsarina refused, thereby expressing her doubts as to his own identity. The arrival of haughty, contemptuous Marina, and the False Dimitri's own shortcomings and errors upon which Shuisky seized in plotting the conspiracy, caused his star to fall as quickly as it had risen.

All the details of character and circumstances proved inspirational in the Schiller, Hebbel, and Musorgsky-Pushkin dramatizations of the pretender's story. In 1804, Friedrich Schiller began to write a drama *Demetrius, or the Blood Wedding in Moscow*. Although it was destined to be his swan song and remained unfinished, the two completed acts as well as numerous extant sketches, plans, and character delineations constitute a magnificent torso, fully indicative of the author's intentions. Friedrich Hebbel, who at one time considered completing Schiller's drama, in 1858 finally decided to write his own play, based on the same historical and legendary material. Curiously, Hebbel, like Schiller, did not live to finish his *Demetrius*. At his death in 1863, four acts were finished and the fifth was begun. Characterizations and the plot were fully realized and developed and only the imaginable denouement was missing.

The musical masterpiece based on this bloody era of Russian history is Musorgsky's *Boris Godunov*. Using Pushkin's loosely constructed "romantic tragedy," which is more interesting historically than dramatically, Musorgsky's libretto eliminated numerous characters, retaining only those absolutely necessary to depict the action. Concentration on the protagonists makes them vividly come to life.

Schiller's False Dimitri, like Oedipus, is a tragic hero. He is an unconscious pretender who innocently and confidently becomes a leader, then abruptly learns that he is deceiving the people and has himself been deceived. While in the service of Marina's father, he is discovered to be the rightful heir to the Russian throne. With his supporters he reaches the Russian frontier and stops, aware of the havoc he will cause: "I can still turn back. No sword is yet out of its scabbard. No blood has been shed. Over these beautiful meadows peace still reigns, and with the horrible weapons of war, I now seek to ravage them! King of kings, guide my heart. Into your hands I commend it."

In a convent Marfa is informed that her son is alive. She is willing to acknowledge him since he will avenge Boris' crime. In the meantime, in Moscow, Boris rules, stern and proud, loved and respected. Within him gnaws his guilt, pivoted to a climax by the pretender's appearance. An absolute noble monarch to the end, he atones for his offense by taking poison.

When the pretender is established in Moscow, the tragedy breaks in upon him. He is told by the scheming reward-seeking monk that he is not really Demetrius. "You have pierced the heart of my life!" the pretender cries out, "You have taken away all faith in myself." And like Othello in his farewell after having heard Iago's revelations, Demetrius continues bitterly, "Farewell, courage and hope; farewell, you joyous self-confidence! Joy! Trust and faith!" Unwittingly caught in a net of lies, he is at odds with himself: "I am an enemy of the people, I and the truth are parted forever!"

The pretender begins to think of the future and his impending doom, "What? Shall I explain the mistake to the people? Shall I unmask myself as an impostor?" Like Macbeth he "must go ahead. I must stand fast and yet I can no longer do it through my own inner conviction. Murder and blood must keep me in my place."

He will not relinquish the falsely won crown. On the contrary, he will fight to retain what is not rightfully his own. Unlike Oedipus, who bowed to destiny, he challenges his fate, inviting catastrophe.

The formerly happy, confident, and innocent youth strikes down the informer and changes into a desperate tyrant.

Demetrius goes through with the marriage to Marina who, instead of loving and comforting him, taunts him that she never really believed he was the tsarevitch. He has been neglecting Marfa, but when the conspirators burst in upon him, he flees to her. Quietly and sadly she turns away from the pretender, "It is not he. . . ." There is no further escape; his end is inevitable.

Although the circumstances are similar, Hebbel's Demetrius emerges quite differently. Hebbel was certain that if Schiller had completed his tragedy, he would not have depicted Demetrius as an impostor, because the hero, as such, would have rendered the tragic effect impossible. Hebbel invents a new motif: Demetrius is a bastard of Ivan, the son of a servant who gave birth at the same time as the Tsarina Marfa. For the story of the child's escape he uses the historical theory that the tsarevitch's playmate or substitute was saved. Hebbel was strongly influenced in his characterization of Demetrius by the description of Prosper Mérimée, who pictures the pretender "boldly playing his part, with an incomprehensible presence of mind, without possessing more to support the fraud than the diamond cross which turned the head of Prince Wisniewiecky, and which probably was stolen. Thus I picture the impostor, who knew how to win a throne, and perhaps perished in his triumph only because instead of possessing all the characteristics of a usurper, he had some merits for which one loves a legitimate prince." Hebbel points out that humaneness and manliness can provoke disaster and tragedy.

At Mnishek's court, before Demetrius believes himself to be the rightful tsar, the contrast between his humble origins and his noble bearing is emphasized. He is a proud, stubborn, and defiant youth:

> I'd rather sit upon the naked earth
> Than on the peasant's chair, prefer to drink
> From a cupped hand, than from the servant's dish,
> And rather search for berries for my hunger,
> Than that I revel where the beggar drinks!

When he claims the throne, the hero grows into a responsible and conscientious leader. The limelight always concentrates on him.

Schiller stirs sympathy for several minor characters—for Boris when he drinks poison, for Xenia whose purity and nobility atone for her father's crime—thus accentuating Demetrius' wrongdoings. Hebbel does not let Boris die on stage. Two citizens discuss his death, wondering whether it was natural or suicide. Even after he gradually learns the truth, Hebbel's Demetrius remains royally self-contained and just in his decisions. First the monk Gregory demands a reward. Then the real mother of Demetrius, Barbara, is granted an audience. "One can be the real son of the tsar," he reflects painfully, "and yet a dog, a bastard on the side." And he questions Mnishek who interrupts the interview with Barbara because of urgent state matters, ". . . whom do you seek? Not the tsar of all Russians! A breath blew him back into empty nothingness. . . . Morning broke in, the old woman there pushed open the shutters, and my mask I take off again."

Demetrius' initial impulse is to tell the truth to the boyars. Mnishek convinces him that it is his duty to carry on the work he has begun. Marfa enters hurriedly. Shuisky is to be executed for treason by order of the tsar. She pleads for his life. Thrown back into the reality he himself has created, Demetrius is called upon to act immediately. He pardons Shuisky, for where is the tsar whom he had insulted and hoped to overthrow? Demetrius realizes that he must continue to wear his mask, in spite of his conscience. He is ready to be crowned tomorrow, with Marina as tsarina:

> But this, my carnival, I shall never
> Stain with blood, no offender
> I'll punish, since I myself am the worst.
> The joke therefore must not endure too long. . . .
> I am the captain of a vessel
> That shipwrecks; quick, into the lifeboat,
> Then I'll kindle the ammunition chamber.

Demetrius foresees his imminent end, but he is resigned to meeting it unflinchingly, unlike Schiller's protagonist, who desperately contends with his fate.

Musorgsky's and Pushkin's False Dimitri is altogether different from Schiller's or Hebbel's. In *Boris Godunov* the interest is divided among several characters, of whom Boris and the False Dimitri are the most important. Yet in the opera in particular, the deepest sympathy is aroused by the Russian people, first ruled by the remorseful murderer Boris, then the shrewd impostor Dimitri, and finally the intriguing traitor Shuisky.

In comparison to the romanticized and idealized hero of Schiller and Hebbel, the Musorgsky-Pushkin False Dimitri is unembellished and harsh, even though Pushkin describes him as "wise, affable, cunning, and pleasing to all men." Gregory Otrepiev, a novice in a monastery, hears the story of how Boris had the young tsarevitch murdered. Because he is of the same age as Dimitri would have been, he decides to impersonate him and avenge his death. Having revealed himself as Dimitri, this vainglorious pretender is spurred on by an equally ambitious Marina. His passion for her leads him to blurt out to her the truth of his humble origin. When she calls him "lowly adventurer" and "peasant slave," he roughly chides her a "false arrogant Pole," whom he will laugh at when he reigns as tsar "in majesty unchallenged." He will enjoy seeing her at his feet "tortured by the loss of an empire, servile and cringing!" She goads him to seize the throne and forget Marina who loves him. Finally, this unheroic pair patch up their quarrel, expecting to be reunited in Moscow as tsar and tsarina. Rather than the False Dimitri, it is the repentent Boris who, as he dies, wins sympathy.

There are some variations between the Pushkin drama and the Musorgsky opera. With cold realism, Pushkin pictures the pretender's gradual approach to Moscow. At the end he has not yet arrived, but the boyars ruthlessly kill the innocent young Feodor and his mother, then inform the horrified crowd that both took poison. "Why are ye silent?" the people are asked. "Cry, long live Tsar Dimitri Ivanovitch!" In the opera, there is no bloodshed. Dimitri simply arrives with his entourage, promising justice and protection. He does not know yet that Shuisky is conspiring against him. Here the dark premonition of what is to pass is voiced by the simplest of the people, the simpleton: "Flow, flow tears. Weep, ye honest souls. Soon the enemy will come and darkness will fall. Woe, then, to Russia! Weep, Russian people, weep, hungry people!"

The Schiller, Hebbel, and Musorgsky-Pushkin dramatic treatments actually present three different pretenders as variously described by historians. The False Dimitri of the Russian dramatist and composer is the conscious impostor, an escaped monk and adventurer utterly deluded by his good fortune. Hebbel's Demetrius, on the other hand, is a romantic hero, generous and noble, in Levesque's words, "If he was not born for the throne, it seems that he was at least qualified to ascend it." Schiller's tragic protagonist is a mixture of the two, a deceived deceiver, both hero and villain, grappling with his destiny.

Friedrich von Schiller (1759–1805), oil painting by Franz Gerhard von Kuegelgen. *The Roy Bernard Co., Inc.*

Giacomo Puccini (1858–1924).
Ballerini & Fratini

Scene from Schiller's *Turandot:*
the Emperor of China and his
daughter; in the background, on
poles, the cutoff heads of suitors
who failed to guess her riddles.
The Roy Bernard Co., Inc.

Scene from Gluck's *Orfeo ed
Euridice. The American Swedish
News Exchange, Inc.*

Christoph Willibald von Gluck (1714–1787), painting by Duplessis, 1773. *Roy Bernard-Archiv*

An ancient Hebrew coin, picturing the lyre, dating from the Bar Kochba Revolt (132–133 A.D.). *The Bezalel Jewish National Museum.*

A modern Israeli coin with a lyre, modeled after the ancient coins. *Israel Office of Information*

The island of Delos where Apollo was born. *Royal Greek Embassy, Press & Information Service*

An illustration from a medieval Hebrew manuscript, featuring two youthful musicians with their instruments. *The Bezalel Jewish National Museum*

An eighty-eight-year-old Spanish gypsy, playing and singing in Barcelona. *Opera News*

Georges Bizet (1838–1875). *French Embassy Press & Information Division*

An etching of a gypsy caravan by Jacques Callot, 17th century. *Opera News*

A Yugoslav gypsy. *Opera News*

Hindu gypsy women and children at a well. *Opera News*

Gypsies at the entrance of their home in Seville. *Opera News*

King Francis 1 of France (1494–1547), prototype of the Duke of Mantua in Verdi's *Rigoletto*.

Château de Chambord on the Loire, built by King Francis I, later occupied by Louis XIV and XV; scene of the premiere of Molière's *Le Bourgeois Gentilhomme. French Government Tourist Office*

Scene from Musorgsky's *Boris Godunov:* Marina (Nell Rankin) is wooed by the false Dimitri (Albert Da Costa), who promises to make her Empress of Russia, *Metropolitan Opera Assn., Inc.*

Part Six
Myth and Reality:
The World of Wagner

THE FABLED SWAN

AT THE CRUCIAL MOMENT IN WAGNER'S *Lohengrin*, THERE APPEARS A
boat drawn by a white swan and bearing a knight in splendid shining
armor. Three times the call has gone forth for a gallant champion
to arise and defend the blameless Elsa; at the third call her prayer is
heard and answered by Lohengrin's arrival.

The mystery of Lohengrin and his origins is explained as the story
unfolds in words and music; the swan turns out to be Elsa's young
brother Godfrey, maliciously transformed by the scheming Ortrud.
Upon his reassuming human shape, a dove of the Holy Grail takes
the swan's place and draws away the boat bearing Lohengrin.

With its plumage of pure whiteness, its proud beauty, grace, and
calmness, the swan has long been considered a symbol of light,
warmth, and growth. From earliest times, the bird was associated
with godliness and known as a messenger of the gods of light. In
Greek mythology Nemesis turned herself into a swan to flee from the
pursuing Zeus. In a later, more generally accepted version, Zeus
transformed himself into a swan to win Leda, who became the
mother of Helen and the twins Castor and Pollux. Swans continue
to play a part in ancient Greek literature and are known as companions of a god (probably Apollo). In the *Phaedo*, Plato has
Socrates say, "Swans sing most beautifully at the approach of death
because they know they are going to the god whose ministers they
are." In the *Republic*, Plato lets the soul of Orpheus choose the life
of a swan.

In the Germanic myths, too, the swan is a prophetic bird and its
melancholy song portends approaching death. References to swans
are plentiful. In the *Edda*, one of the Valkyries, Swanhwit, wears

211

swan-feathers. The *Wielandsage* tells of three young maidens who made swan dresses for themselves, put them on, and flew off. In the *Gudrunsage*, tidings of her approaching rescue are brought to her by an angel in the guise of a swan. The daughters of Aegir, god of the sea, change into swans. In the story of Urda's well, the gods' favorite trysting place, two beautiful swans, who are supposedly the ancestors of the entire swan race, float pure and white on the holy water, remaining silent until shortly before their death. Another fable tells of a swan swimming on a lake high in a hollow mountain. The swan carries a gold ring in its bill. If it should drop the ring into the water, it will signify the end of the world. According to one interpretation of the legend, the swan is the symbol of God, the ring in its bill the world, and the lake eternity. Last but not least, there is the angel in the shape of a swan who guides Lohengrin in the *Wartburgkrieg* and the *Lorengel*.

Certain god-like creatures in German mythology loved to assume the shape of swans, especially the Valkyries (maidens of battle and destiny) and wood and water spirits. They were then called swan-maidens and usually acquired the gift of prophecy. Through loss of their swan-shape, they could be forced into human marriage. In a Bavarian poem of the fourteenth century by Friedrich von Schwaben, doves took the place of swans. In Grimm's version, the swans became ravens.

Transformation of the swan-maidens usually took place by means of a veil, necklace, or other garment of a swan's plumage. As long as the swan-maidens possessed this power, they retained their youth and freedom. If, however, a mortal gained possession of their means of transformation, they lost the precious gift and were equal to human beings, or often at the mercy of their evil scheming.

The origin of swan legends, according to Jacob Grimm, lies in nature mythology. Primitive man was much interested in the frequent changes in the heavens, for which he had no scientific explanation. Ominously threatening black clouds with their disturbingly still watchfulness or swiftly racing movement, as well as flashing lightning and powerful winds, became beasts in his susceptible, superstitious mind. A cloud would soar through the gray sky like an eagle —or at night like a raven. If it sailed across a calm, sea-blue sky, the white cloud was likened to a swan. As such vivid imagery and descriptions were passed down through generations, they intensified and grew in man's imagination. At later stages, he saw human forms in the powers of nature. Swans in folk tales became swan-maidens, the personification of everything calm, gentle, fair, and good. On the other hand, stormy clouds were envisioned as panting steeds on which the Valkyries rode into battle.

Common to several German tribes was the ancient folk myth of a boy who drifted from an ocean or large inland sea toward land and there became the patriarch of their oldest ruling family. Later versions added that a swan drew the knight in his boat. Such swan-knight legends flourished in the Middle Ages, thriving on the romantic spirit of the time, the ideals of chivalry, and reverence for womanhood. Thus the swan assumed a new character and became a favorite theme of court epics. The most popular story is of a handsome, noble young knight, sent by divine decree on a mission of redress and protection, conveyed in a small boat drawn by a swan to whom alone his destination is known. In the French romances, the swan is a transformed human being with supernatural intuition, while the knight he bears in the boat is his own human brother. German accounts explain the swan as an angel sent by God; the knight he guides is a knight of the Holy Grail.

Similar features exist in both French and German versions. Somewhere on the lower Rhine dwells a lady of high degree in dire need of a protector. A fair knight appears in a boat drawn by a swan with a gold or silver chain. The swan delivers him to the right place and departs. The knight becomes the lady's champion, frees her, and consequently weds her (or her daughter, if they are mother and daughter) with the condition that she never demand to know his name or origin. They marry and the hero becomes the founder of a new dynasty. Children are born and eventually the prohibited question is asked. The swan, about whom nothing has been mentioned or become known during his absence, reappears to call for the knight, who bids his wife farewell, leaving her a horn with magic power (or a ring or sword). He departs with the mysterious swan and is never seen again.

Several ruling houses along the lower Rhine and neighboring

streams claim the swan-knight as their ancestor, among them Cleves, Geldern, and Brabant. On a steep incline in the middle of the town of Cleves stands a former castle, the *Schwanenburg*, with a "swan tower" built in 1439. In Cleves, too, a monument was erected in memory of the swan legend several years after Wagner had written his *Lohengrin*.

The origin of the swan-knight legend is analogous to that of swan-children and goes back to the nature myths of recurring seasons, growth and decay, summer and winter, life and death. Symbolizing the approaching winter and its destructive effects on vegetation, children turn into swans, and knights depart in boats. The life of children as swans and the knight's sojourn in an unknown land suggest the inertness of nature in the icy bonds of winter. In turn, the recovery of human form and the appearance of the champion suggest the reawakening of spring, the happy bright days ahead, and finally the joy and warmth of summer. The distressed lady who is saved by the champion sometimes becomes a double symbol of spring: when the accounts deal with a mother and daughter, the mother is the *terra mater*, the daughter the virgin May Queen.

The association of swans with the seasons dates back to the Celtic god of light and warmth, Lugus. Long before the Christian era, the sand-filled Rhine-bed and its submerged coast were well suited as a resting place for swans on their migratory flights north and south. The Celts, impressed with the birds' beauty and grace, their radiant whiteness and plaintive song, as well as the coincidence of their coming and departure with that of their principal god of light and warmth, naturally identified the swans as messengers of the god. Germanic Batavians, who migrated into this region, adopted the legend and attributed it to their own god of the sky, Tius (Tuesday), with one change in the number of swans. Instead of a large flock, or the customary seven, three, or two used in tales, they chose one swan to attend their god.

It was the French who first introduced a written version of the swan-knight legend. In it, Helias, one of the seven children of the folk-tale tradition, is born to a swan-maiden mother, and is later to become the grandfather of the celebrated Godfrey of Bouillon (born 1061), leader and hero of the First Crusade.

Allusion to Godfrey's descent from a swan is made in the twelfth century by the Crusade's historian, Guillaume, Archbishop of Tyre, in his *Historia belli sacri*. This is also the approximate date of *Le Roman du chevalier au cygne* manuscripts and the *Dolopathos* by Jean de Haute Seille.

With its pagan background, the poetic story retains elements of mythology, magic, and sorcery. Early versions show a slight Christian influence, which becomes more pronounced in later years.

Modeling their knighthood on the French, the Germans also imitated them by working the swan-knight material into epics and romances, weaving into them their own national and domestic ideals. According to the Germans, the knight is of a different origin and significance. He becomes a Christian, a symbol of divine dependence on human love and faith, and of selfless service to mankind. He is a Grail knight; his ancestors are Grail kings. The Grail kingdom is accessible only to those who profess complete faith in God and are steadfast and true. This German swan-knight actually has no connection with the folk-tale swan-children but carries the title of swan-knight only because a swan guides him.

The earliest written German account was penned twenty years after the French by Wolfram von Eschenbach, who attributes the myth to Loherangrin, son of Parsifal, king of the Grail. A ballad rather than an epic, it is told with simplicity, dignity, and poetic diction. Stressing high rank, nobility, and beauty, true to the romantic spirit of the day, the poem also has spiritual significance, reflecting the religious zeal of the age caused primarily by the Crusades.

Shortly after Wolfram, Konrad von Wuerzburg (died 1287) wrote the story under the title of *The Swan-Knight*, placing it in the reign of Charlemagne. His swan-knight is nameless and homeless, and it is in his version that the houses of Cleves and Geldern are the knight's descendants. Otherwise the poem resembles Wolfram's.

Written some twenty years after Wuerzburg's account, a long tedious section of the *Wartburgkrieg* is devoted to the swan-knight. Based on Wolfram's version, the setting is the tenth century under the reign of King Henry the Fowler. Here the hero is a knight of the Grail, of lofty origin and invincible, yet simultaneously human and fallible. The spiritual essence of earlier versions recedes as superstition and magic gain in importance. A religious element is conspicuous but formal rather than truly spiritual and confined to attendances at the minster. Mention of the pope and clergy becomes significant. The knights wrangle endlessly as to who should be the champion of the heroine.

The *Lorengel* appeared about 150 years later, as did several other fifteenth-century prose accounts, but there was no further development of the swan-theme.

It was not until four hundred years later that Richard Wagner's *Lohengrin* added new dimensions to the legend. Although based principally on the *Wartburgkrieg*, it also draws material from the other versions. Wagner's prime concern was to make the characters human with real emotions. He created dramatic situations; his characters are alive; their joy and sorrow, their heroism or viciousness are convincing. His opera is national in setting and character, medieval in background. Above all, Wagner succeeded in expressing dramatically and musically the basic theme of the swan-knight myth as it had evolved so beautifully from its primitive beginnings: the theme of divine longing for human love, founded on absolute trust and faith.

UNDER THE RHINE

ACCORDING TO RICHARD WAGNER'S *Der Ring des Nibelungen*, THE world fell into three distinct divisions of which the Rhine River was the significant central dividing line. Beneath the waters of the Rhine lived the dwarfs whose race, in Wagner's words, "came into being . . . out of the womb of night and death . . . dwelling in Nibelheim, that is, in gloomy subterranean clefts and caverns. They are known as the Nibelungen; feverishly, ceaselessly, they burrow through the bowels of the earth like worms in a dead body; they anneal and smelt and forge hard metals." The face of the earth, level with the river, was inhabited by giants (in Riesenheim) and the rather unimportant human race, while above the earth and Rhine, in heaven among the clouds, was Valhalla, the domain of the gods—who, on occasion, chose to walk on earth.

It was around the Rhine River that Norse mythology had its roots and flourished. Since mythology, as well as history, religion, philosophy, or science, seeks to refer to and establish its beginnings in the origin of man and his world, it is natural that a prime common factor to all should be water, an accepted significant element of creation. As in Genesis "the spirit of the Lord hovered over the waters," so in Greek philosophy water was declared to be the basic element of all things; in Norse mythology lifeless glaciers began to melt, thus setting in motion the process of creation of life. The warmth that melted the ice was propitious to life. Out of it was born the first giant, Ymir, and out of Ymir was created the world.

The general concept of the world was that of an island which had come forth from the waters; daily the sun seemed to rise from the water's depth—constantly, miraculously, without fail—playing

217

upon and gilding the rippling waves with its warm, rich glow. It did not take much effort for man's imagination to picture golden treasures buried untouched at the bottom of the waters. With its unique quality of liquidity and pliancy, water was able to assume the shape of all things. No element could claim its hermetic and mysterious superiority and powers, apparently unlimited and endless like eternity, and capable of generative forces like the gods themselves, especially when, as rain, it fell upon the land and was absorbed by dry, thirsty earth. Water was most mysterious and prone to imaginative speculation.

Man, believing that the earth had risen from the waters and watching the sun rise every day, easily associated the fiery ball with gold. He invented the idea of a golden treasure at the bottom of the waters—pure, beautiful, and harmless as long as it remained slumbering and untouched in the watery depth, but inviting restlessness and discord as soon as it was disturbed and reached the light.

According to the *Edda*, after the gold had been brought to the surface of the water, the timelessness of the gods was at an end, their peaceful, innocent existence a thing of the past. There awakened an unquenchable lust after might, wealth, and visible proof of this immeasurable richness—in the shape of castles (Valhalla) and costly, artistically wrought vessels and decorations crafted of the gold. Competition, strife, and guilt began.

Wagner adopted and adapted these beginnings for the opening of his great music drama. In the first scene of *Das Rheingold* there is conveyed the symbolic timelessness and eternity of water, the Rhine, its calm and undisturbed peacefulness before the discovery and rape of the gold. The first leitmotiv, of the Rhine, musically implies the primordial element, the deeply hidden, untold forces of the water, their restless movement and swelling, seeking realization, expression, and shape, the longing to burst through a confining shell, to become and to be. The first sounds of the sportive Rhinemaidens —speaking for the Rhine—are indistinguishable and merely a part of the language of nature. No touch of unhappiness, no cry of pain has yet been heard in this intangible and indefinable state of timelessness that can conceive of no beginning or end.

But then appears the intruder from the outside, Alberich the

Nibelung, from Nibelheim (or Nebelheim, which means literally "home of mist"), kingdom of the dwarfs in the earth beneath the Rhine. Alberich's origins are lowly. Norse mythology in its explanation of creation tells of his ancestors, the worms within the earth—actually the worms in the flesh of Ymir, the original giant who came to life when heat melted the ice. In the *Edda*, when the gods were seated on their heavenly chairs, musing in deliberation and judgment, they considered the possible fate and consequences of dwarfs coming to life in dust and earth, like maggots in meat. The heavenly rulers decided that dwarfs should have a human shape and the understanding and intellect of man. But they were to remain living within the earth and subterranean caverns. Consequently, although dwarfs received life in the flesh of the primordial giant, their form, the extent of their thinking ability, and their destiny were determined by the gods.

In contrast to man walking upon the earth, dwarfs in the dark cavernous regions below were short and ugly, with over-large heads, compact figures, and wizened skin. Unlike all other mythological beings, they lived a long but relatively normal human life—were born, grew old, and died. They were known to be exceptionally skilled, deceitful, thievish, and cunning, but also helpful and grateful in return for good deeds, though dangerously vindictive after having suffered an insult. Alberich, furious because the Rhinemaidens had escaped his amorous advances and teased him, quickly renounced love and instead stole the gleaming gold to fashion for himself the ring which would make him master of the world.

Another characteristic which distinguished the dwarfs from all other mythological creatures was their frequently close contact with man and his world—unlike giants and gods—while simultaneously they preserved a close affinity with all aspects of nature. Man fostered his cordial relationship with these gnomes and, hoping that their exceptional gifts would become apparent in his children, named them after dwarfs. Names like Albuin, Albwin, Albigardis, Albheida, and Albhilt were common; Tacitus also mentioned a seeress named Albruna.

The dwarfs were known primarily for their craftsmanship. In the depth of the earth, amidst caverns and rocks, they built magnificent

great halls which they decorated with metallic treasures and art-
work, and where they forged unusual weapons. Norse mythology
relates that for the gods they provided those implements required
to run the world. Odin (Wotan) owned a spear which never failed
to give him victory (until Siegfried shattered it) and a miraculous
golden ring which every ninth night yielded eight similar rings. For
Thor the dwarfs had fashioned a hammer which never missed and
always returned to its owner of its own accord. Freyr had received
the air-and-cloud ship that folded up like a cloth. One of the dwarfs'
greatest treasures was the *Tarnhelm* or *Nebelkappe*, made by Mime
for Alberich, which served Siegfried to win Brünnhilde for Gunther.
It was a cloak not only rendering its wearer invisible but also endow-
ing him with supernatural physical strength. Whoever owned it
became king of the dwarfs and all their wealth.

Most famed and representative of the dwarfs and their outstanding occupation—although they were known to excel also in music
and dance—was, of course, Mime, a master in his craft. His name itself indicated wisdom (from the Latin *memor,* thinker); he also was
called Regin, meaning "counselor." But his wisdom leaned heavily
toward shrewdness and cunning. Out of his dark smithy in the forest
was to emerge the bright fearless hero, Siegfried, who, alone and
miraculously surpassing even Mime's skill, forged his own true
hero's sword, Nothung. With its help, Siegfried was able to kill the
dragon and unwittingly won the fateful gold, which Alberich had
craftily stolen from its original owner, the Rhine.

While the gold, cursed by Alberich, passed from one hand to the
next, precipitating destruction and the annihilation of the gods, the
Rhine River mourned its loss. The Rhinemaidens implored Siegfried to restore to them the treasure—which had been theirs to guard
and had been ruthlessly stolen—and with it the Rhine's former
eternal peacefulness. But neither he nor Brünnhilde, nor anyone else
who has once owned the evil-bringing gold, will part with it wil-
lingly. The gods are doomed. Flames mount from the funeral pyre
on which in death Brünnhilde's and Siegfried's love finally triumphs.

As the mighty Rhine River swells at the end of *Götterdämmerung,* extinguishing the flames, Hagen makes one ultimate desperate
attempt to snatch the gold (the symbolic ring), but the Rhinemaid-

ens grasp him in the act, pulling him into the depth below. Jubilantly they reclaim their treasure, which will be cleansed of the curse by the waters of the Rhine, as Brünnhilde admonishes

> Ye in the flood
> wash it away
> and ever keep pure
> the gleaming gold,
> the glowing star of the Rhine
> once stolen to your bane!

Once more tranquility is restored. The Rhine resumes its natural, continuous course, as though naught had ever disturbed it—majestically, powerfully, and eternally secretive and timeless. Its calm surface indicates no sign of the strife that began beneath it, no echo of the turbulence of subsequent events. It is rather for posterity to conjecture about the gold that still rests, slumbering peacefully, at its bottom—or about the dark, busy kingdom of dwarfs, deep below in Nibelheim.

BRÜNNHILDE'S HERITAGE

AFTER CENTURIES OF HISTORICAL, MYTHOLOGICAL, AND POETIC INFLU-
ences, it was Richard Wagner who, in fusing various elements of
Valkyrie myths, refined the material and achieved the highest artistic peak of its development in his heroically conceived figure of
Brünnhilde. In Wagner's *Der Ring des Nibelungen*, Brünnhilde
emerges as a supernatural young warrior maiden torn between duty
to her godly father, Wotan, and her own sympathies; a defiant, subsequently penitent and yet proud daughter; a passionate woman in
her emotions, which break forth with all their force in her love for
the hero, Siegfried; a proud woman avenging her honor and choosing to die with her lover. Clothed in Wagner's dramatic libretto and
music, she attains poetic heights of German womanhood.

Far from this idealized concept was the historic background of
the Valkyries (choosers of the dead). As in all folklore and mythology, it is difficult to determine their exact beginnings; but the
extent of a people's civilization, its dominant characteristics and
way of life give us definite clues. Since the life of barbaric North
German tribes consisted mainly of wars and battles, we know that in
such a restless nomadic life, instead of merely guarding the hearth,
women became their men's companions as warriors and conquerors.
They fought side by side with the men, sharing an equality born of
necessity rather than freedom of choice. They assumed warlike
characters: courage was their prime and most highly esteemed
virtue. The men admired and paid homage to these traits of valor
and fearlessness in their women, so that eventually an exaggerated
glorification was bound to occur. With heroic deeds in battle, the
women helped to shape their people's history.

The "Marius" of Plutarch's *Lives* tells of women fighting in battle. Romans found the bodies of armed German women in the battle-fields, and Marcus Aurelius in his triumphal march included ten "Gothic Amazons." While the barbaric German's ideal of woman-hood was beauty and faithfulness, in hours of need she was expected to assume more masculine characteristics of leadership, stalwart-ness, and even brutality, so that she could defend herself and her own with a sword.

Although women were not rulers of large empires, in instances of tribes like the Vikings, where a kingdom usually consisted of a ship or a fleet of ships, a woman occasionally assumed command. The history of the Vikings (it will be remembered that the name itself means "warriors") cites examples of daring wives and daughters in charge of ships. Tenth-century Irish annals record the arrival on the coast of Ireland of a Norman fleet, whose last ships belonged to a red-headed woman. Proud, adventurous daughters of reigning kings or tribesmen not only defended their belongings and people but also their maidenhood until, conquered by a "hero," they once again assumed the gentler and more subservient qualities associated with their sex.

These heathens created their religion—or myths and superstitions —in accordance with their own way of life. Their mythology, too, was one of endless, bloody slaughter, peopled with heroes, villains, and evil spirits. The recorded myths as we know them actually had their beginnings long after this period, when the activity of valiant women, the historical "shield-maidens" (*Schildmädchen*), had ended. It was then that they became typical figures in Nordic poetry. What had been stark reality in the eighth and ninth cen-turies lived on in romanticized mythological versions in the twelfth and thirteenth, when European literature began to blossom. The popularity of these stories is evidenced by their great number.

Such figures of historic origin had no distinct connection with the basic concept of Valkyries. Early Anglo-Saxons knew of a spirit, dark and demonic, whose glance proved fatal to him who looked upon her. Another apparition was supposed to cause lameness to warriors. Common to Indo-Germanic tribes was not only the belief

in Odin (Wotan) but also in a number of lesser deities, among them
the goddesses of destiny. Supernatural female figures of fate held a
similar place in Greek myths and Sanskrit poetry. The *Merseburger
Zaubersprüche* (magic formulas), documents of ninth-century German origin, speak of goddesses determining the fate of armies and
the outcome of battles, pointing to the early attributes of the Valkyries.

In man's imagination the idea of heroic, warlike women was not
far removed from that of goddesses of war; the concepts comple-
mented each other and consequently merged into one. In a life of
battles there were also innumerable dead. Was this truly their end,
or was there another existence, an after-life, for the slain heroes?
Their souls went to Valhalla, Odin's great hall, where their women,
their equals on earth, joined them in death. Thus the historical
king, his army, and the heroic women of his time slowly gave rise
to Valhalla and Valkyrie myths. Odin and Valhalla, supernaturally
associated with war and battle, attracted everything to do with the
business of fighting in actual life. Without sacrificing their former
independence, female war deities became attached to Odin, fusing
with the early Nordic heroines in Valhalla.

On the activities of Valkyries, the Merseburg document reports
in one instance that they are occupied on the battlefield in three
groups of three each. One group ties up the prisoners, the second
wards off the enemy, and the third, with the magic formula "Escape
from the bonds, flee from the enemies" (*Entspringe den Banden,
entfahre den Feinden*), loosens the fetters of imprisoned warriors.
The Valkyries were generally pictured on horseback but also appeared in the guise of swans. They were associated with swan-
maidens (typical of old Nordic poetic fantasy) and those destiny-
makers, the Norns. Valkyries might assume the shape of swan-maidens, but the latter were not necessarily Valkyries. Moreover, where
Norns may have had a hand in wars, Valkyries, exclusively concerned with battles, were absolute messengers of death. In this
sense they also differed from witches and female giants, evildoers
who were more diversified. On the other hand a bright, helpful,
protective, and loving feminine spirit was never called Valkyrie. It

is understandable that in the people's mind Valkyries became associated with crows, eagles, and ravens, the traditional molders of fate and harbingers of death. The raven, Nordic bird of fate, was considered not only an apparition or sign but the actual cause of an enemy's fall. Like the Valkyrie, the bird had a secret power to obtain exactly what he desired.

The Valkyrie was invisible and showed her face only to the dying; or she appeared after death, on the battlefield, after the fighting was over. Pictured thus, she gradually became the godly figure who helped warriors to Valhalla. Eventually she emerged as a new creature who protected the hero but at the same time offered herself to him as a reward for his protection. Here a strictly feminine quality slowly crept into her make-up. Without the thought of death, only a beautiful armed maiden remains. Although the Valkyrie continued to be a harbinger of death, she no longer felt joy in causing it; she was carrying out an unfathomable decree and led the sacrificed hero to the heights of glory and honor in Valhalla, where she laid aside her "shield-maiden's" armor to serve him food and drink. Here she resembled the historical Nordic woman sharing the man's glorified after-life. A godly sublimity surrounded her; she had become a "wish-maiden" (*Wunschmädchen, Wunschtochter*) of Odin; she had attained the supreme step in her development without sacrificing her vocation. The dark evil-bringer was replaced by a tragic heroine.

The genus *Valkyrie* actually is Brünnhilde (fighter in armor), as most of the Valkyrie sagas are woven about her and their development is drawn primarily from hers. She is unique among her sisters: she embodies all the characteristics of her kind. Although there are references to Valkyries throughout the course of mythology, it is Brünnhilde who recurs as a fully realized character. It is she who represents the German's ideal of his women. Numerous Valkyries are cited—Chlotilde (famous fighter); Siglint, Sigidrud, Sighilt (victorious one); Hildegund (battle); Thrud (strength); Herfiotur, Heeresfessel (frightens the army)—but Brünnhilde is a true mover of events. It is after her that the *lectulus Brunihildae* (Brünnhilde's rock) is named. Identified by this name in a document dated

1221 is a huge rock on the Feldberg, near Frankfurt, where she is said to have slept.

The fully shaped Valkyrie or Brünnhilde myth appears in a number of different but related sagas. The *Edda* and *Walsunga Saga* agree that Odin had an effect on Brünnhilde's destiny. She defied him, giving victory to the wrong one, and is punished. Still dressed in her armor as she comes from battle, she is banished to a rock where she is to remain asleep, surrounded by a protective magic fire, until awakened by a hero who dares to brave the flames and claim her as his own. No more is she to ride in battle, no more mete out victory or death or serve the heroes in Valhalla; after her awakening, marriage is to be her destiny.

In the German *Nibelungenlied*, Brünnhilde's character has undergone a change. Although her sinister strength has remained, she no longer retains the sublimity she possessed in the *Edda*. Her earlier meeting with Siegfried is almost forgotten; she has only to avenge the deception practiced on her. There is nothing of her secret passion for Siegfried, and after her vengeance she simply steps into the background of the poetic tapestry, whereas in the *Edda* she can no longer bear to live. Thus the most moving moments are gone: Brünnhilde's talk with Sigurd after her secret has become known (retained only in the *Walsunga Saga*) and her proud end. The *Nibelungenlied* has no reference to the tragic grandeur of her character as evidenced in the *Edda* by her great love for Sigurd, the necessity to demand his death to restore her honor, her last speech with the instructions for the double funeral, and her ultimate prophecy. Here her personality is merely supernatural and strange; she is a figure of strength in her shining armor, but her power is dependent on her virginity.

Wagner ingeniously combined the most dramatic qualities of the Valkyries from all sources to make Brünnhilde a true heroine, typifying the best of Valkyrie myth and Germanic history. In three of the *Ring* operas she is a major character: her scenes are basic and outstanding, on the highest level of poetry and music. Wagner's Brünnhilde is the heroic Nordic woman of history, reminiscent of the darkly foreboding supernatural spirits of the early myths and similarly the shaper of destinies—yet through a higher power

(Odin, Wotan) unable to decide her own. This Brünnhilde is not the pale, passive maiden of the *Nibelungenlied* but has once again assumed the stature she enjoyed in the *Edda* and *Walsunga Saga*. Although her fate in poetic mythology is to bring death, making her primarily an evil spirit, Wagner has recreated her as a heroine who wins our sympathy and commands our emotion.

WORMS AND THE NIBELUNGENLIED

ALTHOUGH RICHARD WAGNER COMBINES CHARACTERS AND SITUATIONS in *Der Ring des Nibelungen* from various sources of Norse mythology and legend, recreating them to suit his dramatic purposes, the original tales and locales remain discernible. In *Das Rheingold* Wagner introduces us to the world of gods, dwarfs, giants, and Rhinemaidens—dwellers of the heavens, the underworld of caves and rocks, the earth, and the waters, respectively. In *Die Walküre* and *Siegfried,* supernatural elements conflict with human protagonists against the wild natural backgrounds of anonymous woods, rocks, and caverns. It is not until *Götterdämmerung,* however, that supernatural beings and nameless wild locales make way for a human cast and geographical sites.

Götterdämmerung seems to concern ordinary mortals in spite of the opening scene of the Norns, the reappearance of the Rhinemaidens, Siegfried's extraordinary prowess and attributes, Brünnhilde's godly ancestry, and the half-dwarf, half-human origin of Hagen. Possibly the basic reason for the touch of reality and true human drama in this last opera of the *Ring* is its locale. Although Wagner merely refers to a stronghold on the Rhine, we are given a specific geographical area and are able to conjure up a definite scene where the action unfolds. The original German *Nibelungenlied,* much of which has been absorbed, with Wagner's variations, into *Götterdämmerung,* goes even further and names an ancient city as the center of its story: Worms on the Rhine. Thus the imaginary picture has found a definite focal point.

The city of Worms, situated twenty-five miles south of Mainz and twenty miles northwest of Heidelberg, has a long and famed history. It was here that the Frankish kings in the eighth century established a royal palace where Charlemagne and later emperors frequently held court. In 1122 Worms was the scene of the concordat which ended a long controversy between emperor and pope. In 1495 Maximilian I proclaimed "perpetual peace" (*Ewiger Landfriede*) at the Diet of Worms. Martin Luther stood in Worms before Charles V in 1521 to defend his doctrine. Worms embraced Protestantism four years later and suffered severely during the Thirty Years' War. The city's historical background for the *Nibelungenlied*, however, dates back further.

Worms already existed in the days of Roman rule, which lasted until 413, when Jovinus permitted the Burgundians under King Guntar to settle on the left bank of the Rhine. Here they founded a kingdom, with Worms as its capital city. Soon the Burgundians rose in revolt against the Romans, who hastily employed the Huns to suppress the rebels. From this period dates the city's association with the *Nibelungenlied*, often referred to as the German *Heldenlied* (Hero's Lay). The original consists roughly of Siegfried's exploits as a youth, his death, and the subsequent revenge of Kriemhild (Gutrune) upon her brothers and Hagen, who had treacherously murdered him. Whereas Wagner's treatment ends with Siegfried's death, the *Nibelungenlied* devotes a lengthy section to the revenge, in which the widowed Burgundian queen weds Etzel (Attila the Hun, according to history), plots for years, and eventually carries out the gruesome downfall of her brother's house and kingdom. With the suggestion of a parallel between the story of the *Nibelungenlied* and the fifth-century history of the city, Worms gained the distinction of being the chosen site of northern mythology.

The name itself—Worms—has a legendary connotation quite in harmony with the Siegfried stories. According to one popular version, the city takes its name from the many evil and destructive worms who used to live there, whom Siegfried killed and in whose blood he bathed. With the rise in popularity of Nordic myths, the Worms coat of arms, which had formerly pictured St. Peter with his key, now became a dragon (or *Lindwurm*) with a key in its claws. The key to heaven's gate, that is, turned into the key with which "horned" Siegfried unlocked the *Drachenfels* or *Drachenstein* (Dragon's Rock) to free Kriemhild from the dragon—one of the hero's numerous exploits not used by Wagner.

A naïve account of how Worms received its name was told by the secretary of the Jewish congregation there, the oldest in Germany, already extant at the beginning of Christianity. Published in Amsterdam in 1696 and entitled "Why the city is called Worms, and why a key is its coat of arms," this is the tale in brief: At one time, long ago, when Worms was a great and renowned city, a huge monstrous dragon (or worm) lay outside its wall, constantly devouring humans and animals. It laid waste the fields; the inhabitants could neither plant nor reap, and soon there was famine in the city. If, every morning, one human being was thrown to the dragon, it would be quiet for the rest of the day. Daily a lot was cast to choose the next victim. There lived in the city three giants, brothers, who owned a smithy and were well known locksmiths. They fashioned a harness of iron so that if the lot should be cast for one of them, he would be protected. The city was ruled by a queen; one day a lot was drawn bearing her name. One of the brothers gallantly offered himself in her stead: were he to conquer the dragon, his reward would be the throne of the realm. The dragon promptly swallowed the locksmith, but the man successfully fought and killed the beast and emerged safely from its body. The locksmith saved the city from the scourge and became king; since then it has been known as Worms and its coat of arms has been a key.

Since time does not differentiate between legend and history, it is difficult to distinguish reality from dreams, experience from fancy. The age of the actual city as well as the mere association of its name with destructive worms or dragons made it fertile ground for the growth of appropriate myths. Already in the *Edda*, the Siegfried legend has its setting on the Rhine. The route of the hunt on which Siegfried is to meet his death in the *Nibelungenlied* is from Worms, on the left bank of the Rhine, across the river to the Odenwald. Similarly, the argument between Brünnhilde and Kriemhild (Gutrune) takes place at the historic northern gate of the Cathedral of Sts. Peter and Paul.

From such positive identification with legend, Worms proudly created its own landmarks, enhancing the stories and attempting to clothe them with greater credibility and historic reality. The city claimed a *Hagengasse* (Hagen Alley), *Brünnhildewiese* (Brünnhilde Meadow) and *Brünnhildegraben* (Brünnhilde Ditch). As early as the fifteenth century, documents mention the names of buildings and inns containing the word "giant" (*Riese*), while as late as 1689, when the French under Mélac almost completely destroyed the city through fire, a report tells of giants who used to live in Worms and the finding of their bones. No doubt these were archaelogical discoveries of fossil remains; but in the imagination of the people, heroic Siegfried had become a giant.

Worms' most renowned landmarks of the *Nibelungenlied* are the Siegfried relics: his grave, his lance, his rock. Siegfried's grave (in the original he was buried rather than burned), also called the *Riesengrab* (Giant's Grave), was supposedly situated between the Church of St. Cecilia and the prayerhouse of St. Meinhard in the outskirts of Worms. In the fifteenth century, belief in such a grave was so prevalent that Emperor Frederick III, while in Worms, requested the gravemaster to dig for Siegfried's bones. Dig they did until they struck water, but they found nothing save a head and several limbs. A conflicting source, dated 1488, describes the episode: "The emperor found no sign of the body. . . . Everything written about Siegfried and his sword and lance is fiction." If there was such a grave, marking the burial-place of a legendary rather than an actual person, it was probably destroyed by the great fire of 1689.

Siegfried's lance, according to sixteenth-century sources, was a sixty-six-foot spruce tree used as a beam for the cathedral. A seventeenth-century report tells of a huge rock which in the *Nibelungenlied* Siegfried hurled across a square in Worms; identified as this rock is a large stone located next to a gate near the cathedral.

Further proof identifying Worms with the *Nibelungenlied* was a painting at the Mint, on the market place, of Siegfried's lethal fight with the dragon, whose body also hung suspended from iron chains. On the city wall was said to have been a picture of a giant. Finally there was the Church of St. John (*Johanniskirche*), sometimes called the *Siegfriedskapelle,* part of which was demolished in 1807 and yet in 1824 still was referred to as the *Siégfriedskapelle*. Of the cathedral and the lion sculpture on its eastern gate, Sulpiz de Boisserée, visiting Worms in 1808, noted in his diary, "This tends to give the edifice an antique and rare character. Involuntarily, one connects with it thoughts of the dark legends about Siegfried and those ancient, bloody, terrible fates of the Nibelungen."

After 1689, the old legends lost their appeal. Worms, once the rich storehouse of Siegfried stories and relics, was stripped of its legends. None of the great German classic poets, painters, or composers seemed attracted to the Nibelungen material. It was not until the oppression of foreign rule and wars of liberation reawakened German patriotism, and the romantic school demonstrated its love for the colorful heroics and sentiments of the Middle Ages, that renewed stimulation was aroused at the turn of the nineteenth century by the old tales which claimed Worms as their setting. At the site of the former Mint was sculpted Siegfried's first arrival in Worms. Pictured with him were Gunther, Kriemhild, and Brünnhilde. A *Siegfriedbrunnen* (Siegfried Fountain) was erected just outside the city.

Not only in the plastic arts but in literature and music as well, there was a revival of interest in the *Nibelungenlied*. Friedrich Hebbel wrote his great three-part tragedy *Die Nibelungen*, consisting of *Der gehörnte Siegfried* (Horned Siegfried), *Siegfrieds Tod* (Siegfried's Death) and *Kriemhilds Rache* (Kriemhild's Revenge), following closely the plot of the original. Lastly, Wagner composed his *Ring des Nibelungen*, altering the narrative and characters but at the same time presenting them in a new light and restoring to Worms, too, its former glory as the dramatic scene of the *Nibelungenlied*.

THE LOVE POTION

FROM THE PIVOTAL LOVE-POTION SCENE, AND THE LOVE POTION ITSELF,
evolves the drama of *Tristan und Isolde*. In Gottfried von Strassburg's original poem, which remained unfinished, it is Queen Isolt
who prepares a magic drink. Secretly entrusting it to her niece,
Brangäne, she tells her that this is a potent love potion to be
guarded well and given to her daughter, also called Isolt, and King
Marke upon their marriage.

Accompanied by Brangäne, the young Isolt sets out on her voy-
age to meet her unknown husband-to-be; she is not at all eager to
marry Marke, and Tristan seeks to comfort her. When many of the
women are overcome by seasickness, the ship pulls into port and
all go ashore. Tristan remains aboard with Isolt. Only a few young
waiting-maidens are about. Tristan asks for wine. An unsuspecting
maiden brings the love potion to Tristan and Isolt. Brangäne returns
to the scene, blanches at the sight of the empty vessel but remains
silent and merely throws the flask into the sea. Tristan and Isolt of
course fall in love. Isolt begs Brangäne to take her place with King
Marke during the wedding night; silently bearing the heavy burden
of her guilt, Brangäne agrees.

In Gottfried's poem, as in Wagner's drama, Marke does not learn
of the fatal potion until is it too late. Thus in this version the *Minnetranc* is essentially a tragic mistake. In Wagner, however, Isolde is
herself aware of the magic potions: she demands the death potion
for herself and Tristan. Brangäne, who alone knows of the love
potion, in desperation substitutes it instead, so that the redeeming
death-draught which Isolde has chosen to lead her out of an un-
bearable world of agony and shame serves only to intensify her suffering.

233

The idea that Tristan and Isolde's love antedates the love potion—that it grew out of their first meeting—is not unknown to later versions of the legend, when in all probability the faith in magic potions had paled. Originally, minstrels believed that the lovers' passion resulted from the *Minnetranc* alone. Magic drinks played a significant part in the old romances; thus Siegfried is given a special brew by Hagen to forget Brünnhilde. In their results, the forgetfulness drink of Siegfried and the love potion of Tristan and Isolde are closely linked. Both cause the eventual death of those who drink them.

Wagner's presentation, outwardly traditional, recounts the love of Tristan and Isolde simply as the result of the potion. Previously she was bitterly incensed against Tristan while he, seemingly indifferent to her, kept his distance, ignoring rather than seeking her as his prototype did on the journey in Gottfried's poem. But from their behavior toward each other, especially Isolde's, it is apparent that the germinating seed of love had already taken root in the hidden corners of their souls. It is feelings of guilt that have kept Wagner's Tristan away from Isolde throughout the trip. He has offered to bring King Marke a bride; but he loves her himself. This knowledge must remain hidden, or he would turn traitor against his master, uncle, and friend. In addition, there exists between him and Isolde a blood feud: he has slain Morold, whom she was to marry—a relationship intensified by Wagner, for in Gottfried's poem Morold was only Isolde's uncle.

Isolde loves the knight who killed her betrothed. Ashamed of her feelings, and at the same time insulted that he avoids her, she rages against him. Added to hatred and love is her humiliation: boldly the hero returned to ask her hand in marriage for his old uncle.

In building up this scene forcefully toward the climactic love potion, Wagner utilizes Brangäne to represent the traditional point of view. In her simplicity she does not grasp those words of Isolde's which hint at her love; when Isolde relates that the Tantris she nursed and the hero Tristan are one and the same person, Brangäne is so surprised and impressed by the discovery that the deeper insight important to this narrative escapes her. Again, when her mistress reflects that

> Unloved
> to see this glorious knight
> constantly close to me
> how could I support such anguish?

Brangäne misunderstands, believing that Isolde fears Marke may not love her. These mistakes lead her to suggest the love potion, with which, should Marke not naturally love Isolde, she would bind him to her.

At this crucial moment, Brangäne takes the love potion from the casket containing the magic draughts and balms that Isolde's mother gave them for the journey. But Isolde brusquely waves it aside: she knows a better potion. Brangäne recoils in horror; the listener, on the other hand, is hardly surprised at Isolde's choice. She could only choose death in this turmoil of her distress. The one revelation is that she has marked the flask to be able to recognize it, which would seem to prove that hers was not a momentary decision. One gathers that as soon as Tristan, whom she loved, had arrived and stated his mission, she secretly resolved to die rather than bear the insult of being wooed by him as John Alden was to woo Priscilla.

Wagner next exploits his device psychologically. Isolde reasons that Tristan's death and her own will avenge that of Morold and simultaneously justify her love. Tristan, by accepting Isolde's challenge to die with her, silently admits his own guilt, his love. Clearly these two are meant for each other, bound together not only by their unexpressed love but a common friendship with death. They drink the potion. Any other impending threat would have served Wagner equally well, but he chose the drink as a motivating agent because of its striking irony. Brangäne, in her ignorance, of all available magic potions chooses the one that will precipitate the unavoidable tragedy. Tristan and Isolde, stripped of every reserve, rapturously reveal their love in the belief that all will shortly be over. Forgotten are Tristan's thoughts of friendship, loyalty, honor; who can hold it against him if, with the expectation of momentary death, he throws caution to the wind? Isolde's anger, hatred, and shame dissolve into nothingness in the supposedly brief period of life still remaining.

The traditional point of view is upheld when, at the very end of the tragedy, King Marke is informed about the fatal drink and its consequences: the lovers were simply under a spell. Although in Wagner the *Minnetranc* of Gottfried's poem loses some of its original significance, it does not lose in importance. There is, of course, stark tragedy in the earlier versions of the story, where the draught is drained lightly and carelessly, turning the refreshing cup of wine on a hot summer day into a magic brew that empoisons innocent victims. But in Wagner's drama the tragedy is foreseen by hero and heroine alike; both seek death to escape from an already existing situation. His hero and heroine are complex and problematic before they drink the potion, which they expect will solve their troubles. Their tragedy is brought on, and comes to a climax, from within them.

In the legends—especially in Gottfried's tale, where she is related to Isolt—Brangäne is described as "proud" and "free." She is likened to the moon, Isolt to the golden dawn and the sun. In these early versions of the story, Brangäne's role is negligible after the drinking of the love potion. One of the poets who continued Gottfried's unfinished masterpiece tells us that she died of grief over her cousin's plight. As soon as her function in the story ceases, without much ado she disappears from it.

Wagner's even development and consistent treatment of her character, and her part in the drama, are more satisfactory to a modern audience. She is not only the uncomprehending spectator of the intricate conflict leading to the love-potion scene; she also becomes the agent who causes the draught to be drunk. Although Isolde has considered death before, it is Brangäne who brings out the casket and suggests a magic potion. The love philtre is drunk here not as a result of Brangäne's carelessness but because of her quick decision and action. Finally, she does not disappear from the drama. It is she who, at the end, confesses everything to the king, prompting him to sail after the fleeing lovers, eager to forgive them. But it happens too late, for Tristan and Isolde have at last found the love-death they sought, in vain, in a potion.

UNDER AN OPEN SKY

OF ALL OPERA COMPOSERS, IT IS UNQUESTIONABLY RICHARD WAGNER whose work is most strongly and poetically imbued with the phenomena of nature. To quote Nietzsche's succinct appraisal, "Wagner takes the dawn, forest, fog, chasm, mountaintop, night's eeriness and moonlight, and understands their secret desire: they too, long to be expressed in sound." While such romantic composers as Schumann, Dvořák, and Sibelius express their love of nature through symphonic music, Wagner reveals a spirit of harmony and communion with the physical universe through his music dramas. The forces of nature are powerful agents throughout his work, whether he is concerned with human beings, the animal world, mountains, the changing seasons, or night and day. All Wagner's dramas take place essentially out of doors; the few indoor scenes remain almost unnoticed, because the basic motives of the elements hover over them, and are quickly succeeded by scenes under the open sky—in the forest, near the ocean or river, in the garden or street.

At the very beginning of *The Flying Dutchman* there is a furious storm, tempestuously tossing Daland's ship and forcing it to seek harbor. The opening scene of *Tannhäuser* takes place within a mountain, the Venusberg; the second scene is set in a beautiful valley, suffused with sunlight, where a shepherd sings a welcome to the sweet month of May; still later, Wolfram addresses his praise to the evening star. The mythological *Ring* encompasses with grandeur the vastness and loveliness of nature in innumerable examples—the scenes of the Rhinemaidens and Alberich in *Das Rheingold;* Siegmund's love song and Sieglinde's jubilant response, *"Du bist der Lenz,"* from *Die Walküre;* the Forest Murmurs in *Sieg-*

237

fried; the Rhine Journey and final cataclysm in *Götterdämmerung.*
Tristan und Isolde opens on a "water" scene, with winds blowing
the sails of the ship. The second-act love scene takes place in a garden on a lovely summer night. The religious drama *Parsifal* conveys
a strong feeling of nature in the youthful hero's innocent and fearless way of life in the forest, as well as in the supernatural aspect
of Klingsor's tropical garden and the primitive figure of Kundry.

All these music dramas, removed from reality through magic, a
curse, or transformations, feature natural phenomena in their development. Wagner's characters grow out of mythology, the primitive origins of which are closely related to nature. Historically,
man's imagination translated certain natural phenomena into symbols from which beliefs and customs gradually evolved; the work-
ings of nature began to guide human life through their beauty or
awesomeness. Wagner succeeds in creating music drama out of
this elemental combination of nature and mythology.

Only one of his works, *Die Meistersinger,* stands somewhat apart.
Wagner's comic opera is highly romantic but also down-to-earth,
even though it too is based on a great nature festival abounding
with myth and superstition. In this work nature plays her most important role; the opera is permeated with a sunny, summery atmosphere of joy interspersed with nostalgia. The entire action centers
about the feast-day of St. John, celebrated since the fourth century
as the birthday of John the Baptist but in later years considered
little of a religious holiday. Because most Christian holidays were
intended to supplant heathen rites, they were appropriately instituted on the dates of primitive celebrations. St. John's Day replaced
the pagan observation of Midsummer Night and Day, on June 23rd
and 24th.

In *Die Meistersinger,* the fusion of church and nature festival
is beautifully expressed in word and music. The opening scene of
the opera, with its chorale, sets the tone for *Johannistag,* St. John's
Day; after this the action is devoted completely to secular rejoicing
at the warmth and perfume of spring just turned into summer. This
is the day largely associated with heathen cults, but there is little
reference to such practices. The only echo of dancing about or
leaping over fires on St. John's Eve is the marvelous riot scene at

the end of the second act, where David's attack on Beckmesser sets off general confusion. There is a contagious feeling of midsummer intoxication here; moreover, the beating of Beckmesser might be compared to the ancient custom of burning effigies to ward off evil and illness.

As for the remainder of the opera, appreciation of nature is expressed in sheer lyricism, beginning with Pogner's address:

> *Nun hört, und versteht mich recht!*
> *Das schöne Fest, Johannistag, ihr wisst,*
> *begeh'n wir morgen*
> *auf grüner Au', am Blumenhag*
> *bei Spiel und Tanz im Lustgelag,*
> *an froher Brust geborgen,*
> *vergessen seiner Sorgen,*
> *ein Jeder freut sich, wie er mag.*

> Now hearken to what I say!
> The lovely feast of St. John's Day,
> You know, we keep tomorrow
> On meadow green, with flowers gay,
> With game and dance and merry play,
> With gladness till the morrow,
> Forgetting all our sorrow,
> Each one rejoices as he may.

Walther von Stolzing's daring song before the masters, which kindles Beckmesser's wrath, is a long, rhapsodic outpouring on the reawakening of spring and summer after the "long winter's night." The "fields are freed from frost" and resplendent as summer returns. All the forest echoes to the swelling call of spring.

Act II, with its mild summer-evening atmosphere, enjoys a poetic setting of linden and lilac. Joyously the apprentices sing. During the twilight hour Hans Sachs, at his workbench in front of his door, muses on how the lilac's scent—"so mild, so strong, so full"—charms him and inspires him to poetry. Others too, in different ways, are inspired by the pervading midsummer magic: an ardent Walther arrives to abduct Eva; an awkward Beckmesser comes upon the scene with his lute to serenade her. While the lovers find refuge

under the heavy foliage of the linden tree, Beckmesser unsuspect-
ingly serenades Magdalene and arouses David's jealousy. All are
caught in the spell nature casts on the minds and emotions of men
that special evening. Even the watchman at the end of the act, coming upon a now deserted alley, peaceful and bright in the full
moon's glow, shakily warns against specters and spooks.

With the dawning of Midsummer Day, the inebriated passions
of the night before are past. Walther relates his dream—which is
to be his Prize Song—to Hans Sachs. Softly he sings of a beautiful
garden beyond all reality, an incomparable tree with golden fruit,
a wondrously fair woman who offers him the fruit from this tree of
life. While Sachs fits her shoe, Eva hears the final stanzas of the
song, in which Walther likens her to the stars and sun. In the last
scene, the Prize Song receives its proper hearing during the festivities on the meadow near the Pegnitz, outside Nuremberg. After the
humiliation of poor Beckmesser—so insensitive to nature's poetry,
so utterly lacking in sense of humor—a happy ending is in tune with
the day of St. John.

Hans Sachs' words in his great philosophical aria on the madness
of the world, "*Wahn, Wahn, überall Wahn,*" summarize the opera's
mood in terms of nature. Eloquently he visualizes the transition
from Act II to Act III:

> *Gott weiss, wie das geschah?*
> *Ein Kobold half wohl da!*
> *Ein Glühwurm fand sein Weibchen nicht,*
> *Der hat den Schaden angericht.*
> *Der Flieder war's—Johannisnacht—*
> *Nun aber kam Johannistag.*

> God knows how it befell!
> An elf did cast the spell.
> A glowworm could not find his mate;
> 'Twas he who caused the harm and hate,
> The lilac, too—Midsummer Night—
> But now has dawned Midsummer Day.

THE MAKING OF A HERO

PARALLEL WITH WAGNER'S MASTERY ON AN EVER GRANDER SCALE OF the music, poetry, and theatrical aspects of his music dramas, there also becomes apparent the gradual idealization and eventual perfection of his hero. From the earthbound Flying Dutchman to the earth-absolving seeker of divinity, Parsifal, the Wagnerian hero grows in a sweeping ascent from sinner to redeemer. Indeed, there is a linking of all his dramas and struggles, from which finally emerges the only perfectly harmonious being, in whom no conflict exists.

One over-all hero embodies the development, in character, motives, and meaning, from the Dutchman to Parsifal. Either he seeks a form of redemption, as atonement for his own inadequacy or wrongdoing, or his character in some measure contains that godly purity and selflessness which brings the ideal to erring human beings. It is compassionate love that offers salvation; Wagner strives to present human perfection, from the redemption of an individual to the redemption of all mankind. Symbol of an idea rather than a true human being, the hero grows more and more complex, through his creator's own searching, until Parsifal steps forth at last with utmost simplicity, trust, and calmness, surrounded by an aura of divine light.

The first picture of the hero is that of the troubled, accursed Dutchman, destined to sail the seas until he finds a woman who will love him faithfully unto death. His sad fate—the eternal, self-consuming longing for salvation—arouses compassion; Senta, who does love him, proves it by dying for him, whereupon the Dutchman is saved from the curse he has inflicted upon himself. In Tannhäuser the pattern recurs. Again we have the erring human hero, who longs to be redeemed from a degrading passion by a lofty, pure love. Yet there is a difference: Wagner for the first time introduces a religious motive. Tannhäuser appeals to the pope; he humbles himself before God. The motive of divine redemption comes to the fore with particular fervor at the end of the opera when, through the intercession of Elisabeth, his transgressions are forgiven.

Lohengrin reverses the situation. This hero no longer seeks the selfless love of a human being through whom he is finally saved: he himself becomes a symbol of godly grace and compassion. He is not a redeemer but a tool, a messenger sent to rectify human error—the aloof, untouchable hero in shining armor.

In *Der Ring des Nibelungen* the motives become more involved. Siegfried, a pure, fearless hero with similarities to Lohengrin, yet must pass like Tannhäuser and the Dutchman through worldly human temptations before he is completely liberated in death. It is in Wagner's next hero, Tristan, that the love-longing of Lohengrin comes to full expression. But its object is unattainable in life, the solution can only be tragic, and Tristan—less godly than Lohengrin or Siegfried, more human like the Dutchman, most like his brother Tannhäuser, hopelessly ensnared by his passion—is predestined from the beginning to the love-death.

Like Tristan, Hans Sachs is a human figure, but built on a superior level, with the heroic qualities of a Siegfried and the calm, tender strength of a Lohengrin. In Sachs the romantic love-longing is, in noble restraint, self-denied. While the poetic and philosophical Nuremberg shoemaker, surrounded and acclaimed by the multitude, summarizes the ideals of love and wisdom in human manhood, Parsifal, standing alone, reaches beyond humanity for the divine in compassionate love.

As Wagner's hero develops, his music aptly diminishes in descriptiveness and turns introspective. Inner thoughts and motivations rather than obvious actions determine the dramas. That the composer thought of all his works as a unified whole is exemplified by the fact that at one time he intended his Parsifal, as the wandering Black Knight, to meet the mortally wounded Tristan in the third act of *Tristan und Isolde*. All motivations of significance in Wagner's own life culminate in Parsifal, the symbol of the purification of a man's soul. In his words to Liszt, as influenced by Schopenhauer's thought, "In all my relations to the suffering world, I feel led and guided by one thing alone—compassion."

With Siegfried, Wagner stated his theme of a fearless hero; with Parsifal he goes further, creating a fool who bears within him the godly innocence of a pure heart. What is meant by such a "fool"? Kant defines him as one who sacrifices a thing of value for purposes that are worthless—for example, exchanging one's happiness within the home for what seems brighter outside. Such a fool is Parsifal, who leaves his mother to run after the "glittering men, sitting on beautiful beasts," who one day passed in the forest.

While Siegfried's background is well known, Wagner draws a veil of obscurity over Parsifal's origins, thus comparing him to Christ rather than creating him as a "hero." His father Gamuret, dying in battle in Arabia, named his son; his mother Herzeleide (Heart's Sorrow) raised the boy in the forest. Siegfried, too, was raised in the lonely wilderness. Parsifal, who knows his mother, is not much concerned about having left her. Siegfried, on the other hand, constantly wonders about the "dear mother" he never knew. Both fearless Siegfried and foolish Parsifal are unaware of the existence of weapons. As Kundry mocks Parsifal's ignorance, so the dwarf Mime is shocked at Siegfried's lack of fear. Yet because of this fearlessness, Siegfried is the only one able to forge his sword; similarly, Parsifal tells of his bow and arrow: "I made it myself/To drive the savage eagles from the forest."

Not only do Siegfried and Parsifal achieve their means independently, as the result of free development of their personalities, but the strength of their weapons sends them out to wildly boyish deeds. Siegfried tests his sword in overcoming the dragon; Parsifal wantonly shoots a swan. Gurnemanz's reprimand makes a profound impression on him. Parsifal recognizes the wrong of his action and—unlike Siegfried, who goes on to further heroic deeds—casts away the arrows and breaks his bow. This is the beginning of abnegation, of sacrificing his own personality for a holy cause. Not through prowess but humility and compassion will Parsifal be able to understand the secret of the Last Supper.

From the slaying of the dragon and the shooting of the swan, the paths of Siegfried and Parsifal diverge widely. The four dramas of the *Ring* treat ideals of the present and near future and the active, outer, material life. *Parsifal* is concerned with the more distant future, the ultimate age, difficult to attain, and the inner, spiritual experience. The *Ring* deals primarily with might and power, gained through earthly possessions. Like the Dutchman's rash oath to win over the elements, Tannhäuser's guilty passion, and Tristan's doomed, adulterous love, the avarice of the *Ring* is a transgression to be redeemed only in death and annihilation. Lohengrin, sent by a higher order, must sadly depart because the world is not ready for heroic perfection. Parsifal alone gains the redemption longed for by all others.

Siegfried breaks the spear of might with which Wotan opposes him; then he yields to temptation by Brünnhilde. Parsifal is awakened first: Kundry tempts him with a kiss and memories of his mother. But at that precise moment he is struck with the realization of Amfortas' suffering. As though mortally wounded himself, he clutches his heart. This sudden knowledge enables Parsifal to win the spear that inflicted the wound and is destined to heal it. When Wotan loses the spear of might against Siegfried's fearlessness, the threatening dusk of the gods is imminent. Parsifal wins the spear of love, and with it the Holy Grail and Amfortas' redemption.

In both the *Ring* and *Parsifal* it is the third generation that carries out a mission. Wotan, the god, rules the world with all his power. Titurel has the Grail in his keeping. Wotan is opposed by the dwarf Alberich, who stole the Rhinegold. Titurel's enemy is the magician Klingsor, eager to wrest the Holy Grail from its guardian. Wotan's son, Siegmund, and Titurel's son, Amfortas, seek higher goals but succumb before they are able to achieve them; using their fathers' weapons, both fail. It is only in the next generation— through Siegfried and Parsifal, raised alone and pure in the forest wilderness—that the final work can be realized. Where Siegfried is diverted and can act only with Brünnhilde, Parsifal is merely awakened to compassion and stands self-sufficient as the perfected ideal. Because he is a "pure fool" who learns through understanding what another has experienced and suffered, he is able to turn from a thoughtless child of nature into a redeemer.

Richard Wagner (1813–1883), portrait by Lenbach. *The Roy Bernard Co., Inc.*

Tureen from the swan service, porcelain of Meissen, model by J. J. Kaendler, 1737–1741. *Opera News*

Platter from the swan service, porcelain of Meissen, model by J. J. Kaendler, 1737–1741. *Opera News*

Scene from Wagner's *Lohengrin:* the hero's arrival, with the swan in the background. *Lauterwasser-Roy Bernard*

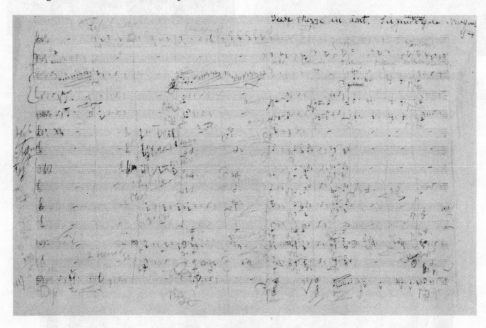

Wagner's original sketch for *Das Rheingold:* Flosshilde mocks Alberich. *Opera News*

Siegfried awakens Brünnhilde in the third act of Wagner's *Siegfried. German Tourist Information Office*

Neptune on a sea monster by Severo da Ravenna, late 15th century. *Opera News*

Hylestad stave church, Norway, 12th century; portal with scenes from the Sigurd legend. *Universitetets Oldsaksamling*

Swedish rune stone from the Viking era, picturing a maiden offering a drinking horn to a warrior, and two men in a boat. *The American Swedish News Exchange, Inc.*

Swedish rune stone from the Viking era, Gotland, circa 900 A.D., featuring a mythological animal. *The American Swedish News Exchange, Inc.*

Scene from Wagner's *Walküre:* Brünnhilde and her sisters. *German Tourist Information Office*

A Viking burial mound from the Iron Age, circa 1000 A.D., in the central Swedish province of Dalsland. *The American Swedish News Exchange, Inc.*

Engraving of Martin Luther (1483–1546). *S. Berges*

Lindenfels in the Odenwald, as seen from the Nibelungen Road. *German Tourist Information Office.*

The Lindelbrunnen in the Odenwald where, according to legend, Siegfried was slain by Hagen. *German Tourist Information Office*

above right. Isolde (Martha Moedl) holding a chalice with the love potion. *Festspielleitung Bayreuth*

A mural dated 1388, from Runkelstein Castle in Bolzano, South Tyrol, depicting a scene from the Tristan legend. *Roy Bernard-Archiv*

A miniature from a 15th-century manuscript, picturing King Marke killing Tristan. *Roy Bernard-Archiv*

Hans Sachs (1494–1576), woodcut by Hans Brosamer, 1545. *Roy Bernard-Archiv*

Beckmesser (Karl Schmitt-Walter) and Hans Sachs (Hans Hotter) in a scene from the third act of Wagner's *Meistersinger. Lauterwasser-Roy Bernard*

The riot scene from the second act of Wagner's *Meistersinger*. *Festspielleitung Bayreuth*

The Dutchman (George London) and Senta (Leonie Rysanek), who, faithful to him "unto death," redeems him, in Wagner's *Flying Dutchman. Ilse Buhs-Roy Bernard*

The Hall of the Grail, with the knights in attendance while Parsifal watches, from Wagner's *Parsifal*, in the Bayreuth production of 1876. *Roy Bernard-Archiv*

SELECTED BIBLIOGRAPHY

Librettos and scores of operas mentioned and discussed as well as English and foreign-language standard reference works are not included in this bibliography.

A PEOPLE'S OPERA

Bekker, Paul, *The Changing Opera*, tr. Arthur Mendel, W. W. Norton and Company, New York, 1935.

Howes, Frank Stewart, and Hope-Wallace, Philip, *A Key to Opera*, Blackie and Son, Ltd., London, 1939.

Scholes, Percy A., *A Miniature History of Opera*, Oxford University Press, London, 1931.

THE UNANSWERED QUESTION

Brandl, Willy, *Richard Strauss Leben und Werk*, Breitkopf & Haertel, Wiesbaden, 1949.

Panofsky, Walter, *Richard Strauss*, R. Piper & Co., Munich, 1965.

Strauss, Richard, and Krauss, Clemens, *Briefwechsel*, ed. Götz Klaus Kende and Willi Schuh, C. H. Beck, Munich, 1963.

Strauss, Richard, and Zweig, Stefan, *Briefwechsel*, ed. Willi Schuh, S. Fischer Verlag, Frankfurt/Main, 1957.

VENETIAN PIONEER

Ambros, A. W., "Francesco Cavalli," *Neue Zeitschrift für Musik*, Vol. LXV, Leipzig, 1869, pp. 313–315.

Hjelmborg, Gjørn, "Aspects of the Aria in the Early Operas of Francesco Cavalli," *Natalicia musicologica*, ed. Hjelmborg, Wilhelm Hansen, Hafniae, 1962.

Kretschmar, Herman, "Die Venetianische Oper und die Werke Cavallis und Cestis," *Vierteljahrschrift für Musikwissenschaft*, Jahrgang 8, Leipzig, 1892, pp. 1–76.

Wiel, Taddeo, "Cavalli," *The Musical Antiquary*, Vol. IV, London, 1912, pp. 1–19.

THE ENDURING CHARM OF PERGOLESI

Grout, Donald, *A Short History of Opera*, Columbia University Press, New York, 1947.

Radiciotti, Giuseppe, *G. B. Pergolesi, vita, opere, ed influenza su l'arte*, Edizione Musica, Rome, 1910.

THE IDEAL BELOVED

Bekker, Paul, *Beethoven*, tr. M. M. Bozman, J. M. Dent, London, 1925.

Engelsmann, Walter, *Goethe und Beethoven*, B. Filser, Augsburg, 1931.

Rolland, Romain, *Goethe and Beethoven*, tr. G. A. Pfister and E. S. Kemp, Harper & Brothers, New York, 1931.

Sonneck, Oscar G. T., *The Riddle of the Immortal Beloved*, G. Schirmer, New York, 1927.

NAPOLEON OF OPERA

Abraham, Gerald, "The Best of Spontini," *Music and Letters*, Vol. 23, London, 1942, pp. 163–171.

Dorn, Heinrich, *Aus meinem Leben, Ritter Gasparo Spontini*, B. Behrs Buchhandlung, Berlin, 1870.

Niecks, Frederick, "Gasparo Spontini," *Monthly Musical Record*, Vol. 42, London, 1912, pp. 29–30, 57–58.

Prout, Ebenezer, "Some Forgotten Operas: Spontinis La Vestale," *Monthly Musical Record*, Vol. 35, London, 1905, pp. 102–106, 122–126.

MELODY MAGICIAN

Fraccaroli, Arnaldo, *Donizetti*, Mondadori, Milan, 1945.

Gavazzeni, Gianandrea, *Gaetano Donizetti, vita e musiche*, Fratelli Bocca, Milan, 1937.

SICILIAN ORPHEUS

Fraccaroli, Arnaldo, *Bellini*, Mondadori, Milan, 1945.
Lloyd, William A., *Bellini*, Sisley's, London, 1908.

ROSSINI'S FRENCH OPERETTA

Toye, Francis, *Rossini, A Study in Tragi-Comedy*, W. W. Norton & Co., Inc., New York, 1963.
Weinstock, Herbert, *Rossini*, Alfred A. Knopf, New York, 1968.

THE MAN MEYERBEER

Becker, Heinz, *Der Fall Heine-Meyerbeer*, Walter de Gruyter & Co., Berlin, 1958.
Dieren, Bernard van, "Meyerbeer," *Down Among the Dead Men*, Oxford University Press, London, 1935, pp. 142–174.
Kapp, Julius, *Giacomo Meyerbeer: eine Biographie*, Schuster & Loeffler, Berlin, 1932.
Schucht, Jean F., *Meyerbeers Leben und Bildungsgang*, H. Matthes, Leipzig, 1869.

BENVENUTO BERLIOZ

Barzun, Jacques, *Berlioz and His Century*, Meridian Books, The World Publishing Co., New York, 1956.
———, *Berlioz and the Romantic Century*, 2 vols., Little, Brown and Company, Boston, 1950.
Berlioz, Hector, *Evenings in the Orchestra*, tr. C. R. Fortescue, Penguin Books, Baltimore, 1963.
———, *Memoirs*, tr. Rachel and Eleanor Holmes, ed. Ernest Newman, Dover Publications, Inc., New York, 1966.
———, *A Selection from His Letters*, ed. and tr. Humphrey Searle, Harcourt, Brace & World, Inc., New York, 1966.
Cellini, Benvenuto, *Autobiography*. Available in Italian and English editions.
Goethe, Johann Wolfgang von, *Faust*, Part I. Available in German and English editions.
Shakespeare, William, *Romeo and Juliet*. Available in any Shakespeare collected works edition.

Turner, W. J., *Berlioz: The Man and His Work,* J. M. Dent and Sons, Ltd., London, 1934.

Virgil, *The Aeneid.* Available in Latin and English editions.

Wotton, Tom S., *Hector Berlioz,* Oxford University Press, London, 1935.

IN WAGNER'S SHADOW

Cornelius, Carl Maria, *Peter Cornelius,* 2 vols., Gustav Bosse Verlag, Regensburg, 1925.

Sandberger, Adolf, *Leben und Werke des Dichtermusikers Peter Cornelius,* C. F. Kahnt Nachfolger, Leipzig, 1887.

GOTHIC SWAN SONG

Cleland, E. M., "The Humour of Offenbach," *Musical Opinion,* London, Sept. 1940, pp. 523–24; Oct. 1940, pp. 8–9.

Gray, Robert, "When Offenbach Came to Town," *Musical America,* New York, Sept. 20, 1913, p. 29.

Hewett-Thayer, Harvey W., *Hoffmann: Author of the Tales,* Princeton University Press, 1948.

Hoffmann, E. T. A., *Tales of Hoffmann,* G. G. Harrap, London, 1932.

——, *The Serapion Brethren,* tr. Alexander Ewing, George Bell, London, 1908.

Kracauer, Siegfried, *Offenbach and the Paris of His Time,* Constable, London, 1937.

Moss, Arthur and Marvel, Evalyn, *Cancan and Barcarolle,* Exposition Press, New York, 1954.

Reik, Theodor, *The Haunting Melody,* Farrar, Strauss & Young, New York, 1953.

NO OPERA, NO WIFE

Brahms, Johannes, and Billroth, Theodor, *Letters from a Musical Friendship*, tr. and ed. Hans Barkan, University of Oklahoma Press, Norman, Oklahoma, 1957.

Geiringer, Karl, "Brahms as a Reader and Collector," *Musical Quarterly*, Vol. 19, New York, 1933, pp. 158–168.

———, *Brahms, His Life and Work*, tr. H. B. Weiner and Bernard Miall, G. Allen & Unwin, Ltd., London, 1936.

Henschel, George, *Personal Recollections of Johannes Brahms*, R. G. Badger, Boston, 1907.

Kalbeck, Max, *Johannes Brahms*, 4 vols., Wiener Verlag, Vienna, 1904–1914.

Widmann, Josef Viktor, *Johannes Brahms in Erinnerungen*, Gebrüder Paetel, Berlin, 1898.

TCHAIKOVSKY AND HIS OPERAS

Newmarch, Rosa, *Tchaikovsky, His Life and Works*, J. Lane, New York, 1900.

Stein, Richard H., *Tschaikowskij*, Deutsche Verlags-Anstalt, Stuttgart, 1927.

Tchaikovsky, Modeste, *The Life and Letters of Peter Ilich Tchaikovsky*, J. Lane, London & New York, 1906.

ARABELLA'S FATHERS

Brandl, Willy, *Richard Strauss, Leben und Werk*, Breitkopf & Haertel, Wiesbaden, 1949.

Hofmannsthal, Hugo von, *Selected Prose*, tr. Mary Hottinger and Tania and James Stern, Bollingen Series XXXIII, Pantheon Books, New York, 1952.

Strauss, Richard and Hofmannsthal, Hugo von, *Briefwechsel* (Gesammt-ausgabe), ed. Franz and Alice Strauss, Atlantis Verlag, Zürich, 1952.

Strauss and Hofmannsthal, *Correspondence, 1907–1918*, Alfred A. Knopf, New York, 1927.

KOECHEL LISTING . . .

Köchel, Ludwig, *Chronologisch-thematisches Verzeichnis sämmtlicher Tonwerke Wolfgang Amade Mozarts,* J. W. Edwards, Ann Arbor, Michigan, 1947.

Pulver, Jeffray, "Köchel," *Musical Times,* London, 1911, Vol. 52, No. 817, pp. 169–70.

Schrott, Ludwig, "Ein unbekannter Weltberühmter," *Zeitschrift für Musik,* Regensburg, Jan. 1950, p. 94.

GENOVEVA—A FORGOTTEN OPERA

Abert, Hermann, *Robert Schumann,* Harmonie, Berlin, 1903.

Hebbel, Friedrich, "Genoveva," *Sämmtliche Werke,* Vol. I, Hoffmann und Campe, Hamburg, 1891.

Niecks, Frederick, *Robert Schumann,* J. M. Dent, London, 1925.

Schauffler, Robert Haven, *Florestan,* Henry Holt & Co., New York, 1945.

Servières, Georges, "*L'Unique opéra de Robert Schumann,*" *Épisodes d'histoire musicale,* Fischbacher, Paris, 1914.

Wörner, Karl H., *Robert Schumann,* Atlantis Verlag, Zürich, 1949.

THE DEVIL'S DOMAIN

Goethe, Johann Wolfgang von, *Dichtung und Wahrheit.* Available in German and English editions.

——, *Faust,* Part I. Available in German and English editions.

Mannhardt, Johann, W. E., "Der Baumkultus der Germanen," *Wald-und Feldkulte,* Part I, Berlin, 1877.

Steele, Francesca Maria, *Life of St. Walburga,* H. Cranton, London, 1921.

DUMAS, SON OF DUVAL

Dumas, Alexandre, *La Dame aux camélias,* Cadot, Paris, 1848. Available in English translation.

Saunders, Edith, *The Prodigal Father,* Longmans, Green & Co., London and New York, 1951.

THE MARRIAGE OF NORTH AND SOUTH

Bacchelli, Riccardo, "Verdi e Shakespeare," *Rassegna Musicale,* Rome, July 1951, pp. 201–3.

Brünner, E., "Verdi und Shakespeare," *Allgemeine Musikzeitung*, Jahrgang 64, Berlin, 1947, pp. 129–31.

Istel, Edgar, "Verdi und Shakespeare," *Deutsche Shakespeare Gesellschaft*, Berlin, Jahrgang 53, Jahrbuch 1917, pp. 69–124.

Ruppel, K. H., "Verdi und Shakespeare," *Schweizerische Musikzeitung*, Zürich, Jahrgang 95, No. 4, April 1955, pp. 137–41.

Shakespeare, William, *Hamlet, Macbeth, King Lear, Othello, The Merry Wives of Windsor*, and *King Henry the Fourth*, Parts I and II. All available in any Shakespeare collected works edition.

NO NAME FOR IAGO

Allen, Ned. B., "The Source of Othello," *Delaware Notes*, Series 21, Newark, New Jersey, 1948, pp. 71–96.

Cinthio, G. B., *Hecatommithi*, E. Neuchino and G. B. Pulciani, Venice, 1608.

Dukas, Paul, "Otello de Verdi," *Les Ecrits de Paul Dukas sur la musique*, Société d'éditions françaises et internationales, Paris, 1948, pp. 220–25.

Knowles, Dom David, "Honest Iago," *Downside Review*, London, May 1931, pp. 326–36.

Muir, Kenneth, "The Jealousy of Iago," *English Miscellany*, Vol. II, Rome, 1951, pp. 65–83.

Shakespeare, William, *Othello*. Available in any Shakespeare collected works edition.

Taylor, John Edward, *The Moor of Venice, Cinthio's Tale and Shakespeare's Tragedy*, Chapman & Hall, London, 1855.

THE ABYSS OF REALITY

Blaukopf, Kurt, "New Lights on Wozzeck," *The Saturday Review*, New York, Sept. 26, 1953.

Büchner, Georg, "Woyzeck," tr. Theodore Hoffmann, *The Modern Theatre*, Vol. I, ed. Eric Bentley, Anchor Books, New York, 1955.

Klein, John W., "Some Reflections on Wozzeck," *Musical Opinion*, London, May 1952, pp. 465–67.

Reich, Willi, *A Guide to Alban Berg's Opera: Wozzeck*, tr. Adolph Weiss, League of Composers, New York, 1931.

Stefan, Paul, "Wozzeck, an Atonal Opera," *Modern Music*, New York, 1926, pp. 38–40.

THE THREE RIDDLES

Bolte, Johannes, *Anmerkungen zu den Kinder- und Hausmärchen der Brüder Grimm*, 5 vols., Dieterich'sche Verlagsbuchhandlung, Leipzig, 1913.

Frazer, Sir James G., *Folklore in the Old Testament*, 3 vols., Macmillan & Co., London, 1919.

Ginzberg, Louis, *Legends of the Jews*, The Jewish Publication Society, Philadelphia, 1910.

Gozzi, Carlo, *Turandot, Princess of China*, a chinoiserie in 3 acts, by Karl Vollmoeller, tr. Jethro Bithell, T. F. Unwin, London, 1913.

Jolles, André, *Rätselforschungen*, Germanica, Halle/Saale, 1925.

Pétis de la Croix, François, *Les Mille et un jour*, P. Coup, Amsterdam, 1713–31. Available in English translation.

Petsch, Robert, *Spruchdichtung des Volkes*, Max Niemeyer Verlag, Halle/Saale, 1938.

Schiller, Friedrich von, "Turandot," *Werke*, Vol. V, G. Grote'sche Verlagsbuchhandlung, Berlin, 1904.

ORPHEUS AND HIS LYRE

Finesinger, Sol Baruch, *Musical Instruments in the Old Testament*, Johns Hopkins University, Baltimore, 1926.

Frazer, Sir James G., *The Golden Bough*, 12 vols., Macmillan & Co., London, 1911.

Sachs, Curt, *The History of Musical Instruments*, W. W. Norton, New York, 1940.

Saint-Saëns, Camille, "Lyre et cithare," *Encyclopédie de la musique et dictionnaire du conservatoire*, Part I, Librairie Delagrave, Paris, 1913, pp. 538–40.

CARMEN'S ANCESTORS

Bercovici, Konrad, *The Story of the Gypsies*, Cosmopolitan Book Corp., New York, 1928.

Block, Martin, *Gypsies; Their Life and Their Customs*, tr. Barbara Kuczynski and Duncan Taylor, D. Appleton-Century Co., New York, 1939.

Borrow, George, *The Zincali, An Account of the Gypsies in Spain*, J. Murray, London, 1888.

Brown, Irving, *Nights and Days on the Gypsy Trail Through Andalusia and on Other Mediterranean Shores*, Harper & Brothers, New York and London, 1922.

De Peyster, John W., *Gypsies*, E. & G. Goldsmid, Edinburgh, 1887.

Heister, Karl von, *Ethnographische und geschichtliche Notizen über die Zigeuner*, Gräfe & Unzer, Königsberg, 1842.

Leland, C. G., *Gypsy Sorcery and Fortune Telling*, T. F. Unwin, London, 1891.

Mérimée, Prosper, *Carmen*, M. Levy, Paris, 1875.

ANTECEDENTS OF THE MANTUAN COURT

Hackett, Francis, *Francis I*, W. Heinemann, London, 1943.

Hugo, Victor, *Le Roi s'amuse*. Available in French or English complete editions of Hugo's plays.

Kemble, Frances Anne, *Francis the First*, a historical drama in 5 acts, J. Murray, London, 1832.

Putnam, Samuel, *Marguerite of Navarre*, Coward-McCann, New York, 1935.

Shellabarger, Samuel, *The King's Cavalier*, Little, Brown & Co., Boston, 1950.

THE FALSE DIMITRI: HERO OR VILLAIN?

Hebbel, Friedrich, "Demetrius," *Sämmtliche Werke*, Vol. VI, Hoffmann & Campe, Hamburg, 1891.

Mérimée, Prosper, *Épisode de l'histoire de Russie, les faux Démétrius*, C. Levy, Paris, 1897.

———, "Mémoires contemporains relatifs au faux Démétrius," *Mémoires historiques* (*inédits*), F. Bernouard, Paris, 1927.

Pantenius, Theodor, *Der falsche Demetrius*, Velhagen & Klasing, Bielefeld, 1904.

Pushkin, Alexander, "Boris Godunov," *The Poems, Prose and Plays of Alexander Pushkin*, The Modern Library, New York, 1936.

Schiller, Friedrich von, *Demetrius*, Goethe-Gesellschaft, Weimar, 1894.

Ustryalov, Nikolai G., *Die Geschichte Russlands*, Vol I, J. G. Cotta, Stuttgart, 1840–43.

THE FABLED SWAN

Frey, Anna L., *Swan-Knight Legend*, George Peabody College for Teachers, No. 103, Nashville, Tennessee, 1931.

Jaffray, Robert, *The Two Knights of the Swan*, G. P. Putnam's Sons, New York, 1910.

Heinrichs, Richard, "Die Lohengrin-Dichtung und ihre Deutung," *Frankfurter zeitgemässe Broschüren*, Frankfurt, Vol. 24, pp. 157–212.

Rank, Otto, *Die Lohengrinsage*, F. Deuticke, Leipzig, 1911.

UNDER THE RHINE

Drews, Arthur C. H., *Der Ideengehalt von Richard Wagners dramatischen Dichtungen*, E. Pfeiffer, Leipzig, 1931.

The Elder or Poetic Edda, tr. O. Bray, Viking Club, London, 1908.

Gólther, Wolfgang, *Handbuch der germanischen Mythologie*, S. Hirzel, Leipzig, 1895.

Newman, Ernest, *The Wagner Operas*, Alfred A. Knopf, New York, 1949.

BRÜNNHILDE'S HERITAGE

Doepler, Emil, *Walhall, die Götterwelt der Germanen*, M. Oldenburg, Berlin, 1900.

The Elder or Poetic Edda, tr. O. Bray, Viking Club, London, 1908.

Golther, Wolfgang, *Studien zur germanischen Sagengeschichte*, Königliche Bayerische Akademie der Wissenschaften, Abhandlungen, Vol. XVIII, Munich, 1890, pp. 399–504.

Grimm, Jacob L. K., *Deutsche Mythologie*, Dietrich, Göttingen, 1844.

Grimm, Wilhelm K., *Deutsche Heldensage*, C. Bertelsmann, Gütersloh, 1889.

Krappe, Alexander H., "The Valkyries," *Modern Language Review*, Vol. 21, London, 1926, pp. 55–73,

Neckel, Gustav, *Walhall; Studien über den germanischen Jenseitsglauben*, F. W. Ruhfus, Dortmund, 1913.

The Nibelungenlied, tr. Margaret Armour, J. M. Dent, London, 1908.

The Volsunga Saga, tr. William Morris and Eirikir Magnusson, Norroena Society, London, 1907.

WORMS AND THE NIBELUNGENLIED

Kranzbuehler, Eugen, *Worms und die Heldensage*, Stadtbibliothek, Worms, 1930.

Lange, Georg F., *Geschichte und Beschreibung der Stadt Worms*, C. G. Kunze, Worms, 1837.

The Nibelungenlied, tr. Margaret Armour, J. M. Dent, London, 1908.

THE LOVE POTION

Strassburg, Gottfried von, *Tristan und Isolt,* tr. August Closs, Blackwell, Oxford, 1944.

Weston, Jessie L., *The Legends of the Wagner Dramas,* D. Nutt, London, 1903.

Wirth, Moritz, *König Marke,* Gebrüder Senf, Leipzig, 1882.

Wolzogen, H. P. von, *Guide Through the Musical Motives of Richard Wagner's Tristan und Isolde,* G. Schirmer, New York, ca. 1889.

UNDER AN OPEN SKY

Müller, Karl H., "Richard Wagner und die Natur," *Die Musik,* Berlin, July 1940, pp. 325–29.

Rudder, May de, "La Musique dans la nature, sa place dans l'oeuvre de Richard Wagner," *Le Guide Musical,* Vol. 50, Paris, 1904, p. 843.

THE MAKING OF A HERO

Eschenbach, Wolfram von, *Parzival,* tr. Jessie L. Weston, D. Nutt, London, 1894.

Gross, Felix, *Die Wiedergeburt des Sehers,* Amalthea-Verlag, Zürich, 1927.

Pfordten, Hermann L. von, *Richard Wagners Bühnenwerke in Handlung und Dichtung,* Trowitzsch & Sohn, Berlin, 1922.

Weston, Jessie L., *The Legends of the Wagner Dramas,* D. Nutt, London, 1903.

INDEX

Abélard and Héloïse, 143
Abraham ben Meir ibn Ezra, 186
"Abscheulicher! Wo eilst du hin?", 51
Achmed I, Sultan of Turkey, 200
Adam, Adolphe, 77
Adami, Giuseppe, 182
Adriano in Siria (Pergolesi), 51
Aeneid (Virgil), 95
Agnes von Hohenstaufen (Spontini),
  62
d'Agoult, Countess Marie, 156
Aguado, Alexandre, 78
Die ägyptische Helena (Richard
  Strauss), 131, 132, 135
"Ah m'abbraccia" (Bellini), 74
Aida (Verdi), 30, 147
Albrecht, Fieldmarshal, Grand Duke
  of Teschen, 138
Album for the Young (Schumann), 145
Alceste (Gluck), 103
Alcidor (Spontini), 62
Allgemeine Musikzeitung, 140
Allgeyer, Julius, 116
Alt, Karl, 153n.
Alto Rhapsody (Brahms), 118
Anacréon (Cherubini), 59
Andersen, Hans Christian, 143
Andrea Chenier (Giordano), 29
Andrea del Sarto, 197
Andromeda (Manelli), 42
Angiolini, Gaspare, 25
Anna Bolena (Donizetti), 67
Antony and Cleopatra (Shakespeare),
  99
Arabella (Richard Strauss), 131–136
Ariadne auf Naxos (Richard Strauss),
  131, 132
Arianna (Monteverdi), 24
Aristophanes, 108
Aristotle, 177

Arnim, Bettina von. *See* Brentano,
  Bettina
Arthur legends, King, 144
Attila the Hun, 229
Auber, Daniel François, 78, 94, 118

Bahram Gur, King of Persia, 189–190
Balakireff, Mili, 124
Un ballo in maschera (Verdi), 30
Balzac, Honoré de, 91, 156
Barbaja, Domenico, 73
Barbe-bleue (Offenbach), 108
Barbier, Jules, 88
Der Barbier von Bagdad (Cornelius),
  103–104, 105, 106–107
Il barbiere di Siviglia (Rossini), 26,
  27, 77
Basmanov, Peter, 200
Bayreuth Festival, 118
Beatrice di Tenda (Bellini), 74
Béatrice et Bénédict (Berlioz), 99–100
Beer, Wilhelm, 83
Beethoven, Ludwig van, 16, 54–57, 66,
  72, 77, 86, 87, 88, 89, 90, 101, 115,
  118, 119, 139, 143, 147, 148–149
  Eighth Symphony, 77
  Ninth Symphony (Choral), 57, 87
  F Major Quartet, Opus 18, No. 1,
    90
  C Minor Quartet, Opus 18, No. 4,
    144
Bel canto, 34, 85
Belisario (Donizetti), 27, 67
La belle Hélène (Offenbach), 108
Bellini, Vincenzo, 27–28, 67, 68, 70,
  71, 72–75, 83
Belmontet, Louis, 74
Bendemann, Eduard, 144
Benvenuto Cellini (Berlioz), 87–89,
  97–98, 103

Berg, Alban, 16, 171–174
Berlioz, Adéle, 89
Berlioz, Hector, 13, 59–60, 61, 77, 86–101, 102, 103, 104, 105
Berlioz, Louis, 97, 100
Betly (Donizetti), 67
Bianca e Fernando (Bellini), 72, 73
Bible, 178, 187, 188
Billroth, Theodor, 116, 119
Bizet, Georges, 118
Blumenthal, Oskar von, 109
Boieldieu, François, 59, 61, 78, 118
Boisserée, Sulpiz de, 232
Boito, Arrigo, 29, 164, 169
Book of the King (Firdusi), 182
Borgias, 43
Boris Godunov (Musorgsky), 203–204, 206–208
Bouffes-Parisiens (Paris), 98, 110
Bouilly, Jean Nicolas, 55
Bradley, Andrew Cecil, 168, 169
Brahms, Johannes, 68, 113–119
Brautlieder (Cornelius), 105
Brecht, Bertolt, 172
Breitkopf and Haertel, 140
Brentano, Bettina, 54, 102
Brühl, Count Karl von, 63
Brünnhilde, 15, 220, 221, 222, 225–227, 228, 230, 244
Brunswick, Therese von, 54
Büchner, Georg, 16, 171–173, 174
Bülow, Hans von, 105
Bulthaupt, Heinrich, 116
Busenello, Giovanni Francesco, 44
Busoni, Ferruccio, 183
Byron, George Gordon, Lord, 143

Caccini, Francesca, 46
Caccini, Giulio, 43, 46
Caius Marius (Plutarch), 223
Calderón de la Barca, Pedro, 116, 143
Caletti-Bruni, Gian Battista, 41, 42
Le Calife de Bagdad (Boieldieu), 78
Callas, Maria Meneghini, 30
Calzabigi, Ranieri, 25
Il campanello di notte (Donizetti), 70
Capriccio (Richard Strauss), 32–37
I Capuleti e i Montecchi (Bellini), 73
Carcano, Giulio, 163, 164
Carl, Archduke of Teschen, 137
Carmen (Bizet), 15, 118, 133, 147, 189, 193, 194
Carvalho, Léon, 111
Casanova, Giovanni Jacopo, 25
Casella, Alfredo, 30

Casti, Abbate Giovanni Battista, 32
Castrati, 24, 25, 26
Catalani, Angelica, 80
Catarina Cornaro (Donizetti), 69
Catherine de Medici, 196
Cavalleria rusticana (Mascagni), 29
Cavalli, Federigò, 41–42, 47
Cavalli, Pietro Francesco, 41–47
    Requiem, 47
Cellini, Benvenuto, 87, 100, 197
Cervantes Saavedra, Miguel de, 108
Chaplin, Charles, 108
Charlemagne, 215, 229
Charles V, Holy Roman Emperor, 197, 229
Charles VI, Holy Roman Emperor, 51
Charles III, King of Spain, 194
Cherubini, Luigi, 26, 59, 61
Le Cheval bronze (Auber), 78
Chopin, Frédéric, 74, 75, 91, 156
"Chorus of Insects" (Tchaikovsky), 122
Christ, 243
Christina, Queen of Sweden, 46
Chronological-Thematic Catalogue of all Compositions by W. A. Mozart (Koechel), 139–140
Church Fathers, 186
Der Cid (Cornelius), 104, 106
Cimarosa, Domenico, 26, 58, 59, 66
Cinthio, Giovanni Battista Giraldi, 166, 167, 168, 170
Cinyra, 186
Ciro (Cavalli), 45
Cithara. See Lyre
Clapisson, Antoine Louis, 94
Clement VII, Pope, 196
Clementi, Muzio, 80
Coleridge, Samuel Taylor, 168
Commedia dell 'arte, 25, 48
Le Comte Ory (Rossini), 77, 78
Conservatoire (Paris), 60, 87, 94
Conservatorio dei Poveri de Gesù Cristo (Naples), 49
Les Contes d'Hoffmann (Offenbach), 15, 108, 110–111
La conversione di San Guglielmo d'Aquitania (Pergolesi), 49
Corneille, Pierre, 35, 104
Cornelius, Peter, 13, 102–107
The Corsair (Byron), 143
Il corvo (Gozzi), 117
Couperin, François, 35
Courtesans, 156, 157, 158, 159, 160
"Credo" (Verdi), 169–170

Crusades, 77, 200, 214, 215
Cui, César, 123, 127

Da capo aria, 26
Dafne (Peri), 24
Dallapiccola, Luigi, 30
La Dame aux camélias (Dumas), 157–159, 160
La Dame blanche (Boieldieu), 78, 118
La Damnation de Faust (Berlioz), 92–94
Daniel, Book of, 186
Dantan, Jean Pierre, 75
Danton's Death (Büchner), 171
Daphne (Richard Strauss), 32
David, Félicien, 84
David, Ferdinand, 81
David, King, 187, 188
Davidov, Karl, 124
Dehn, Siegfried Wilhelm, 103
Delestre-Poirson, Charles-Gaspard, 76
Demetrius (Hebbel), 203, 205–206, 207, 208
Demetrius, or the Blood Wedding in Moscow (Schiller), 116–117, 203, 204–205, 206, 207, 208
Dent, Edward J., 24
Les Deux Journées (Cherubini), 59
Les Diamants de la Couronne (Auber), 94
Diane de Lys (Dumas), 159
Diane de Poitiers, 196
Diet of Worms, 229
Dimitri Ivanovitch, Tsarevitch of Russia, 199, 200–201
Dimitri, The False, 199, 200, 201–203
Dolente immagine di figlia mia (Bellini), 73
Dolopathos (Jean de Haute Seille), 215
Le Domino noir (Auber), 78, 118
Dom Sébastien (Donizetti), 69
Don Giovanni (Mozart), 51, 55, 62, 64, 88, 119
Donizetti, Gaetano, 27, 28, 65–71
  Requiem for Bellini, 70
Donizetti, Virginia, 68–69, 83
Don Pasquale (Donizetti), 27, 69, 70
Dorn, Heinrich, 63
Dragon (Lindwurm), 220, 229–230, 231, 243, 244
Dramma per musica, 42, 43
The Dream on the Volga (Ostrovsky), 121
Drury Lane Theatre (London), 74

"Du bist der Lenz" (Wagner), 237
Duboeuf, Estelle, 99
Dukas, Paul, 169–170
Dumas, Alexandre, fils, 156–160, 161
Dumas, Alexandre, père, 156, 158, 159
Duplessis, Marie Alphonsine, 156, 157, 158
Durante, Francesco, 49
Durazzo, Count Giacomo, 25
Dussek, Johann, 80
Dvořák, Antonin, 237
Dwarfs (Nibelungen), 16, 103, 217, 219, 220, 221, 228, 243, 244

Edda, 104, 181, 211, 218, 219, 226, 227, 230
Egisto (Cavalli), 45
Egmont (Goethe), 56
The Egyptian Helen. See Die ägyptische Helena
Eighty-three Newly Discovered Original Letters of Ludwig van Beethoven to Archduke Rudolf (Koechel), 139
Elektra (Richard Strauss), 131, 132
Elisabeth Christina, Empress of Austria, 50
Elisabetta, regina d'Inghilterra (Rossini), 27
L'elisir d'amore (Donizetti), 67, 70
L'Enfance du Christ (Berlioz), 103
Enrico, conte di Borgogna (Donizetti), 66
Erard, Céleste, 61
Ercole amante (Cavalli), 46–47
Ernani (Verdi), 29
d'Etampes, Madame (Anne de Pisseleu), 196, 197
Eugene Onegin (Pushkin), 125
Eugene Onegin (Tchaikovsky), 120, 121, 125–126, 127, 128
Euridice (Peri), 24
Ezekiel, 178

Fables, 177, 192, 212. See also Legends
Faccio, Franco, 164
"The False Prophet" (Moore), 143
Falstaff (Verdi), 29, 33, 164–165
Faust (Goethe), 45, 57, 85, 87, 92, 93, 94, 143, 144, 150–155
Faust (Gounod), 15, 150, 152–153
Faustini, Giovanni, 44
La Favorite (Donizetti), 68, 69–70
Federico, Gennaro Antonio, 50, 52

Fenesta ca lucive (Bellini), 73
La fenice sul rogo, or La morte di San Giuseppe (Pergolesi), 49
La Fenice (Venice), 26
Feodor Ivanovitch, Tsar of Russia, 199–200
Feodor II, Tsar of Russia, 200
Ferdinand I, King of Naples, 59
Fernand Cortez (Spontini), 61, 62
Ferrand, Humbert, 87
Ferrara, Duchess of (Renata di Francia), 198
Ferrari, Benedetto, 42
Une Fête de Néron (Soumet and Belmontet), 74
Der Fiaker als Graf (Hofmannsthal), 131
Fidelio (Beethoven), 16, 55–57, 90, 118, 148–149
La Fille du régiment (Donizetti), 68
Firdusi, 182, 189–190
Flaminio (Pergolesi), 52
Flaubert, Gustave, 157
Die Fledermaus (Johann Strauss), 132, 134, 135
Der fliegende Holländer (Wagner), 84, 118, 237, 241, 242, 244
Florimo, Francesco, 72, 74
The Flying Dutchman. See Der fliegende Holländer
Folktales, 177, 213, 214, 222. See also Legends and Mythology
Forconi, Alipio, 25
Forest Murmurs (Wagner), 237
Fra Diavolo (Auber), 78
Francis I, King of France, 195–198
Francis I, King of Sicily, 72–73
Francis the First (Kemble), 195
Franck, César, 91
Lo frate 'nnammorato (Pergolesi), 50
Frauenliebe und Leben (Schumann), 105, 148
Die Frau ohne Schatten (Richard Strauss), 131, 132
Frederick I, Holy Roman Emperor (Barbarossa), 41
Frederick III, Holy Roman Emperor, 231
Frederick William III, King of Prussia, 62, 63
Frederick William IV, King of Prussia, 63, 84
French Revolution, 171
Freud, Sigmund, 110
Friedenstag (Richard Strauss), 32

Friedrich, son of Archduke Carl of Teschen, 137
Friedrich von Schwaben, 212
Il furioso (Donizetti), 67
Fux, Johann Joseph, 139

Gade, Nils, 145
El galán fantasmo (Calderón), 143
Garcia, Manuel, 26
Garibaldi, Giuseppe, 65
Gauthier, Théophile, 91
La gazza ladra (Rossini), 26
Der gehörnte Siegfried (Hebbel), 232
Geibel, Emanuel, 116
Gemma di Vergy (Donizetti), 67
Genesis, 187, 217
Genoveva (Hebbel), 144, 147, 148, 149
Genoveva (Schumann), 144–149
George, Mademoiselle (Marguerite Joséphine Weimer), 156
German romanticism, 23, 73, 86, 109, 110, 112, 143, 232
Die Geschwister (Goethe), 117
Gianni di Parigi (Donizetti), 67
Giants, 217, 219, 224, 228, 231
Giasone (Cavalli), 45
Gibby—la cornemuse (Clapisson), 94
Gioconda (Ponchielli), 29
Giordano, Umberto, 29
Gitanos. See Gypsies
Gleichenstein, Baron Ignaz von, 54
Gluck, Christoph Willibald von, 23, 25, 26, 34, 35, 51, 59, 60, 61, 67, 86, 88, 89, 101 102, 103
Godfrey of Bouillon 214–215
Godunov, Boris Fedorovitch, Tsar of Russia, 199–200, 201
Godunov, Irene, Tsarina of Russia, 200
Godunov, Xenia, 200
Goethe, Johann Wolfgang von, 33, 45, 55, 56, 57, 85, 87, 92, 93, 102, 104, 116, 117, 150, 153, 154, 184
Goethes Werke, 153 n.
Gogol, Nicolai Vasilievitch, 124
Gossec, François-Joseph, 60
Götterdämmerung (Wagner), 220–221, 228, 238
Gottfried von Strassburg, 233, 234, 236
Gounod, Charles, 99, 150
Gozzi, Carlo, 117, 181, 182–183
Granville-Barker, Harley, 169
Greco, Gaetano, 49
Gregory, 202
Grétry, André, 60, 78

Grimm, Jacob L. K., 212
Grisi, Giulia, 27, 28, 69
Groth, Claus, 116
Grout, Donald J., 51, 98
Gudrunsage, 212
Guicciardi, Giulietta, 54
Guillaume, Archbishop of Tyre, 215
Guillaume Tell (Rossini), 73, 79
Gunlöd (Cornelius), 104
Guntar, King, 229
Gypsies, 15, 189-194

Habeneck, François Antoine, 77
Hamlet (Shakespeare), 87, 163
Hanslick, Eduard, 91
Harold en Italie (Berlioz), 89
Hasse, Johann Adolph, 49
Hauptmann, Moritz, 145
Haydn, Franz Joseph, 66, 72
Hazlitt, William, 168
Hebbel, Friedrich, 144-145, 147, 148,
    149, 203, 205-206, 207, 208, 232
Hecatommithi (Cinthio), 166-167, 168
Heine, Heinrich, 62-63, 70, 72, 75,
    81, 82, 84, 91, 104, 108, 109
Heldenlied, 229
Heller, Stephen, 91
Henry II, King of France, 196
Henry IV (Shakespeare), 164
Henry the Fowler, King, 215
Herder, Johann Gottfried von, 102
Hérold, Louis, 78
Hertz, Hendrik, 128
Der Hessische Landbote (Büchner),
    171
Heyse, Paul, 116
Hiller, Ferdinand, 81, 92, 144, 145
Historia belli sacri (Guillaume), 215
Hoffmann, Ernst Theodor Amadeus,
    62, 110, 114, 143
Hofmannsthal, Hugo von, 131-136
Holy Grail, 211, 213, 215, 244
Homer, 43, 178, 185
Horace, 187
Hugo, Victor, 67, 161, 195, 196, 198
Huit scènes de Faust (Berlioz), 92
Hummel, Johann Nepomuk, 82

Iliad (Homer), 43
Immortal Beloved, 54
Imperial Theatre (St. Petersburg),
    121, 122, 123, 124, 126, 127, 128
The Impresario (Mozart), 32
L'incoronazione di Poppea (Monte-
    verdi), 24, 44

Inquisition, 192
Intermezzo, 25, 48, 49, 50, 51, 52, 53.
    See also Opera buffa
Intermezzo (Richard Strauss), 32
Iolanthe (Tchaikovsky), 121, 128
Iphigénie en Aulide (Gluck), 59, 61,
    103
Iphigénie en Tauride (Gluck), 61, 103
Isaiah, 109
L'Italiana in Algeri (Rossini), 26, 77
Ivan the Terrible, Tsar of Russia, 123,
    199, 200, 202, 203

Jacob, 186
Jahn, Otto, 140
Jean de Haute Seille, 215
Joachim, Joseph, 106, 117
Joan of Arc (Tchaikovsky), 121, 126-
    127
Job, 164, 187
Job, Patriarch of Moscow, 202
John the Baptist, 238
Joseph, 186
Josephine, Empress of France, 60
Jouy, Etienne, 59, 60, 61
Jovinus, Emperor of Gaul, 229
Jubal, 186
Judah Halevi, 180
Jung, Bertha, 105
Des jungen Kreislers Schatzkästlein,
    113, 115
Jurgenson, Peter, 121

Kafka, Franz, 173
Die kaiserliche Hofmusikkapelle von
    1543-1567 (Koechel), 139
Kant, Immanuel, 243
Kemble, Fanny, 195
King Lear (Shakespeare), 163, 164
King René's Daughter (Hertz), 128
The King's Cavalier (Shellabarger),
    195
Kinnor, 186, 187
Kittredge, George Lyman, 168
Koechel, Ludwig Alois Friedrich von,
    15, 137-140
Königliche Musikschule (Munich),
    105
Konrad von Wuerzburg, 215
Koran, 179
Kossmaly, Carl, 143
Krauss, Clemens, 32, 37
Kriemhilds Rache (Hebbel), 232

Lablache, Luigi, 28, 69

"La donna è mobile" (Verdi), 196
Lafontaine (Louis Marie-Henri Thomas), 158
Lalla Rookh (Moore), 143
Lalla Rookh (Spontini), 62
La Place, Pierre-Antoine de, 77
Laroche, Herman, 123, 124
Lashetchnikov, Ivan Ivanovitch, 122
Last Supper, 244
Legends, 154, 178, 180, 185, 188, 189, 203, 212, 214, 228, 229, 230–231, 232, 234, 236. *See also* Folktales and Mythology
Lehár, Franz, 36, 135
Leipzig Stadttheater, 145
Leis prala, 193
Leitmotiv, 118, 147, 218
Lélio (Berlioz), 103
Liceo musicale (Bologna), 66
Leo, Leonardo, 49, 50
Leoncavallo, Ruggiero, 29
Leonore, or Conjugal Love (Bouilly), 55, 56
"Leonore" Overtures (Beethoven), 56
Lessing, Gotthold Ephraim, 162
Lesueur, Jean-François, 86, 87
Die Liebe der Danae (Strauss), 32
Linda di Chamounix (Donizetti), 69
Liszt, Franz, 84, 91, 92, 94, 95, 102, 103, 105, 106, 145, 146, 156, 194, 243
Die Litterarische Thaetigkeit des Carl Ehrenbrecht, Freiherrn von Moll (Koechel), 139
Lives (Plutarch), 223
Livietta e Tracollo (Pergolesi), 51
Loewen, Johann Friedrich, 153
Lohengrin (Wagner), 102, 144, 211, 214, 216, 242, 244
Lorengel, 212, 216
Louis XII, King of France, 196
Louis XIV, King of France, 46, 47
Louis XVIII, King of France, 62
Louis Philippe, King of France, 74, 83
Louise of Savoy, 195, 197
Love potion, 15, 233–236
Lucia di Lammermoor (Donizetti), 67
Lucidor (Hofmannsthal), 132, 133
Lucrezia Borgia (Donizetti), 67
Ludwig I, King of Bavaria, 156
Ludwig II, King of Bavaria, 105
Lully, Jean Baptiste, 46, 53
Luther, Martin, 229
Lyra, 188
Lyre, 185–188

Macbeth (Shakespeare), 162–163
Macbeth (Verdi), 28, 162, 164
Madama Butterfly (Puccini), 29
Maddaloni, Don Domenico Carafa, Duke of, 51, 52
Maffei, Andrea, 163
Mahler, Gustav, 119
Malfatti, Therese von, 54
Malibran, Maria, 27, 74
Malipiero, Gian Francesco, 30
Mandragora (Tchaikovsky), 122
Manelli, Francesco, 42
Marcello, Benedetto, 24–25
Marfa Nagaya, Tsarina of Russia, 199, 200, 201, 203
Marguerite of Navarre, 195, 197–198
Maria di Rohan (Donizetti), 27, 69
Maria di Rudenz (Donizetti), 67
Maria Padilla (Donizetti), 69
Maria Stuart (Schiller), 143
Maria Theresia, Infanta of Spain, 46
Marino Faliero (Donizetti), 67
Mario, Giuseppe, Cavaliere di Candia, 69
Marot, Clément, 196, 197–198
The Marriage of Figaro. See Le nozze di Figaro
Marschner, Heinrich, 84, 147
Les Martyrs (Donizetti), 68
Marx, A. Bernhard, 51
Mascagni, Pietro, 29
Mattei, Padre Stanislao, 66
Matteis, Domenico De, 49
Maximilian I, Holy Roman Emperor, 229
May Day (May 1st), 154. *See also Walpurgisnacht*
Mayr, Johann Simon, 65, 66
Mazarin, Cardinal Jules, 46
Mazeppa (Slowacky), 144
Mazeppa (Tchaikovsky), 121, 127
Meck, Nadejda von, 120, 122, 126
Médée (Cherubini), 59
Mefistofele (Boito), 29
Méhul, Etienne Nicolas, 60, 61
Die Meistersinger (Wagner), 15, 107, 117, 133, 238–240, 242
Mélac, Maréchal de Camp, 231
Memoirs (Berlioz), 92–93, 94
Menander, 50
Mendelssohn, Felix, 73, 83, 92, 116
Mérimée, Prosper, 205
The Merry Wives of Windsor (Shakespeare), 164
Merseburger Zaubersprüche, 224

Metastasio, Pietro, 25, 48, 51
Meyerbeer, Caecilie, 82
Meyerbeer, Giacomo, 13, 61, 64, 78, 80–85, 89, 97, 104, 127, 146
Michel Angelo (Hebbel), 145
Middle Ages, 65, 179, 180, 213, 232
Midrash, 187
Midsummer Day (St. John's Day), 238, 239, 240
Midsummer Eve (St. John's Eve), 238–239, 240
Les Mille et un jour (Pétis de la Croix), 181
Milton (Spontini), 60
Minato, Niccolò, 44
Le Minêstrel, 111
Minnesänger, 179
Minnetranc. See Love potion
Mnishek, Marina, 200
Mnishek, Yuri, 200
Moïse (Rossini), 76
Molière, Jean-Baptiste Poquelin, 108
Monteverde, Giulio, 75
Monteverdi, Claudio, 24, 41, 42, 43, 44
Montez, Lola, 156
Monumenti antichi inediti spiegati ed illustrati (Winckelmann), 59
Moore, Thomas, 143
Moscheles, Ignaz, 145
Moscow conservatory, 126
Mozart, Wolfgang Amadeus, 15, 32, 54–55, 62, 66, 70, 72, 88, 109, 116, 118, 137, 138, 139, 140
    Requiem, 140
Much Ado about Nothing (Shakespeare), 99
Musik am Oesterreichischen Hofe (Koechel), 139
Musorgsky, Modeste, 203–204, 206–208
Musset, Alfred de, 111, 156
Mythology (Myths), 24, 42–43, 177, 178, 179, 187, 211–212, 213, 215, 216, 217, 219, 220, 222–227, 228, 229, 238. See also Folktales and Legends

Nabucco (Verdi), 29
Nachtlied (Schumann), 145
Napoleon I, Emperor of France, 59, 60, 61, 82, 118
Napoli-Signorelli, Pietro, 50
Napravnik, Edward, 124
Nature, 15, 93, 163–164, 237–240

Nebel (Psaltery), 187
Nebuchadnezzar, King of Babylon, 187
Nerval, Gérard de, 92
Nesselrode, Countess de (Lydia Zakrefsky), 159
Neue Musik (new music), 91, 92, 102
Neue Zeitschrift für Musik, 103
Newman, Ernest, 98–99
Die Nibelungen (Hebbel), 232
The Nibelungenlied, 143, 226, 227, 228, 229, 230, 231, 232
Nicolai, Otto, 84
Nietzsche, Friedrich, 109, 237
Norma (Bellini), 28, 73–74
Nourrit, Adolphe, 76, 77
Novello, Clara, 63
Le nozze di Figaro (Mozart), 55, 118–119, 133
Le nozze di Teti e di Peleo (Cavalli), 42
Nuove musiche, 43
Nurmahal (Spontini), 62
The Nutcracker Suite (Tchaikovsky), 128

Oberon (Weber), 86
Ode to Joy (Schiller), 57
Odyssey (Homer), 43, 144
Offenbach, Jacques, 78, 98, 108–112
Old Testament, 186
L'Olimpiade (Pergolesi), 51
Olympie (Spontini), 61, 62
"On the Extent of Mozart's Musical Productivity" (Koechel), 139
Opera buffa, 25, 26, 27, 49, 50, 51, 52, 53, 67
Opéra bouffe, 108
Opéra comique, 78, 88, 100
Opéra Comique (Paris), 59, 68, 94, 111
Opéra (Paris), 77, 86, 87, 88, 94
Opera semiseria, 60, 88
Opera seria, 24, 25, 26, 48, 50, 51, 52
The Oprichnik (Tchaikovsky), 121, 122–123, 124
Orfeo (Monteverdi), 24
Orfeo ed Euridice (Gluck), 25
Orione (Cavalli), 46
Ormindo (Cavalli), 44–45
Orphée aux enfers (Offenbach), 108
Ostrovsky, Alexander, 121, 122
Otello (Rossini), 27
Otello (Verdi), 164, 166
Othello (Shakespeare), 164, 166, 167–169

Otrepiev, 201, 202

Paër, Ferdinando, 56
Paganini, Nicolò, 89–90, 91
Pagliacci (Leoncavallo), 29
Paisiello, Giovanni, 26, 58, 66
Parables and Riddles (Schiller), 184
Das Paradies und die Peri (Schumann), 148
Parisina (Donizetti), 67
Parsifal (Wagner), 162, 238, 241–245
Pasta, Giuditta, 27, 67
Paul, Jean (Johann Paul Friedrich Richter), 115
Pergolesi, Giovanni Battista (Giambattista), 26, 48–53, 72, 103
Peri, Jacopo, 24, 43
Pericles (Shakespeare), 180–181
Peters, C. F., 146
Pétis de la Croix, François, 181
Phaedo (Plato), 211
Pianetti, Marchese Cardolo Maria, 49
Piave, Francesco Maria, 195
Piccinni, Niccolò, 23, 26, 34, 35, 58
Pindar, 43, 187
Il pirata (Bellini), 73
Pizzetti, Ildebrando, 30
Plato, 211
Plutarch, 223
Polonsky, Yakov Petrovich, 124
Ponchielli, Amilcare, 29
Ponte, Lorenzo da, 81
Il prigionier superbo (Pergolesi), 50
Prima donna, 24, 27
Prima la musica e poi le parole (Casti), 32
Primaticcio, Francesco, 197
La Prise de Troie. See Les Troyens
Prize Song (Wagner), 240
Proverbs, 177
Psalmist, 187
Il pubblico segreto (Gozzi), 117
Puccini, Giacomo, 29, 30, 147, 182, 183
I Puritani (Bellini), 28, 67, 74
Pushkin, Alexander, 125, 127, 203, 206–208

Queen Mab scherzo (Berlioz), 90
The Queen of Spades (Tchaikovsky), 120, 121, 127–128

Rachel (Elisa Félix), 156
Rákóczy March (Berlioz), 93

Rameau, Jean Philippe, 35, 53
Real Conservatorio di Musica (Naples), 72
Reccio, Marie, 95
Il re cervo (Gozzi), 117
Recitativo secco, 24, 25
Reik, Theodor, 110
Reinecke, Carl, 145
Reinhardt, Max, 133
Reinick, Robert, 144
Renaissance, 42, 87, 161, 195, 196, 197, 198
The Republic (Plato), 211
Respighi, Ottorino, 30
Das Rheingold (Wagner), 16, 218–219, 228, 237
Rhine Journey (Wagner), 238
Rhine River, 213, 217, 218, 220, 221, 228, 229
Ricordi, Giulio, 164
Riddles, 177–184
Rienzi (Wagner), 84
Rietz, Julius, 145
Rigoletto (Verdi), 15, 27, 30, 195, 196, 197, 198
Rimsky-Korsakoff, Nicolai, 124
Rinaldo (Brahms), 116
Der Ring des Nibelungen (Wagner), 217, 222, 226–227, 228, 232, 237, 242–244
Rinuccini, Ottavio, 46
Il ritorno d'Ulisse in patria (Monteverdi), 24
Roberto Devereux (Donizetti), 67
Le Roi s'amuse (Hugo), 195, 198
Le Roman du chevalier au cygne, 215
Romani, Giuseppe Felice, 74
Romeo and Juliet Fantasy Overture (Tchaikovsky), 122
Romeo and Juliet (Shakespeare), 90
Roméo et Juliette (Berlioz), 90–91, 97, 98, 99
Ronde des paysans (Berlioz), 92
Ronsard, Pierre, 34
Der Rosenkavalier (Richard Strauss), 131, 132, 133, 135
Rossi, Luigi, 46
Rossini, Gioacchino, 13, 26, 27, 64, 66, 71, 72, 73, 74, 75, 76–79, 83, 85
"The Royal Hunt and Storm" (Berlioz), 98
Rubini, Giovanni Battista, 28, 67
Rubinstein, Anton, 106, 124
Rubinstein, Nikolai, 124
Rückert, Friedrich, 104

Sachs, Hans, 239–240, 242
Sacrati, Francesco, 42
St. John, 238
St. Peter, 229
Saint-Saëns, Camille, 78
Saint Valliers, Seigneur de (Jean de Poitiers), 196
St. Walpurgis (Walburga), 153–154
Sala, Nicolo, 58
Salieri, Antonio, 26, 32, 82
Sallet, Friedrich von, 114
Salustia (Pergolesi), 50
Salzburg Festival, 33
Sammartino, Duchess of, 72
Sand, Georges, 156
Sardanapalus (Byron), 143
Saul, King, 187, 188
Sayn-Wittgenstein, Princess Caroline, 94, 95, 96, 99, 106
Scarlatti, Alessandro, 24, 52
Scharschmid, Franz von, 137, 138, 139
Scheffler, Johannes, 104
Schiller, Johann Christoph Friedrich von, 55, 57, 92, 102, 114, 116, 126, 161, 181–182, 183, 184, 203, 204–205, 206, 207, 208
Schindler, Anton, 55
Schönberg, Arnold, 172
Schopenhauer, Arthur, 243
Schumann, Clara, 92, 106, 114–115, 117, 118, 145–146, 148
Schumann, Julie, 118
Schumann, Marie, 115
Schumann, Robert, 16, 68, 70, 73, 74, 83, 92, 114, 115, 118, 143–149, 237
Scribe, Eugène, 76, 83
Scriptures, 188. See also Bible
Sebald, Amalie, 54
El secreto a voces (Calderòn), 116, 117
Serov, Alexander, 124
La serva padrona (Pergolesi), 26, 49, 50–51, 53, 103
Sforza, Maximilian, 197
Shakespeare, William, 15, 48, 87, 88, 90, 96, 98, 99, 100, 101, 161–165, 166, 167–169, 170, 180
Sheba, Queen of, 178–179, 184, 187
Shellabarger, Samuel, 195
The Shoes (Tchaikovsky), 125. See also Vakoula the Smith
Shpashinsky, Ippolit Vassilevitch, 127
Shuisky, Basil, 200–201
Tsar of Russia, 201, 202, 203
Sibelius, Jean, 237
Siebold, Agathe von, 115

Siegfried (Wagner), 118, 228, 237–238
Siegfrieds Tod (Hebbel), 232
Sigismund III, King of Poland, 200
Simoni, Renato, 182
Singspiel, 116
Slowacky, Julius, 144
Smithson, Harriet, 86–87, 99
Socrates, 211
Sollogub, Count Vladimir, 122
Solomon, King, 178–179, 187
The Song Contest in the Wartburg. See Wartburgkrieg
La sonnambula (Bellini), 28, 73, 74
Sontag, Henriette, 80
The Sorceress (Tchaikovsky), 121, 127
Soumet, Louis Alexandre, 74
Sozumeni, Maria dei, 47
Spohr, Ludwig, 80, 84, 145, 147
Spontini, Gasparo, 13, 26, 58–64, 83, 84, 86
Stabat Mater (Pergolesi), 52, 53, 72
Stigliano, Prince of, 50
Strachey, Lytton, 168
La straniera (Bellini), 73
Strauss, Johann, 36, 118
Strauss, Richard, 32–37, 131–136
Sturm und Drang (storm and stress), 115
The Swan-Knight (Konrad von Wuerzburg), 215
Swans, 185, 211–216, 224, 243, 244
Symphonie Fantastique (Berlioz), 89

The Taking of Troy. See Les Troyens
The Tales of Hoffmann. See Les Contes d'Hoffmann
Talmud, 179, 187
Tamburini, Antonio, 28, 69
Tancredi (Rossini), 26
Taneieff, Sergei, 123, 125
Tannhäuser (Wagner), 237, 241–242, 244
Tasso, Torquato, 65
Tchaikovsky, Antonina, 125–126
Tchaikovsky, Modeste, 122, 127, 128
Tchaikovsky, Peter Ilitch, 120–128, 147
Fourth Symphony, 126
Violin Concerto, 126
Il teatro alla moda (Marcello), 24
Teatro alla Scala (Milan), 26, 29, 30, 73, 74
Teatro Carlo Felice (Genoa), 73
Teatro Costanzi (Rome), 29

Teatro filarmonico (Milan), 68
Teatro Regio (Milan), 46
Teatro Regio (Parma), 29, 30
Teatro San Benedetto (Venice), 26
Teatro San Carlo (Naples), 72
Teatro San Cassiano (Venice), 42, 44, 45
Teatro San Giovanni e San Paolo (Venice), 45
Le Temple de Cupidon (Marot), 196
Théatre de l'Impératrice (Paris), 62. See also Théâtre Italien
Théâtre Feydeau (Paris), 60
Théâtre Italien (Paris), 59, 62, 77
Théâtre Lyrique (Paris), 97
Thirty Years War, 99, 229
A Thousand and One Nights, 104
Tieck, Ludwig, 114
Till Eulenspiegel, 143
Timotheus, 50
Torquato Tasso (Donizetti), 67, 70
Toscanini, Arturo, 30
Tovey, Sir Donald, 98
La Traviata (Verdi), 29, 158
Tristan und Isolde (Wagner), 15, 74, 106, 118, 146, 233, 234–236, 238, 242, 243, 244
Tristan und Isolt (Gottfried von Strassburg), 233, 234, 236
Tritto, Giacomo, 58
Trojan March (Berlioz), 98
The Trojans. See Les Troyens
Les Troyens (Berlioz), 95–99, 100
Les Troyens à Carthage. See Les Troyens
Turandot (Busoni), 183
Turandot (Gozzi), 181, 182, 183
Turandot (Puccini), 182, 183
Turandot (Schiller), 181–182, 183
Il Turco in Italia (Rossini), 26
Turgenev, Ivan Sergeevitch, 116
Turina, Giuditta, 73

Undine (Tchaikovsky), 121, 122

Vakoula the Smith (Tchaikovsky), 121, 124–125
Valhalla, 217, 218, 224, 225, 226
Valkyries, 211, 212, 213, 222, 223, 224–226
Vaselli, Virginia. See Donizetti, Virginia
Verdi, Giuseppe, 15, 27, 28–29, 30, 33, 68, 83, 85, 143, 157, 161–165, 166, 169–170, 196

Requiem, 118
Verhulst, Johannes, 145
Verismo, 29
Verzeichnis aller meiner Werke vom Monath Februarius 1784, bis Monath—(Mozart), 138
La Vestale (Spontini), 59–61, 62, 64, 86
Il viaggio a Reims (Rossini), 76
Victor Emmanuel II, King of Italy, 65
Viel-Castel, Horace de, 157
Vigarani, Gasparo, 46
Villarosa, Marchese di (Carlo Antonio de Rosa), 50
Villars, François de, 51
Vinci, Leonardo, 49
Vinci, Leonardo da, 197
Virgil, 86, 95, 96, 101
Vogler, Abbé George Joseph, 82
Voltaire, François Marie Arouet, 61, 109
"Vous soupirez, Madame" (Berlioz), 100
The Voyevode (Tchaikovsky), 121, 122

Wagner, Richard, 23, 29, 36, 60, 61, 73–74, 83, 84, 85, 88, 91, 92, 96, 102, 103, 104, 105, 106, 109, 115, 117, 118, 143, 144, 145, 146–147, 149, 162, 164, 211, 214, 216, 217, 218, 222, 226–227, 228, 229, 230, 232, 233, 234–236, 237–238, 241, 242–243
"Wahn, Wahn, überall Wahn" (Wagner), 240
Wailly, Léon de, 88
Die Walküre (Wagner), 118, 228, 237
Walpurgisnacht (Walpurgis Night), 15, 150–151, 152–154
Walsunga Saga, 226, 227
Wartburgkrieg, 143, 180, 212, 215, 216
Wassermann, Jakob, 133
Weber, Carl Maria von, 61, 62, 80, 83, 85, 86, 88, 112, 147
Weill, Kurt, 172
Weimar court theatre, 102, 103, 104, 146
Werfel, Franz, 133
Werthes, Friedrich August Clemens, 181
Widmann, Josef Viktor, 113, 117, 119
Wiedemann, 145
Wieland, Christoph Martin, 102
Wielandsage, 212

William Tell. See Guillaume Tell
Willibald, 153
Winckelmann, Johann Joachim, 59
Wisniewiecky, Prince Adam, 205
Witches, 150, 151, 154, 163, 224
Witches' Sabbath, *See Walpurgisnacht*
Wolfhart, 154
Wolfram von Eschenbach, 180, 215
Worms, 228–232
Woyzeck (Büchner), 171–172, 173
Woyzeck, Johann Christian, 173
Wozzeck (Berg), 16, 172, 173–174

Wunnibald, 153

Xerse (Cavalli), 46

Zaira (Bellini), 73
Zampa (Hérold), 78
Die Zauberflöte (Mozart), 116, 117
Zenatello, Giovanni, 30
Zingarelli, Nicola, 72
Zoraide di Granata (Donizetti), 66
Zweig, Stefan, 32